Records of the 1st meeting of the

National League of Professional

Base Ball Clubs

held

the Grand Central Hotel New York

Feb. 2, 1876

O'ROURKE,
Centre Field, NEW YORK.

GORE,
Centre Field, NEW YORK.

RICHARDSON,
2nd Base, NEW YORK.

CONNOR,
1st Base, NEW YORK.

SLATTERY,
Left Field, NEW YORK.

MURPHY,
Catcher, New York.

CRANE,
Pitcher, NEW YORK.

HATFIELD, 3rd Base, NEW YORK.

Constitution.

Article I.   Name.

Name.

This association shall be called, The National League of Professional Base-Ball Clubs.

Article II.   Objects.

Objects.

The objects of this League are,

1. To encourage, foster and elevate the game of base-ball:

2. To enact and enforce proper rules for the exhibition and conduct of the game:

3. To make base-ball playing respectable and honorable:

4. To protect and promote the mutual interests of professional base-ball clubs and professional base-ball players: and

5. To establish and regulate the "Base-Ball Championship of the United States."

Article III.   Membership.

Membership.

This League shall consist of the following named Professional Base-Ball Clubs, namely:

Athletic B. B. Club of Philadelphia, Pa.;

Boston B. B. Club of Boston, Mass.;

Chicago B. B. Club of Chicago, Ills.;

Cincinnati B. B. Club of Cincinnati, Ohio;

Hartford B. B. Club of Hartford, Conn.;

Mutual B. B. Club of Brooklyn, N. Y.;

Louisville B. B. Club of Louisville, Ky.; and

St. Louis B. B. Club of St. Louis, Mo.,

and such other professional Base-Ball Clubs as may from time to

time be elected to membership under the following
rules, namely:

1. No other Club shall be admitted from either of the
cities above named other than the clubs mentioned
except in the event that either of such clubs shall
lose its membership and in no event shall there
be more than one club from any city.

2. No club shall be admitted from any city whose pop-
ulation is less than 75000 except by unanimous vote
of the League.

3 No club shall be admitted unless it shall first have
delivered to the Secretary of the League at least thirty
days before the Annual Meeting a written application
for membership signed by its President and Secretary
accompanied by documents showing that such club
bears the name of the city in which it is located. and
that it is regularly organized and officered and (where
the State law permits it) chartered, and accompanied
also by a pledge that it will keep all its engagements
with the clubs members of the League, and that it
has not in its employ any player who has been dismissed or expelled by the League or any club members
thereof.

4. The voting upon an application for membership shall
be by white and black balls: two black balls shall
be sufficient to exclude the applicant and no club
shall be required under any circumstances to state

"OLD CINCINNATI RED STOCKINGS" of 1869

GEORGE WRIGHT

CHICAGO

A. C. ANSON

GILT EDGE JAY HUGHES

BOSTON

GEORGE W

I . Three-Color Presswork by Walter N. Brunt

GEORGE WRIGHT AN

From a Painting by Carl Dahlg

Colored Plates by Bolton & Strong

E GOLDEN GATE

cuted for S. R. Church

The ball Section 1. The ball must weigh not less than five, nor more than five and one-quarter ounces avoirdupois. It must measure not less than nine, nor more than nine and one-quarter inches in circumference. It must be composed of woolen yarn, and shall be covered with leather. *(It shall not contain more than one ounce of rubber.)*

Furnishing the ball Sec. 2. In all games the ball – or balls – played with shall be furnished by the home club, and shall become the property of the winning club.

A legal ball Sec. 3 No ball shall be played with in any regular match game unless it is of the regulation size, weight, and material, and also have the name of its maker, & the figures indicating its weight and circumference plainly stamped on its cover. Should any ball used in a regular match game prove on examination by the umpire, to be illegal in size, weight, or materials, balls of the same manufacture shall not be used thereafter in regular match games.

Changing ball Sec. 4. When the ball becomes out of shape, or cut or ripped so as to expose the yarn, or in any way so injured as to be unfit for fair use, a new ball shall be called for by the umpire at the end of an even innings, at the request of either captain; should the ball be lost during a game, the umpire shall, at the expiration of five minutes, call for a new ball.

The Bat.

Sec. 5. The bat must be round and must not exceed two and a half inches in diameter in the thickest part. It must be made wholly of wood, and shall not exceed forty-two inches in length.

The Bases.

Sec. 6. The bases must be four in number, and they must be placed and securely fastened upon each corner of a square the sides of which are respectively thirty yards. The bases must be so constructed and placed as to be distinctly seen by the umpire, and must cover a space equal to one square foot of surface. The first, second, and third bases shall be canvas bags, painted white, and filled with some soft material; the home base shall be of white marble or stone, so fixed in the ground as to be even with the surface, and with one corner facing the pitcher's position, said corner touching the intersection of the foul lines.

Positions of the bases

Sec. 7. The base from which the ball is struck shall be designated the home base, and must be directly opposite the second base; the first base must always be that upon the right-hand, and the third base that upon the left-hand side of the striker when occupying his position at the home base. In all match games lines connecting the home and first bases, and the home and third bases, and also the lines of the striker's and pitcher's positions, shall be

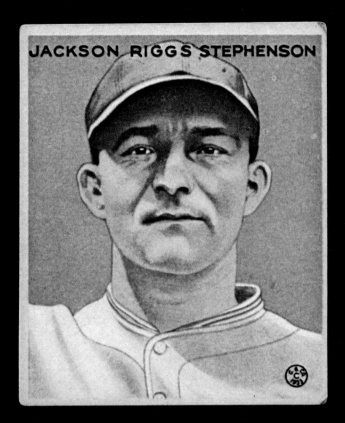

JACKSON RIGGS STEPHENSON

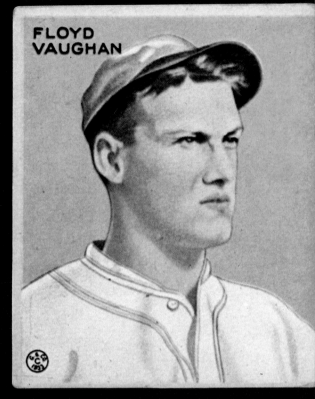

FLOYD
VAUGHAN

ANDY HIGH

BIG LEAGUE CHEWING GUM

EARL
ADAMS

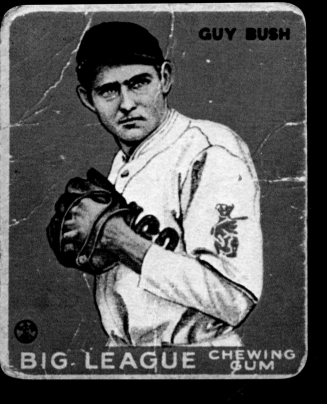

GUY BUSH

BIG LEAGUE CHEWING GUM

RAY BENGE

BIG LEAGUE CHEWING GUM

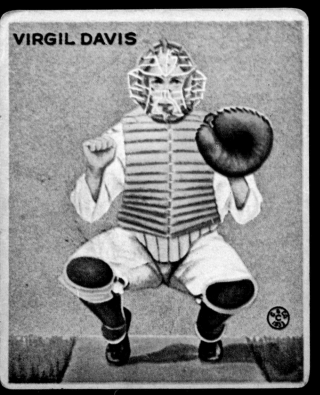

VIRGIL DAVIS

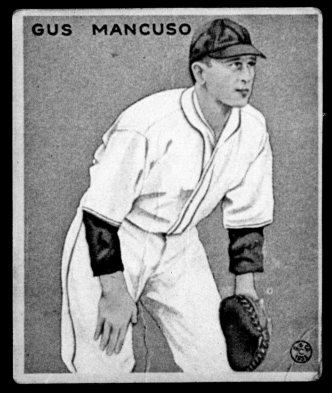

GUS MANCUSO

Athletic Club of Phila. Pa.

Thomas S. Smith President
A.H. Wright Sec'y.
A.J. Reach Manager
Club Rooms No. 45 South 11th St.

Boston Club of Boston Mass

N.T. Apollonio President
Harry Wright Sec'y. No. 39 Eliot St.

Chicago Club of Chicago Ill.

W. A. Hulbert President
A.J. Spalding Sec'y. Room 5. No. 166 Randolph St.

Cincinnati Club Cincinnati Ohio
J. L. Keck Pres.
G. H. Van Voorhis Sec'y. No. 80 Poplar St.

Hartford Club   Hartford Conn.
M. G. Bulkeley   President
B. Douglass Jr   Sec'y

Louisville Club   Louisville Ky.
W. N. Haldeman   President
Chas. E. Chase Vice Pres.   No. 12 Third St.
George K. Speed Sec'y. & Treas.
Jno. C. Chapman   Manager

Mutual Club of Brooklyn N.Y.
Wm. H. Cammeyer   Manager
Union Grounds
Williamsburg N.Y.

St. Louis Club   St. Louis Mo.
J. R. C. Lucas   President
Chas. A. Fowle Sec'y. No. 406 North 4th St.
S. Mason Graffen   Manager.

A Baseball Century
The First 100 Years of the National League

A Rutledge Book
Macmillan Publishing Co., Inc.
New York
Collier Macmillan Publishers
London

RUTLEDGE BOOKS
Fred R. Sammis: Publisher
John Sammis: Creative Director
Jeanne McClow: Editor-in-Chief
Allan Mogel: Art Director
Sally Andrews: Managing Editor
Jeremy Friedlander: Editor
Mimi Koren: Editor
B. G. Murphy: Editor
Jay Hyams: Associate Editor
Arthur Gubernick: Production Consultant
Annemarie Bosch: Production Manager
Elyse Shick: Associate Art Director
Eric Marshall: Art Associate

Henry Berry: Historian
Irv Kaze: Special Consultant
Dave Boss: Special Consultant

Macmillan Publishing Co., Inc., 866 Third Avenue, New York, N. Y. 10022
Collier Macmillan Canada, Ltd.
First Printing 1976
Printed in Italy

Library of Congress Cataloging in Publishing Data
Main entry under title:
A Baseball Century.
   "A Rutledge book."
   1. National League of Professional Baseball Clubs—History.
GV875.A3B37   796.357'64'0973   75-35501
ISBN 0-02-510380-6

*Preceding pages: page 1: first page
of minutes of founding meeting;
pages 2-3: lithograph of painting of New York
National League baseball team, 1888, from back
of schedule and statistics printed by Goodwin
Tobacco Company; pages 4-5: first two pages of 1876
constitution; pages 6-7: mural of early National
League stars; pages 8-9: first two pages of 1876
rules; pages 10-11: baseball cards, Big League
series, 1933; pages 12-13: first eight clubs'
directories as they appeared in original minutes,
1876.*

Introduction

For baseball fans, the celebration of a centennial comes easily. Our game is nourished by numbers, and all of us who have followed it, even if only briefly, have found ourselves transformed into walking memory banks, humming with names, dates, batting averages and earned-run averages, games won, games lost, "magic numbers," final standings, lifetime marks, Series, seasons, decades, epochs. Now we have a new record: the National League is one hundred.

Baseball is the most continuous of all our American sports—the least altered in its rules and strategies and distinctive style. That promising twenty-two-year-old rookie shortstop dressed in brilliant double knits and just now tapping the plate as he steps up to bat in his team's new triple-decked stadium is engaged in a pressing task—hitting the ball, moving up the runner, winning the game. But the size of the plate and the dimensions of the field before him (the distance out to the mound, the distance between the bases), the weight of the ball, the size of the bat, and the rules that govern the various flights and fortunes of this game—all these have remained the same over many decades. The rookie is swinging not only against Don Gullett (let's say), but also—figuratively, in statistics, and in memory—against Sandy Koufax, Dazzy Vance, and Rube Marquard. Possibly stricken with a sudden sense of this burden, he pops up, ending the inning, and then runs out to take up his position in the infield—where knowing fans and the silent statistics will now compare him critically with last year's shortstop, and with Chris Speier and Larry Bowa, and Pee Wee Reese and Rabbit Maranville and Honus Wagner.

Baseball, we have come to appreciate, is both fluid and ordered. It is forever fresh and surprising, continually happening, and yet also fixed in an immense foundation of ancient events and precedents. It is, if you will, a little like history itself, with the vivid, sudden event flaming up at the near end, and the dark, unmoving bulk of the past stretching off away from us at the other. It is surprising, I sometimes think, that baseball is so young.

We come to this game simply—as children, most of us—but we end up belonging to it in complicated ways. Our first cheering is for our home team, for the good guys, and then, almost simultaneously, we find a hero. No subsequent baseball attachment ever quite matches the passionate caring we sustained for that special ballplayer of our youth (growing up in New York, I had two: Hubbell and DiMaggio), and a great many Americans have been transfixed by their first intimation of mortality at the moment when they watched their familiar demigod on some spring afternoon and for the first time saw him hesitate at the plate or labor on the mound, and suddenly sensed that he would not be out there for many more Aprils. Long before this, however—after no more than a year or two of following a player and a team through the summer's lengthy doings—the young fan has begun to understand that something more is involved and that he is now attached in a rather mysterious way to a larger structure, to something that is deep and rooted, with its own history, customs, records, honored names, superstitions, founders, esoterica, and lore. Without knowing it, he has been admitted to a family. He belongs, and if he cares and is lucky enough to go on caring, he can belong for a lifetime.

For me, opening this book is like coming upon a family album stuffed with old letters, wedding invitations, tattered newspaper clippings, graduation programs, and hundreds of snapshots. It can be opened at random, or read right through, or looked at backward, going from now to then. We will find our own family portraits, and then, turning these pages, surprise ourselves with the faces and names of departed, almost forgotten visitors and cousins. Everyone is here. The Brooks and the Gashouse Gang and the Big Red Machine. Gabby and Pie and Sunny Jim. Aaron and Bench and Brock. Mays and Clemente. Jackie Robinson. Spahn and Sain and pray for rain. Stan the Man. The Meal Ticket. Old Diz and Ducky and the Fordham Flash. Big Poison and Little Poison. Rogers Hornsby. Bill Klem. (An umpire, yes. He spent more than five thousand afternoons on the field, far more than anyone else in baseball history, and invented the umpire's essential state of mind: "In my heart, I never called one wrong.") Christy Mathewson. The Dutchman. Frank Chance, the Peerless Leader. Old Hoss Radbourn. Cap Anson. A century of names. It is perfectly all right, I think, if we smile a little as we look at the blurry, posed pictures of some of the old-timers here, in their baggy flannels, cardigan sweaters, boxy caps, and stiff little gloves. Think how a reader of the next volume of this history will laugh in 2076 when he comes upon Willie McCovey's pants and Al Hrabosky's sideburns!

This book should also warm our recollections of some other baseball prodigies—men who illuminated the game not with their play but with their imagination, their will, their passionate selves. Instantly, I think of two such men.

He was short and dumpy, only 5-foot 7, and the weight he carried in later years made him look even smaller. He played the game for sixteen years (his lifetime batting average was .334), but he was made to be a manager. He managed the same club for thirty years. In time he bought a piece of the team, but in another sense he had always owned it. For every day and every game of those thirty years he was unquestionably the largest and most vivid figure on any field where his team was playing. He was a master tactician in a time when runs were scratched out singly, out of luck and speed and connivance. He was too impatient to qualify as a great developer of talent, but he was a marvelous coach and a cold and deadly trader. He kept a distance between himself and his players, and the only two for whom he permitted himself to hold a deep affection both died young and before he did. He had great success, but terrible things happened to his teams on the field—immortal bonehead plays, crucial bases left uncovered, pennant-losing collisions on the basepaths, malevolent bounces off invisible pebbles in the dirt. The bitter, enraged expression that settled on his thick face in his last years was the look of a man who had fought a lifelong, bareknuckled fight against bad baseball luck. They called him Little Napoleon. His name was John McGraw. "The main idea," he said, "is to win."

The other man was a lawyer, a churchman, a teetotaler—a straight arrow who made an early promise to his mother never to play ball or watch it on Sundays, and who kept his promise. He had flowing hair and bushy eyebrows and bow ties that he wore like a flag. He was a rhetorician, a nineteenth-century orator, a front-office man who enlivened trade talks with torrents of polysyllables and quotations from Shakespeare and Pope. Ideas and cigar smoke streamed from him. He thought up baseball tryouts. He put numbers on uniforms. He invented Ladies Day. He had the most discerning eye for young baseball talent that the game has ever known, and it was appropriate that he should have been the man who thought up and perfected the farm system. By the time World War II came along, his club, the Cardinals, had a chain of thirty-two minor league teams that employed more than six hundred ballplayers. Each year, the best of his young phenoms came up to the parent club, crowding its famous roster and forcing so many trades that in time half the dugouts of the National League seemed to be populated with his muscular, Ozark-bred throwers and long-ball hitters whom he had first spotted in some cinder-strewn Appalachian ballyard.

Then he, too, moved along to other clubs, still spouting phrases and ideas. "Judas Priest!" he cried. There was something about him of the traveling medicine-show man, something of W. C. Fields. But his ultimate alteration of the game, the destruction of baseball's color bar, was an act of national significance—an essential remedy that had awaited a man of subtlety and stubborn moral courage to bring it about. He refused to accept awards or plaudits for the deed, since it had only reversed an ancient and odious injustice. It would shame a man, he said, to take credit for that. He was the Mahatma: Branch Rickey. "Baseball," he said, "has given me a life of joy."

Quite a pair of forefathers. Quite a family. Judas Priest! Happy birthday to us all.

—Roger Angell

Hurray for Captain Spalding!

On June 24, 1876, Cap Anson led his Chicago baseball nine to victory over the Brooklyn Mutuals in their successful assault on the National League's first pennant. So ruthless was Anson's team in piling up victories that to be shut out in a baseball game became known as being "Chicagoed." On the same day, some 600 miles to the west, and slightly north, George Armstrong Custer led his men in search of a coalition of Sioux, Cheyenne, and Arapaho. The following day, a Sunday, provided the National Leaguers with a day of rest. Custer was not as fortunate. He found his opponents at Little Big Horn and was summarily "Chicagoed."

It is difficult to realize that when Custer met his fate the National League—and thus major league baseball as we know it today—had been in existence some five months. Somehow Custer's stand seems longer ago than that. But organized baseball did, indeed, begin in 1876 when a loosely knit National Association of Professional Base Ball *Players* evolved into the National League of Professional Base Ball *Clubs*. Then, the pitcher (some still called him "bowler") stood 45 feet away and threw underhand to a batter who was permitted to instruct him just where he wanted the ball pitched. The thrower's success depended on how well he could mix up his speed: the great ones, like Al Spalding, had any number of variances with which they hoped to catch the batter off balance. Most of the fielders had no gloves, and a maskless catcher would frequently stand several feet behind the batter in order to catch the ball on the first hop.

The hitter faced this defense with a strategy diametrically opposed to that of today. The more successful ones concentrated on hitting ground balls through the infield. Even several years after the fielders started to wear gloves—they were usually thin, fingerless pieces of leather, somewhat similar to those worn by today's golfers and baseball batters—the hard ground ball remained the best way to reach first safely. But by the time the nineteenth century ended, the game had changed drastically to a form of baseball that, in most cases, was exceedingly close to the game of today, both off and on the field.

Although some 23 cities had franchises during the National League's first 25 years, the eight teams that constituted the league by 1900 would remain stable for 53 years. These were the cities whose teams attracted particularly ardent fans, called "cranks." Their loyalty, frequently passed down from generation to generation, has

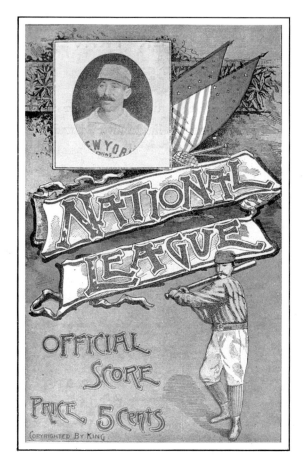

24

Preceding pages: *Elysian Fields game, 16 years before founding of the National League.* Above: *The dominant Chicago nine and a typical scorecard from the time.* Opposite: *Baltimore's Wee Willie Keeler.*

continued to be the lifeblood of the game.

It was an era that spawned the superstar. The King Kellys, Charlie Buffintons, and Willie Keelers were, as a group, the beginning of the fan idolatry that now exists in all sports. They appeared in songs, photographs, poems, and even on the variety stage. Old Judge cigarettes passed out their pictures on cards (if you have a Buck Ewing from the '80 s, it's worth as much as Xerox stock), and youngsters would entice their dads to smoke in order that they might build up collections.

Post-Civil War America saw industrialization of urban areas begin in earnest. Local ball teams filled a void in the humdrum existences of many of the six-day-a-week workers. Incredible as it seems today, the league teams usually were not allowed to play on Sundays, thus prohibiting the large majority of the fans from seeing more than one or two games a year. The situation gave rise to modern sports journalism. If you couldn't see Patsy Tebeau and his Cleveland Spiders, you could at least read about them in the papers. The sports sections of local tabloids began to offer extensive coverage of the teams. While you might work ten hours a day in a Pittsburgh steel mill, you could still find out if Pud Galvin had won another for the Stogies. It was the newspapers that popularized the expression "the national pastime."

In short, these 25 years sophisticated the game, stabilized the National League, and placed professional baseball in a unique position in this country. Baseball no longer dominates the sporting scene, but the game hasn't exactly fallen apart: its vital signs prove it to be hale and hearty. As Mark Twain once responded, "reports of my death are grossly exaggerated."

"To encourage, foster and elevate the game of base ball."

—Constitution of the National League
New York City, February 2, 1876

Someone once wrote, "Organization will be the strangulation of mankind." It worked just the opposite for the National Association of Base Ball Players. Lushing (heavy drinking), hippodroming (throwing of games), revolving (changing from one team to another), failure to complete schedules, and a complete lack of central leadership had the association in a state best described as moribund. Worst of all was the utter domination of the league by the Boston Red Stockings. Harry Wright's New England team had won the pennant from '72 through '75. In the latter year they had amassed the fantastic

record of 71–8, losing not a single game on their home grounds. Of the thirteen teams, only five could play .500 ball. Brooklyn was last with a 2–42 record. Keokuk, Iowa, was next with 1–12. The late baseball historian, Lee Allen, was alleged to have been the only man who knew the name of Keokuk's lone winning pitcher.

The time was perfect for a palace coup, and in William Hulbert, Chicago baseball executive, the game had the man ideally suited to ramrod the insurgents. Raised near the banks of Lake Michigan, he had become a great booster of what had once been Fort Dearborn. "I'd rather be a lamp post in Chicago than a millionaire elsewhere," Hulbert boasted. "I'll take control of the game away from the Easterners." His first move concerned Al Spalding of the Red Stockings, the association's leading pitcher. When Boston made its initial trip to Chicago in '75, Hulbert was there to meet the team.

"Spalding," beseeched Hulbert, "you've no business playing in Boston; you're a western boy and you belong right here. If you'll come to Chicago, I'll accept the presidency of the club and we'll give those easterners the fight of their lives. You can be captain and manager at four thousand dollars a year."

As great a player as Spalding was, he was to prove an even better businessman. "Yes, I'll accept," the star agreed, "and when I come, I'll bring a team of pennant winners with me. I'll get Ross Barnes, Cal McVey, and Deacon White. The people call us 'the Big Four,' but the owners won't pay us very well. A championship team should be paid like champions."

Each player in the association could call his own shots year by year. What he could not do was negotiate with a different club during the season, which was, of course, just what Spalding had done. When the other three also agreed to come to Chicago, the association was in an uproar.

"You seceders," cried the Boston cranks, "your White Stockings will get soiled in Chicago." The Big Four just laughed and played out the season in New England, devastating the rest of the association. Their outstanding play left no room for charges of hippodroming.

No matter what the fans claimed, it was the other club owners who were important. To further complicate matters, Hulbert had also signed the young Philadelphia phenomenon, Adrian Anson. The new Chicago president had pushed the association to the wall. He was convinced that the ruling clique in the East would move against him, and probably suspend his new stars.

Years later, Spalding wrote of Hulbert's countermove, "Mr. Hulbert and myself were in a serious discussion on what we should do. For a few moments I noticed that he was engrossed in deep thought, when suddenly he arose from his chair and said, 'Spalding, I have a new scheme. Let us anticipate the Eastern cusses and organize a new association before the March [1876] meeting, and then we shall see who will do the expelling.'"

It was probably the most important moment in major league history.

The two men went to work. Spalding was installed in Hulbert's home for a month while he drafted a new constitution: alcohol would not be sold on the clubs' grounds; pool selling or gambling of any sort would not be tolerated; all teams would be obligated to play their complete schedule; each franchise would have to represent a city of at least 75,000 people; and, vitally important, it would be a National League of clubs, not players—the owners would have complete control. Mr. Hulbert's league would be run as a business.

Hulbert's next step was to call a meeting of the four so-called Western teams: his own, St. Louis, Cincinnati, and Louisville. They were as fed up with the Easterners as he was. They agreed to go along with his new league.

Armed with power of attorney from the four western teams, Hulbert arranged a meeting with the leaders of Boston, Philadelphia, Hartford, and the Mutuals of Brooklyn to be held at the Grand Central Hotel on Broadway, in New York City, February 2, 1876. Shrewdly, he had arranged to meet with each club alone before facing the entire group.

Legend has it that when he did gather the four club leaders together, he dramatically locked the door, stuck the key in his pocket, and told the group that they couldn't leave until they had heard him out. Actually, his task didn't turn out to be difficult. The Easterners were equally disgruntled with the drawbacks of the association. They, too, were ready for a league that could successfully take advantage of the very rapid growth of a game that Americans were beginning to consider their greatest sport. Hulbert's most telling point was undoubtedly his appeal to their wallets.

"Why should we be losing money," Hulbert asked, "when we represent a game that the people love?"

"Mr. Hulbert," Spalding recorded, "magnificently dominated the whole situation."

One of his smartest moves was not to demand the presidency for himself. The office was given to Morgan G. Bulkeley of Hartford. Bulkeley, later governor of Connecticut and a senator from that state, was just the man to give the league its desperately needed respectability. By the time the day was over, the charter had been drawn. A notice was sent to the media announcing that the eight teams had withdrawn from the association and had formed a National League of Professional Base Ball Clubs. Hulbert had his new league, but his chore was far from over.

Ascending to the presidency in '77, he was faced with a major crisis—what to do with New York and Philadelphia, both of which had failed to make their last western trip in '76. Hulbert didn't hesitate. Even though these teams represented the two most populous areas in the league, they were expelled. The season of '77 found the league down to six clubs.

Then came the hippodroming. Boston had won the pennant in '77 by three games over Louisville in a finish notorious for some incredibly bad playing by the Kentuckians. An investigation proved that their star pitcher, Jim Devlin, and three others had been bribed. Once again Hulbert moved fast—the four were exiled from baseball for life, an especially tough decision for Hulbert because Devlin had been a close friend for many years.

Still another dilemma arose that involved Cincinnati and St. Louis. Both cities were heavily populated with Germans from the European

revolutionary upheavals of '48. They liked their baseball on Sundays, for 25 cents, and accompanied by liberal quantities of beer. Still no wavering from Hulbert. No beer, no Sunday ball, and the price remained a half dollar. Perhaps Mr. Hulbert wasn't always right in his unilateral decisions but, until his early death in 1882, his steadfastness furnished the fledgling National League with much needed backbone.

Morgan Bulkeley, really little more than a figurehead for the league, has been given a plaque at Cooperstown. One hundred years later, none exists for William Hulbert.

There was no comment from Kelly as the detective told Spalding how much whiskey Mike had consumed. It was only the informer's report on the lemonade that infuriated the star.

"It's a dirty lie," protested Kelly, "I never had a damned lemonade in me life."

To measure the Chicago teams of the '80s, you have to start with the amazing man whose commanding presence was always felt, Adrian ("Cap") Anson. (Spalding played one great year in the National League before retiring himself to the executive office, where he could more easily run the affairs of the ball club as well as those of his mushrooming sporting equipment business.) Anson batted .356 the first year of the National League and was still able to hit .285

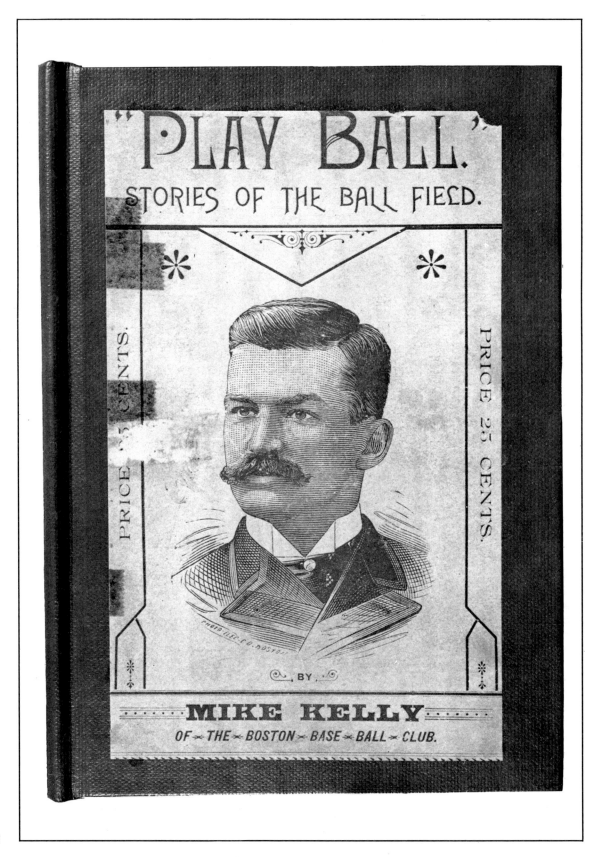

Mike ("King") Kelly was the game's first genuine superstar.
He wrote a book about his exploits on the field (above)
and was even immortalized in song by Maggie Cline (opposite).

in '97, 21 years later. During this span Anson saw the game change tremendously and its season of roughly 66 games more than double. When he finally called it quits, professional baseball had truly arrived as the national game. In the slang of the time, the Cap had "seen the elephant," meaning that a man had done it all.

It was as a player and manager for Chicago in the '80s that he made his mark. Playing mostly as a first baseman (he also played everywhere else), he led his nine to pennants in '80, '81, '82, '85, and '86. And what a team it was! Add Fred Pfeffer, Tommy Burns, and Ned Williamson and you had an infield justifiably called "Chicago's Stone Wall." In '84 Williamson hit 27 home runs, a record not broken until a guy named Ruth came along 35 years later. Behind the plate was the colorful "Silver" Flint. They had trouble getting Silver to wear a mask ("I can't breathe with the damned thing," he protested), and didn't have much more luck with a glove. Years later, Flint was knocked cold in a train wreck. He woke up to find a doctor trying to set all his fingers.

"What the hell are you doing?" asked Flint.

"Why, all your fingers are broken," came the reply.

"Nah," laughed Silver, "I got them that way catching for the Chicago White Stockings."

Those whom Flint was catching were no slouches. Larry Corcoran was the bellwether at the beginning, and John Clarkson was the hero of '85 and '86. Corcoran specialized in no-hitters, tossing three between '80 and '84. Clarkson turned in 53 victories in '85.

And then there was "King" Kelly—Michael J. Kelly, to be exact.

Like the businesslike Anson, who, always in control, was the methodical leader of the nine, catcher-outfielder Kelly was the charismatic star, the Babe Ruth of his day. It was Kelly the lads followed down the street, and Kelly who was always "setting them up" in the finest bistros in the land. He trod the vaudeville halls in the off-season, playing to full houses wherever he appeared. Maggie Cline (of "Throw Him Down McCloskey" fame) added "Slide, Kelly, Slide" to her repertoire, leading the nation in singing of the great Mike. When Kelly would reach first base, the whole park would frequently break out in song. As the leading pillager of his day, Mike would often oblige, dashing down to second, employing his patented "Kelly Spread," the nineteenth century version of the hook slide.

Kelly was not above subterfuge. Too "hung over" to play one day, King was sitting on the

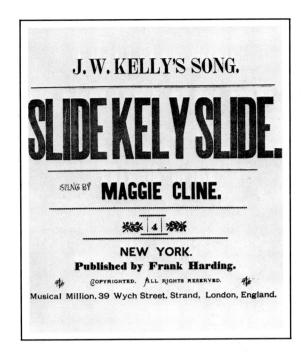

J. W. KELLY'S SONG.

SLIDE KELY SLIDE.

SUNG BY **MAGGIE CLINE.**

❈❈❈ | 4 | ❈❈❈

NEW YORK.
Published by Frank Harding.

(COPYRIGHTED. ALL RIGHTS RESERVED.

Musical Million, 39 Wych Street, Strand, London, England.

bench when an opposing batter hit a foul fly out of the reach of his teammates on the field. "Kelly now catching for Chicago," thundered Mike as he ran over and speared the ball. Playing the outfield in another game, he realized that the fast-falling darkness would soon end the contest. With two outs and the tying run on third, a long fly was hit in King's direction. Kelly ran back, feigned a catch, and nonchalantly began to trot in. The game was called—Kelly had won another for Chicago.

"Who is that old fossil trying to tell me how to hit?" inquired an irritated rookie, Billy Rogell, at a Red Sox training camp in the mid '20s.

"His name is Hugh Duffy," came the reply, "and he once hit four thirty-eight."

While Boston finished on top of the National League no less than eight times during the first quarter century of the league, its real claim to a dynasty occurred during the nineties. Led by the brainy Frank Selee, the Beaneaters captured the flag from '91 through '93, and then repeated in '97 and '98. Looking back, it's impossible to determine which one of those teams was the strongest. One thing is certain: several great and colorful ballplayers wore the Beaneaters' spangles during the halcyon days of the National League in Boston.

The pitching ace was unquestionably Charles ("Kid") Nichols. During each of the pennant-winning years (plus two others) the Kid won over 30 games. Nichols never developed a curve—working with a smooth overhand delivery, he relied on speed and control. He was particularly effective against Baltimore, nearly driving their manager, Ned Hanlon, crazy.

"You always know what the Kid is going to throw," Hanlon lamented, "but he beats you anyway."

At the plate, Boston was led by 5-foot 7-inch Hugh Duffy, possessor of the highest single-season batting average in major league history. Hughie had knocked around the baseball world for five years before joining the Beaneaters—an early example of how great baseball minds can go astray.

In 1888, Duffy had belonged to Cap Anson, but the great Pop hadn't been interested. "Hughie, you fall about five inches and twenty-five pounds short of major league size," Cap said. "The boys will eat you alive."

It was the league pitchers who were eaten alive, particularly in '94, when Duffy hit .438. "I never thought much of it at the time," chuckled an aging Duffy fifty years later. "If I'd known how many people were going to say, 'Yeah, but that's the year when walks counted as hits,' I wouldn't have done it." (1887 was the only year when walks counted as hits—Tip O'Neill hit a very inflated .492.)

Duffy's pal in the outfield was Tom McCarthy, the second member of "the Heavenly Twins." "McCarthy was the heavenly one,"

Duffy always maintained. "He was the smartest player I ever saw." Perhaps he was. It was McCarthy who was responsible for changing the rule governing when a player may leave his base after a fly ball. Tom would let the ball hit his glove, then juggle it as he ran into the infield. He wouldn't take full possession until it was impossible for any runner to advance.

Boston's second base combination during most of this time consisted of Bobby Lowe and Herman ("Germany") Long, complete opposites: Lowe was quiet, Long gregarious. "Germany talks enough for both of us," answered Bobby when he was once asked why he was so quiet.

But Bobby wasn't quiet one afternoon in 1894, at the Boston Congress Street grounds. He led off the third inning with a home run, and followed with another as the Beaneaters batted around. He hit another homer in the fifth and his fourth in the sixth, the first time four home runs had been hit in a league game. The fans went wild. They stopped the game and showered $160 worth of silver on Bobby. Fame is fleeting. When Lowe came up in the eighth, all he could do was single.

"What's the matter, Bobby?" a heckler asked. "Getting weak?"

Fred Tenney and Jimmy Collins joined the team at the corners for the championships of '97 and '98, Tenney straight from the Brown University campus and Collins from the sandlots of

Above: *Beaneaters "brainy" manager Frank Selee and the team's 30-game winner, Charles ("Kid") Nichols. Opposite:* Ned Hanlon, the originator of inside, or "Oriole" baseball.

Buffalo, New York. Fred hit over .300 seven times for the Beaneaters, and Collins has been considered the greatest third baseman of all. He was the first to develop the quick, bare-handed pick-up-and-throw movement on slowly hit balls. Another who had arrived for the last two winning seasons was outfielder "Sliding Billy" Hamilton. At first glance the record book calls Hamilton the greatest base stealer of all time. But much of Billy's career spanned that time when an extra base taken on a hit was scored as a stolen base. His averages of .343 and .369 are not inflated, however; Billy's bat was a tremendous asset for the last two great years of the Beaneaters.

Selee's part in all this was strategical. "Frank was a great judge of players," acknowledged Bobby Lowe, "and a grand planner. But once the game started, he let us more or less develop our own plays."

No one was more aware of this than Selee. When once asked what he felt was the reason for his success, Frank replied, "My success in baseball has been due, in part, to the consistent people I have associated with." Or, as Casey Stengel quipped sixty years later, "I could never have done it without my players."

"Mr. Keeler, how can a man your size hit four thirty-two?"

"Simple," replied Wee Willie, "I keep my eyes clear, and I hit 'em where they ain't."

The movement of Chris Vonderhorst's Baltimore team into the National League in 1892 could hardly be called earthshaking. The combined powers of the Greek oracles, Macbeth's witches, and Bridie Murphy could not have predicted what the move would mean to baseball—yet it caused a revolution that rivals those begun by Babe Ruth's home runs and the advent of black players.

Baltimore's start was anything but auspicious. Finishing twelfth in a twelve-team league in '92 did not foster optimism, nor did the hiring of a journeyman manager named Ned Hanlon. But it was during the years of '92 and '93 that Ned began the maneuvering that terminated in one of baseball's greatest turnabouts.

Hanlon's first move was to dispose of his predecessor, former player-manager George ("Rip") Van Haltren. Ned sent Rip to Pittsburgh for a twenty-year-old rookie, Joe Kelley. Trading an established star for an unknown was no more popular eighty years ago than it is today, but the team was so bad that no one cared.

Then Hanlon turned down a deal—as smart

a move as many of the trades he made. Cap Anson had been watching a certain eighteen-year-old utility infielder of Hanlon's, and he approached Ned with a proposition.

"I notice you're not playing that fighting young rooster, John McGraw," stated Anson. "I'll give you Jim Ryan for him."

"No thanks, Cap," returned Ned. "He's one rooster I want to keep."

Next came a transaction with Louisville that showed Hanlon to be either an absolute genius or the luckiest cuss in baseball. He sent his hard-hitting shortstop, Tim O'Rourke, to Kentucky for weak-hitting (.222) Hughie Jennings. The cranks couldn't believe this one, but the Orioles started to play better ball. When the season of '93 ended, they were four notches higher in the standings.

Before the start of the next season, Hanlon pulled one more surprise, his coup of coups. Twenty-one-year-old Willie Keeler had hit over .300 wherever he had played, but he had a problem that had caused such sages as John Montgomery Ward and Charlie Ebbets to turn their backs. It wasn't that Keeler was short—many of the players were short. Willie was a runt. Whenever anyone would point out that he was 5 feet

*Dan Brouthers poses for a publicity shot that used a
ball suspended by wire. Brouthers came to Baltimore in 1894
in a trade that also brought the Orioles Willie Keeler.*

4 inches, the wee one would laughingly rise to his full height and bellow, "The hell you say. I'm five feet four and one-half inches." His height didn't bother Hanlon—when the manager made his move to acquire aging, but still hard-hitting, Dan Brouthers from Brooklyn, he nabbed Keeler as a throw-in.

When opening day arrived in '94, Hanlon fielded a lineup containing no less than six future Hall of Famers: McGraw, Keeler, Kelley, Jennings, Wilbert Robinson, and Brouthers. All but Brouthers would form the heart of the Orioles for the next half decade, a period that is now referred to as the real beginning of inside, or Oriole, baseball.

With assists from the rules committee and the groundkeeper, Baltimore began the march to greatness. A recent league ruling had moved the pitcher's mound from 50 feet to 60 feet 6 inches from the plate, prompting Hanlon to drill his batters on bunting. Tom Murphy, custodian of the field, was then instructed to grow the grass as high as possible near the foul lines. Every effort would be made to keep the bunts fair.

Starting the season against Giants' ace Amos Rusie, McGraw laid one down toward the high grass, reaching first easily. The magician with a bat, Wee Willie, was next. McGraw faked a steal on the first pitch, establishing the fact that it was the shortstop's job to cover second base. Then McGraw went down for real, and Keeler handsomely poked one through the hole at short. While the Orioles did not invent this play, they perfected it.

With another assist from Mr. Murphy, the infield was kept as hard as a rock, which made for uncommonly big bounces—high enough to allow the Orioles to reach first safely. Swinging down on the ball, the hitters developed the knack of bouncing the ball off either the plate or the cementlike infield. They engulfed poor Rusie that opening day with "Baltimore Chops." It also appeared to Amos that every time an Orioles player reached first, he'd move on. Before the season ended, six of the regulars had racked up thirty or more steals.

It wasn't only on offense that Baltimore startled the Giants. A promising New York rally was killed by a perfectly executed cut-off play (an Orioles invention), while another died when catcher Robinson magnificently faked a throw to second only to turn and nail the other runner at third.

"This isn't baseball they're playing," lamented Monty Ward, Giants manager, "it's an entirely different game. I'm going to bring them up before Young [league president]."

He never did. Baltimore swept the Giants four straight, warming up for a big series with the defending champion Boston Beaneaters. When Nichols faced them in the ninth, with a 3–1 lead, it appeared that they had met their match. Then John and Willie did their thing. Nichols blew up, and Baltimore pushed across 14 runs. Incredible as it seems, McGraw and Keeler pulled their hit-and-run play against Boston 13 consecutive times before they were stopped.

Not all of the Orioles' strategy was within the rules, and sometimes it boomeranged. One of their nifty tricks was to instruct their dependable Mr. Murphy to let the grass grow extra long in strategic places in the outfield. They would then cache extra balls in these pockets of meadow. During a game with St. Louis, "Buttermilk" Tommy Dowd hit one toward the gap, only to be thrown out at second by Joe Kelley. A short time later Orioles' outfielder Steve Brodie heaved the original ball into third.

"What the hell's going on?" roared old Buttermilk. "These rogues have a fake ball." Indeed they did, and this time the Orioles had to forfeit a game.

Another beauty was McGraw's belt trick. John would frequently insert his hand inside the belt of a runner tagging up at third—the delay would be long enough to keep the man from scoring. It didn't work with Pete Browning. Unbeknownst to McGraw, he had unfastened his belt, and McGraw ended up facing the crowd with Pete's belt in his hand, while Browning, desperately clinging to his pants, crossed the plate.

As the season progressed, it became obvious that the Orioles were a changed nine. If the team had a problem, it was on the mound. During the five-year stretch from '94 to '98, only Bill Hoffer could put strong seasons back to back. Still, it's easy to see how they would win without great pitching—the '94 batting averages were: McGraw, .340; Keeler, .367; Kelley, .391; Brouthers, .344; Jennings, .332; Brodie, .369; Reitz, .306; and Robinson, .348. It was this hitting that won 24 of the last 25 games in September, and the pennant.

"We would've won all twenty-five," complained McGraw, "if Robbie hadn't slipped going after a foul fly. The clumsy ox."

It was the same story in '95 and '96; they placed second in '97 and '98. By the turn of the century, inside, scientific baseball had been firmly established. The do-or-die Orioles' style dominated the game until Ruth & Co. overshadowed it with the long ball.

In 1927, Wilbert Robinson, then managing Brooklyn, witnessed the Yankees' sweep of the Pirates in the World Series. An enterprising scribe cornered the jovial Robinson. "How do you think the old Orioles would have done against this Yankees team?" the writer asked.

The now rotund Wilbert nostalgically studied the question, shook his head, and mused, "They would have murdered us!"

"The saloon and the brothel are the evils of the baseball world at the present day."

—Henry Chadwick, 1889

Do 60 wins in one season seem preposterous? It happened in 1884, the year Charlie ("Old Hoss") Radbourn saved the day. With Charlie Sweeney, Radbourn was trying to pitch his Providence Grays club to the pennant over Charlie Buffinton and the Boston Beaneaters. Buff was a Fall River lad, and the race intensified that summer whenever Providence and Boston met.

Sweeney, a colossal "lusher," went on a toot in August. It ended with a dunking in Narragansett Bay to bring him around. The Grays' manager, Frank Bancroft, began to read Sweeney the riot act, and Charlie countered with the time-honored "go boil yer shirt." He then quit the team, and joined St. Louis in Frank Lucas' Union Association. The Grays seemed doomed, but up stepped the Old Hoss.

"Do you want to win the pennant?" Radbourn asked.

"You're damn right," Bancroft roared back.

"Then let me pitch all the rest."

"Go ahead," said Bancroft, "you're the best we have."

And pitch he did—the last 27 games in a row, winning 26, including a 1–0, 16-inning job against Buffinton when a home run went through a hole in the fence at Boston. His feat gave Providence the flag, and the opportunity to meet the New York Metropolitans of the American Association.

Touted as the first fully sanctioned post-season playoff, it ended up a romp for Old Hoss. The first two games he bettered the Mets' ace, Tim Keefe, 6–0 and 3–1. "He's too much for me," lamented Tim. "I want to umpire the next one." He did, and watched Radbourn finish off the Mets, 12–2.

It wasn't exactly baseball as they play it now (it took six balls for a walk and four strikes for a strikeout), but it was the game as they played it then, and Radbourn won the 60.

34

Above: *The fiery and brilliant John McGraw.* Opposite left: *Pitcher Radbourn batted fourth for his team.* Opposite right: *The period's outstanding catcher, Buck Ewing.*

BUFFALO.	OFFICIAL SCORE CARD, JULY 7, 1884.	THURSTONE & CO.'S
RED STOCKINGS.	1 2 3 4 5 6 7 8 9 10 At Bat. R. H R T.B. P.O. A. E.	**Great Drug House**
O'Rourke — l f		420 Main St., Next to Erie Co. Sav. B'k.
Rowe — c		Store doors open all night, with competent clerks in attendance to compound prescriptions.
Richardson — 2 b		
Brouthers — 1 b		**Chase & Comstock**
White — 3 b		LEADING HATTERS,
Lillie — r f		249 Main St.
Force — s s		SOLE AGENTS YOUMANS'
Myers — c f		Celebrated Hats.
Galvin — p		THE NEW
Runs.		"GENESEE"
Totals.		C. ZOBELMAN, Proprietor.
Earned Runs.	Game began.	
1st Base on Errors.	1st to Bat.	CLARENDON HOTEL, Saratoga Springs, N.Y.
Umpire. BURNS.	**ALTMAN & CO., CLOTHIERS,** 68, 70 and 72 Seneca, cor. Ellicott Sts. The only manufacturers who retail clothing and furnishing goods in Buffalo.	
PROVIDENCE.	OFFICIAL SCORE CARD, JULY 7, 1884.	**MICHIGAN CENTRAL**
BLUE STOCKINGS.	1 2 3 4 5 6 7 8 9 10 At Bat. R. H R T.B. P.O. A. E.	"The Niagara Falls Route —TO—
Hines — c f		Detroit, Toledo, Chicago And all points west.
Farrell — 2 b		"DINING CAR ROUTE."
Start — 1 b		General Office, Buffalo, 37 Exchange St.
Radbourn — p		
Irwin — s s		TAKE THE
Denny — 3 b		**West Shore Route** —FOR—
Carroll — l f		NEW YORK, BOSTON And all points east.
Gilligan — c		CITY OFFICE, 3 Exchange Street.
Radford — r f		
Runs.		**Dennis' Natatorium.**
Totals.		Gentlemen and Ladies'
Earned Runs.	Game ended.	**Swimming School.** The finest bathing accommodations in the city.
1st Base on Errors.	Score—B P	Putnam and Simons Baths. Everything new and first-class. Baths 25 cts., including suits, lockers, etc. Only five minutes' walk from Hall Grounds.
PROVIDENCE Tuesday and Wednesday.	**STANDING OF CLUBS TO DATE.** First figures indicate games won; second figures, games lost. Boston, 38-12; New York, 32-20; Chicago, 24-26; Cleveland, 20-29; Prov'nce, 36-14; Buffalo, 25-23; Philad'l'a, 16-38; Detroit, 11-40 EVERY SATURDAY—"CHILDREN'S DAY."	James Allen and Wadsworth Streets.

"*My big fellows! My Giants! We are the people!*"

—New York manager Jim Mutrie, 1885

New York returned to the National League in '83, replacing the bankrupt Troy franchise. John Day, the team's owner, also controlled the Mets in the American Association, which allowed him to maneuver players from one team to another to suit his purposes.

While the Troy team had never amounted to much, it did boast some stars who would shine brightly for New York. Two were the twin right-handed aces "Smiling Mickey" Welch and Tim Keefe. Welch may have been the greatest beer drinker of his day. With his famous couplet, he actually credited the suds for his success:

"Pure elixir of malt and hops,
Beats all the drugs and all the drops."

Keefe, the more sober of the two, designed the Giants' uniform—black with white lettering, the same uniform that John McGraw used in the next century for his World Series team of '05. There was also the hard-hitting first baseman, Roger Connor, and most important of all, the catcher, Buck Ewing.

"Jim Mutrie was our manager," explained a venerable Mickey Welch in the 1930s, "but Buck was our captain and really ran the team on the field." Actually, as it was on most teams, Mutrie was the business manager and Ewing acted as a manager does today.

Ewing was also the charismatic leader, New York's first sports superstar. In '85, Buck came to bat in the tenth inning of a scoreless game. After singling, he stole second and third and then faced the crowd. "It's getting late," he announced. "I'm going to steal home and we can then all have dinner." He did just that. Someone made a gaudy lithograph entitled "Ewing's Famous Slide," which soon adorned most of New York's saloons.

With Keefe and Welch winning 59 games between them, aided by the brainy Montgomery Ward and durable "Orator" Jim O'Rourke, Ewing's Giants won the flag in '88 over Anson's White Stockings. The next year saw the Giants repeat in one of early baseball's great pennant races. The Beaneaters had become a factor again, and they chased New York down to the last game of the season. On the final day, Boston's John Clarkson tried to win his fiftieth game of the season, but ran out of fuel. New York's Hank O'Day (later a famous umpire) had beaten Cleveland, winning the pennant. Buck calmly walked over to Jim Mutrie and smashed his top hat.

35

Postseason baseball started as far back as '82 with an aborted attempt between the winners of the National League and the American Association to establish a real national champion. They tried just about every formula imaginable, including a wearisome 15-game affair in '87 between Detroit and Chicago, played in various cities throughout the country. The next year it was ten games between New York and St. Louis. Amazingly enough, they played the last two games at St. Louis after the Giants had won the series, lame duck affairs that amassed a total of 1,123 paying customers. All in all, they tried eight such World Series that never really captured the imagination of the country.

The one exception was in 1886, the only series won by the association; it is the one whose formula most closely resembles the highly successful World Series of today. The ingredients were there—the last of Cap Anson's great White Stockings teams and Charlie Comiskey's colorful St. Louis Browns, to play a best-of-seven series.

Kelly and Anson had batted .388 and .371, finishing first and second in the National League. It was Mike's best year—"the King" scored an unbelievable 155 tallies in 118 games. Project that into a modern season, and you have over 200 runs. John Clarkson had picked up 36 wins while Jim McCormick had 29; Jocko Flynn was low man with 24. The team was considered so good that they didn't particularly want to play St. Louis. They'd just win four straight, not make much money, and impress no one. Then Anson and Spalding came up with a unique idea; they'd play all right, but on their terms.

"Oh, we'll play you, but under one condition," Anson informed Comiskey, "that the winner take every penny of the gate."

Charlie was crushed. He couldn't see any way that his eccentric boss, Chris Von der Ahe, would agree to such a proposal from the White Stockings.

Much to Comiskey's surprise, Chris accepted. "Sure, ve vill play them fellows and show them ve are ze boss. No club is goot enough to beat my Brownies."

Von der Ahe was one of baseball's great characters. With a nose like W. C. Fields' and a thirst to match, he was a caricature of the music hall German comedians of the period. He once belabored his fellow American Association club owners for scheduling so many of his home games when it rained.

"I don't vant to be greedy," complained Chris, "but next year I vant ze goot games in St. Louie vhen it doesn't rain. Let it rain in Zinzinnati or on that dumkopf Vonderhorst [Baltimore's owner] for ze goot games. Not in St. Louie."

If Chris was something out of a comic opera, his team wasn't. Led by Comiskey at first base, they had won the association by 12 games and featured such stalwarts as Tip O'Neill, 41-game winning Dave Foutz, and Arlie Latham, "the Freshest Man on Earth." The baseball cranks may have looked at them as hopeless underdogs, but it was a sentiment the Browns didn't share.

With the temperamental Clarkson in complete control, Chicago made the bucket shops look good by "Chicagoing" St. Louis in the first of the three to be played at Chicago, 6–0. Then came the shocker: led by O'Neill's two home runs, the Browns jumped all over Jim McCormick, 12–0.

"We just had an off day," jeered Anson. "Watch tomorrow." The Cap seemed right as Chicago blasted out an 11–4 win, which featured a tremendous home run by Kelly. Chicago moved to St. Louis with a 2–1 lead. If they'd known what awaited them, they would have stayed home.

Playing before their heavy beer drinking and vociferous St. Louis fans, the Browns awoke with a fury, easily capturing the next two games. The stage was set for the final bout, one of the most famous contests in the history of baseball. With his back to the wall, Anson came back with Clarkson; Comiskey used Bob Caruthers.

"Anson was as grim as a Western gunfighter as he warmed to the task," wrote a scribe of the period. He gave it all he had to stave off an incredible humiliation for his league. Even the gregarious Kelly was humorless as he carped on every decision that went against Chicago.

Chicago pecked away at Caruthers, taking a 3–0 lead into the eighth. Then the Browns came to life as they scored their first run. The tension continued to mount when they put men on first and second, bringing the 10,000 spectators (a huge crowd for the '80s) to their feet. Up to the plate stepped their hero, Arlie Latham.

The scrappy third baseman waved to the crowd and thundered, "Don't get nervous, folks, I'll tie it up." And that's just what he did, tripling to left field. The fans were now hysterical, crushing derbies and breaking canes as they pleaded for still another run. But Latham died at third and the game went into extra innings. After holding Chicago in the tenth, the Browns moved in for the kill. Curt Welch opened the

THE MONARCHS OF THE SPHERE.

The Browns were the only American Association team to defeat a National League team, and their owner saw to it that they were appropriately glorified.

inning by sticking his shoulder in front of a pitch and starting for first base.

"Oh, no," admonished Kelly, "that black-guard is always doing that." The umpire agreed and called Welch back.

"I'll show that lusher Kelly," the infuriated Curt screamed to the crowd. He followed his boast with a single over second. An error and a sacrifice later, Curt was standing on third with only one out. The crowd hushed as Clarkson looked at Welch, faced the plate, and let fly a high, inside pitch. Kelly leaped but could only deflect the errant pitch; in came Welch with what will always be known as the "$15,000 slide." The "beer and whiskey boys" had humbled the mighty National League.

The impact of the series on the country was tremendous. Never before had so much interest been shown a sporting event. Cranks all over the country crowded telegraph offices for the results; saloons and poolrooms employed "the chalk with which you mark the base ball score" to keep their patrons informed; papers brought out sports extras for three cents; people in Boston and Detroit showed as much interest in the game as they would have if their own cities had been involved.

No one was happier than Chris. He went out and had a statue of himself made. (It was eventually placed on his grave.) Later years were tough on Chris—he lost just about everything. But for the season of '87 he could drive his players around in open barouches with brightly colored blankets on the horses proclaiming, "St. Louis Browns, Champions of the World."

"Mr. Chairman and Gentlemen, I claim the right of addressing a few words to this League."

—Albert G. Spalding
National League meeting
December 11, 1901

When it comes to early National League history, it can truly be said that Al Spalding was "a man for all seasons." He had been there at the birth, and had been the star on the league's first pennant-winning team. As Chicago manager and executive, he had been a guiding light in all league decisions. It was Spalding who had first taken the players around the world, and Spalding who had engineered the first big player sale (King Kelly to Boston for $10,000). When the no-holds-barred struggle was waged against the competing Players' League in 1890, he directed the "war committee" to a victorious conclusion. After all, it was Spalding baseballs they were playing with—his stake in the league was a little higher than that of anyone else.

Thus, when the National League faced a double-barreled threat—the American League and syndicated baseball—at the turn of the century, it was left to Albert to step in once again and render yeoman service.

By the annual meeting of December, 1901, the National League had to face the fact that Ban Johnson's rival league was a fait accompli. Realizing that many of their stars would jump to the new league (Cy Young, Nap Lajoie, and Willie Keeler were already gone), one group's solution was to "syndicate" baseball. Paced by the highly controversial Giants owner, Andrew Freeman, four teams (New York, Boston, St. Louis, and Cincinnati) pushed to form a baseball trust. The league, led by Freeman, would then hold all the stock in the clubs and pay out yearly dividends. The players themselves could be moved around at the owners' will, being used wherever they seemed to be needed—in short, the teams would lose their real identity.

"Freeman is a baseball traitor, a baseball marplot," challenged Spalding. "In fact, a baseball impossibility. I must get him out of the National League." And in one of the game's most dramatic hours, that is exactly what he did.

Although no longer active in the management of the Chicago club, and having no real right to address the club owners, the now highly successful sporting goods manufacturer burst in on their crucial syndicated baseball meeting in New York City, the last month of 1901. To Spalding, Freeman's plan meant the demise of the league as he knew it; he faced the group with his plea.

"This National League has two fathers: one, William A. Hulbert—God bless his memory—and the other, myself. Twenty-six years ago this month, I spent thirty days in Mr. Hulbert's house with him, writing the first constitution; and I claim, because of that, because of the fact that I have been unanimously elected an honorary member of this body, that I have the right to speak to its councils."

As it was when Oliver Cromwell walked in on the "Rump Parliament," no one present would dare to throw him out. He continued to plead his case:

"We have a very sick patient here—as I read in the papers—a very sick patient. I think it is time that somebody asked some questions to find out what has brought it to this condition. Emaciated in form, pulse weak, heart fluttering; and yet we see a few motions of the muscles that indicate that life is not extinct. Gentlemen, as an honorary member of this league, if it is to die, I propose to stay by that corpse until it is buried. I sincerely hope that I am misinformed."

Barney Dreyfuss, Pittsburgh owner, nominated Spalding for the presidency, splitting the league into two factions; Freeman's group lined up against Brooklyn, Pittsburgh, Chicago, and Philadelphia, which opted for Spalding. Over the next three days they balloted and each time it was the same—four for Spalding and four to continue Nick Young as president.

Then, at one o'clock in the morning of December 14, the Spalding backers made their move. Young and the Freeman group had departed, when Colonel Rogers of the Philadelphia team addressed the remaining baseball magnates: "Once a quorum, always a quorum," stated the good Colonel. "I nominate Albert Spalding." Naturally, it carried. Spalding was awakened and told the news. He immediately proceeded to Young's room and demanded the league files. The drowsy "ex-president" told him he was crazy, but as they argued, porters carried out the records.

The next morning, as expected, only the four pro-Spalding members attended the first meeting. Freeman, however, had sent his secretary and codelegate to find out what was going on. The minute the Freeman representative put one foot in the room, Spalding declared a quorum and the meeting proceeded.

Spalding's position was challenged. Injunctions were filed and counterfiled. Weeks went by as the battle continued in courts. People began to worry about what would happen to the season of '02.

Spalding played his last trump in March. He offered to resign if Freeman would get out of baseball and take the trust scheme with him. Spalding's ruse worked. He had traded a job he didn't want (and didn't really have) for the elimination of syndicated baseball. Freeman sold, and with him went his scheme to turn the National League into a private holding company. Peace was established with the American League, and the real history of the major leagues as we know them today began. The National League faced the twentieth century united.

Account and box score of first National League game, won by Boston over Philadelphia 6–5. Teams committed 26 errors and earned only 3 of their 11 runs.

40

"I Think We Had More Fun . . ."

41

And there used to be a ball park,
Where the field was warm and green,
And the people played their crazy game
With a joy I've never seen.
And the air was filled with wonder,
From the hotdogs and the beer,
Yes there used to be a ball park
Right here.

Joe Raposo's lyrics, as sung by Sinatra, evoke a sense of longing, in general terms for times past, more specifically for ball parks to which today's symmetrically steeled, artificially turfed stadiums bear no resemblance. Of the twelve teams that make up the National League in 1976, only two, the Montreal Expos and the Chicago Cubs, play in what can be properly termed old ball parks, and only one club, the Cubs, considers its home permanent. But if Raposo is sad because of the change in ball parks, the same cannot be said for millions of fans who pay to see baseball played every year in the multi-tiered, multicolored arenas.

The contrasts between today's stadiums and yesterday's ball parks are only one indication of the enormous changes that have taken place during the one-hundred-year history of the senior circuit. Players wear gloves three times the size of a human hand where once they caught with bare skin. A rookie today may hit twenty or thirty home runs his first season; in 1911, a man named Frank Baker hit two of his season's total of eleven in the Series against the Giants and became known forever as "Home Run" Baker. Uniforms today are skin tight, stretchable, light-weight, and sleek. In 1876, the uniform of the day included a bow tie.

To be sure, some things haven't changed all that much. Since the turn of the century the rules have remained more or less the same, the season lasts just about as long, and legendary heroes slumber in Cooperstown while superstars of another generation carry on the work. But there *have* been changes, some necessary, some quite wonderful, some possibly regrettable, and the contrasts are there for us to dwell on.

It is no longer possible for a baseball club owner to virtually defraud a player. It wasn't always thus. For most of the past century, players in the National League, and their American League counterparts as well, have been offered salaries on a "take it or leave it" basis.

Heinie Zimmerman, starting in 1907, played many years for the Cubs. Before his arrival at major league status, he had played just six weeks when his club owner sadly gathered the players around him and announced, "Boys, the ball club is bankrupt. But don't you worry. I'm paying off right now in alphabetical order." By the time the owner reached the J's, he had run out of funds. Zimmerman managed to bum a lift home. A month later, the owner made a financial rally and once again summoned his players. Zimmerman, reporting for work, was greeted by the owner.

"Let's see now, you're Zimmerman, with a Z, aren't you?"

"Not even close," shot back Heinie. "I'm Adams, with an A."

It has only been recently that athletes, in addition to drawing implausibly large salaries, have been able to add to their incomes by endorsements. The baseball agent has become a fact of baseball life. With the coming of the agent, baseball has taken on an image it never had before.

In contrast, Jesse Haines describes the time in the late twenties when he won 24 games for St. Louis and discussed salary terms with the owner, Sam Breadon. "Breadon was a mean one with a dollar," says Haines. "The year after I won twenty-four, I wanted to talk salary with Branch Rickey, rather than Breadon, and even Rickey was no Santa Claus. So I went to St. Louis, Rickey was out of town, and Breadon cornered me. He said he supposed I was there to talk contract and said, 'You had a pretty good year, Jesse. I'm going to give you a five hundred dollar raise.'"

Haines says he felt like "falling through the floor." Ultimately, he came to terms with Rickey, not Breadon, and was rewarded with more than a $500 raise.

Frank McCormick, the big Cincinnati first baseman who was the National League's most valuable player in 1940, made less than $500 in endorsements following his banner year. "I was paid five hundred dollars for a cigarette endorsement that was run all over the country," he says, "but I had to kick back fifty dollars for the man who arranged it. We had speaking engagements, too, but we never got paid. Sometimes we didn't even get expenses. We were glad to keep our name in front of the public."

In contrast, modern ballplayers are paid to such an extent that events like the World Series and the All-Star Game are sometimes inconsequential from the standpoint of added income except for what is added to the overall players' pension fund.

Burleigh Grimes, the old war-horse who broke in with Pittsburgh in 1916, was asked to

Cartoonist Willard Mullin took pains to point
out the spiraling salaries during the 1930s. Only
the best players were offered bonuses, however.

comment on the huge amounts of money paid out today in baseball. Grimes shrugged his shoulders and, without envy, said, "I think we had more fun when I was playing."

Max Carey, Hall of Fame outfielder with Pittsburgh and later Brooklyn, broke into the majors in 1910. When he was asked who scouted him, he laughed.

"Who scouted me?" Max repeated incredulously. "I scouted myself. My mother, in a way, forced me into the game. She complained one day about the problems of feeding five boys on two dollars and fifty cents a week. My father died suddenly, leaving my mother with five sons, aged ten and under. So I started playing sandlot ball for money at the age of fifteen. It helped support the family."

Carey's ultimate big league future was similar in detail to virtually all those of his contemporaries. Max had no agent, no lawyer, no adviser, and no help in his contract negotiations. It wasn't until the National League had under-

gone some fifty years of change that the so-called "scout" was invented. The true baseball agent didn't arrive until still later.

Even in the teenage days of Stan Musial, whose batting style once was described as one that enabled him to "peek at you around corners," luck, rather than any master scouting plan, led to his useful baseball life in St. Louis. Musial, who was to make his hometown of Donora, Pennsylvania, famous, began his playing career in the Penn State League. His manager, Andy Frank, had a friend in the Cardinals' front office, so Frank suggested the Redbirds take a look at the young man.

"Did you receive a bonus when you signed with the Cardinals' organization?" Musial was asked.

"Bonus?" said Musial. "Unheard of in 1940."

It wasn't necessary for Musial to point out that financial standards in Donora, in 1940, weren't quite the same as those in 1975 Ahoskie, Hertford County, North Carolina, where Catfish Hunter made his home.

Musial was a product of the Cardinals' notoriously extensive farm system. An idea spawned by Branch Rickey, the farm system had become the incubator for many major league stars. It was also destined to create controversy. Major league teams would often try to "bury" a ballplayer in some obscure minor league city, even going as far as to order the future star benched (so as not to attract attention to his statistics) until there was room for him on the varsity roster. The Dodgers outsmarted themselves by trying to hide a young Puerto Rican named Clemente in this fashion, but the Pirates found him anyway. Because Brooklyn had failed to place Clemente on their major league roster (so they could keep all the players they already were using), Pittsburgh claimed him. Clemente had some rather remarkable years in the Three Rivers city. Branch Rickey lives in baseball history, not only as a shrewd manipulator of diamond talent, but also as a man who had a "pocketful of teams."

A ritual of major league baseball almost since the birth of the National League, spring training has developed into an ordeal for the majority of the players. It's a bonus only for the fan, because the baseball season never ends. Today, most players think the spring training season is too long. Modern athletes believe a month, at most, beneath the palm fronds, would be sufficient.

Managers and coaches take a different view.

Opposite: *Grover Alexander, after retiring from the National League, continued to apply his trade for a living.*
Below: *Training camps in the 1930s and 1940s* (top) *stressed group practice; those of today* (bottom) *encourage individuality.*

It is the only time of year they can test their market without jeopardizing their chances to win a pennant. As Bobby Bragan, former manager of the Pirates, expressed it, "I always liked spring training because there was no pressure. Coincidentally, it was a boon to married life as well. My wife used to say, during spring training, that there never was any silence at the dinner table because of games we might have won."

It's also a fact that spring training, of itself, has produced many major leaguers who otherwise might not have blossomed as soon as they did. Carl Furillo, the fine outfielder who played 15 years for the Brooklyn Dodgers, thinks spring training was the major factor in his rapid promotion to the varsity. "If it hadn't been for the exhibition games," says Carl, "I never would have had a chance to show what I could do. It might have taken me four or five years, instead of one spring, to become a regular on the Brooklyn ball club."

In baseball's younger days, spring training had just the opposite effect on newcomers.

Although the pitching machine of 1941 was more cumbersome than that of today, the batting practice cage (and the spectators) were basically the same.

Rarely did a newcomer qualify for the varsity, largely because the veterans needed the short time—four weeks at most—to get in shape. Occasionally, a National League club would indulge in two sessions. The New York Giants in the late thirties would assemble at Hot Springs, Arkansas, for two weeks of calisthenics before taking off for Florida, where they would be allowed to don uniforms and swing bats. Harry Cross, a baseball writer covering the Giants in those days, described their visit to Hot Springs with a twinkle. "The Giants arrived in Hot Springs today to take the baths and prepare for the season, just as the Indians (not Cleveland) used to do, years ago, when they would come down to Arkansas to get in shape for their tribal wars."

The airplane, of course, has long since replaced the train as a major league carrier although baseball has, in its time, offered various other means of transportation. Many clubs, in years gone by, frequently traveled by bus, or even car pool.

Whatever the mode of transportation, players would prefer not to use any of them. Griping is a universal trait of all professional athletes. Today's ballplayers complain about the long schedule and the coast-to-coast travel. The Mets in 1975 played ten games at home, flew to Los Angeles, where they immediately began an eleven-day stretch of eleven games on the West Coast, then took a day off to fly to Montreal, where they continued their road trip.

Yogi Berra, then manager of the Mets, insists he would have been able to play a few more years if it hadn't been for the evolution to airplanes. "You could relax on the trains," Berra says. "It was a fun way to travel, and a lot of us would look forward to a road trip. We'd arrive, let's say in Chicago, and feel refreshed."

Berra might be surprised to hear that a number of his predecessors take a different view. This, of course, was when the national railroad system wasn't equipped with today's comforts. Listen to Burleigh Grimes, who played 25 years before Berra:

"Hell, these ballplayers today, complaining about flying. They should have ridden some of the trains we rode. Sometimes we'd end up all night in a day coach, get into a city, and right away have to play a ball game. Remember, if you tried to open a window, you'd get covered with soot; it could get hot as hell, even if we had Pullmans. Air conditioning? We didn't know what it meant."

Jesse Haines, the fine Cardinals' pitcher, who played concurrently with Grimes:

"I'll tell you about travel in my baseball days. I remember playing a doubleheader one August in St. Louis, hot as blazes. When it was over, we had to rush like the devil to catch a train for Boston. You couldn't open the windows or else you'd get covered with cinders. So you just lay there and sweated. When we got to Boston, we had to play a game right away."

Trains did produce something the comparatively short plane ride cannot—a wealth of anecdotal material. One evening, in New York's Grand Central Station, the Dodgers, under Leo Durocher, were boarding their three private Pullman cars when an irate rookie grabbed road secretary Harold Parrott by the lapels.

"How come I'm assigned to an upper berth?" demanded the rookie. "I went four-for-four today as a regular. I thought regulars were supposed to sleep in a lower berth."

Parrott, not wishing to become involved, said he'd talk to Durocher. In a minute, he was back with a solution.

"Durocher says you are to sleep in the upper," Parrott explained. "He says you're not a regular anymore."

Travel by train helped create a camaraderie among the players that in some ways doesn't exist today. Card games of all kinds—bridge, hearts, cribbage, gin rummy—filled the spare time. Manager Joe McCarthy, of the Chicago Cubs, used to employ a bit of gamesmanship while watching his athletes at the card table.

The Cubs, under McCarthy, had a number of devoted cardplayers, not the least among them "Hack" Wilson, a center fielder of renown. Wilson loved to play hearts on road trips and McCarthy, as a kibitzer, would drive him crazy. On one occasion, Wilson made a crafty lead and McCarthy asked, "How come you save all your brains for the card table, Hack?"

Then, when Wilson would make a bonehead play, McCarthy would be the first to suggest that, "It reminds me of the way you play center field."

"You just couldn't beat him," Wilson used to say of McCarthy.

For all his kidding, though, McCarthy loved his big hitter. Speaking recently, McCarthy said of Wilson, "He loved the bright lights, but you could forgive Hack his little escapades because he was always ready the next day. Hell, today they make it a big thing when somebody knocks in a hundred runs. Hack knocked in almost two hundred one year for me. And he was loyal; you never found Hack sticking a knife in the manager's back."

Over the past 40 years accommodations for

*In the 1890s, spectators could sit in the grandstand
or stand beyond the outfield. Not everyone
had a good view since all the gentlemen wore chapeaus.*

ballplayers at hotels have improved to the point where it is possible to state that every major league club travels only first class. This in contrast to baseball's early years, when ten or twelve athletes would be assigned to a room with an equal number of cots. You could open the hotel windows without fear of being buried under cinders, but there was no air conditioning.

George ("Highpockets") Kelly, a National League first baseman from 1915 to 1932, today an octogenarian, had this to say about his playing days: "All our games were during the day—on a real hot one you could lose ten, fifteen pounds. We did drink beer and a lot of it, usually after every game. I can remember trying unsuccessfully to sleep in a hot hotel room in St. Louis with a cold-water towel over my head."

Life in a hotel for a big leaguer was often anything but routine. As Kirby Higbe, a successful National League pitcher would testify, the players were certainly allowed to get away with errant behavior more than today. Kirby recalls a 1940 doubleheader his Phillies played against the Giants in New York.

"I had lost the first game, 1–0, in the eleventh when Harry Danning hit a broken-bat homer off me. We were down to our last inning in the second game, the score tied. 'Doc' Prothro said to me, 'Hurry and warm up. Hold 'em for one inning. I don't want to lose this one, too.

"So I go in. The first batter hits an easy grounder to Del Young at short, and Del nearly takes Mayor La Guardia's head off in the box seats with his throw. The runner goes to second, so I walk the batter. A bunt pushes them over, so I walk the next batter to pitch to Ott. Ott hits an easy, shallow fly to center. The runner isn't even tagging, but Joe Marty catches the ball and unleashes a throw to the screen. I lost both games that day.

"After the game, Doc tells us to go out and get drunk. Hell, he didn't have to tell us. A group of us went up to my room at the hotel and broke into a couple of bottles. Pretty soon Del's had too much to drink and tosses an empty bottle right through the hotel window.

"It wasn't long before a cop was knocking at the door. I answered. 'Yes, officer, what can I do for you?' 'You're Kirby Higbe, aren't you?' he says. 'That's right, officer.' 'Who in hell threw that bottle out the window? Nearly went through the roof of a taxi.' 'Just a bunch of us Phillies, having a little too much to drink.'

"The cop just laughed. As he turned to leave, he smiled and said, 'Hell, I don't blame you. If I were with the Phillies I'd have thrown myself out the window.'"

It has always been true of road trips that ballplayers love to eat up a storm, at the expense of the ball club, of course. Eddie Brannick, for fifty years the "secretary for foreign affairs" of the New York Giants, loved to recall the time

48

Hank Leiber, a huge outfielder, roomed with a player whose home was in Pittsburgh. As a result, Leiber didn't have a roommate during the four-day stay in Pittsburgh. Leiber took full advantage of the situation. In the belief, so Leiber claimed, that the ball club would be charged for his roommate's meals whether they were eaten or not, Leiber enjoyed six square meals a day. Brannick assigned another player to room with Hank when the Giants next visited Pittsburgh.

Ballplayers, like the thoroughbreds they are, have always been bred to play the game on natural turf. The introduction of artificial playing surfaces in many of today's modern parks has changed the game. Many players believe it is a change for the worse. For one thing, artificial turf is hard on the legs. Chris Pelekoudas, a 29-year umpiring veteran, firmly believes that the modern surfaces will shorten the careers of umpires. If so, it must be equally true for players. Most player complaints, however, come from pitchers.

"I don't think there's a pitcher in baseball who prefers AstroTurf over grass," claims Dodgers' star Don Sutton. His pitching mate Andy Messersmith agrees. "Give me good old mother nature every time. AstroTurf gives the hitters a great advantage."

No longer is baseball likely to produce an incident like the one in 1924, when Fred Lind-strom, an eighteen-year-old rookie, was the New York Giants' starting third baseman. The World Series that year involved the Giants and the Washington Senators. In the twelfth inning of the seventh and decisive game, Earl McNeely of Washington hit what was described as a $50,000 double. McNeely's "double" would have been an easy out on artificial turf, but the ball struck a pebble, bounced over Lindstrom's head, and in came the winning run. The pebble was a topic for Hot Stove League discussion the next four months and is still mentioned in any book on baseball's factual legend.

A ball park years ago had its own character and personality. It became as much a part of a fan's life as rooting for the home team. As an example of the affection Brooklyn fans had for their beloved Ebbets Field, one gentleman from Flatbush wrote an endearing poem the day they tore down the place. The poem was called "The Park with a Broken Heart," and one verse went like this:

A Park that has done what a Park should do;
A Park that has sheltered life;
That has put its loving, concrete arms,
* around a*
Dodger fan and his wife;
A Park that has echoed a baseball song;
Held up a rookie's stumbling feet;
Is the saddest sight, when it's coming down,
That ever your eyes did meet.

Without exception, the old ball parks had eccentricities and peculiarities, none of which have been inherited by the geometric stadiums of today.

In Braves Field, hard by the railroad tracks of the Boston & Maine, there was a special bleacher section where a few die-hard fans would sit. One afternoon, exactly 12 fans were counted in this section. The Braves lost the game. A Boston writer, having counted the fans, wrote that their verdict was "guilty." Thereafter, that bleacher section was referred to as "the jury box."

Crosley Field, in Cincinnati, also had its idiosyncrasies. The ball park, situated in the heart of the city, required extra equipment when Larry MacPhail installed lights for night games. Two tall lamp posts stood just beyond the outfield wall. Glare from the lights created a hazard for batters during games after dark. As a result, two ordinary window shades were installed atop the concrete wall in right and left center as a shield for the batters' eyes. In the summer of *49*

Umpires years ago (above) worked as hard as do those of today. At Veterans Stadium in 1975, the men in blue are served refreshments (opposite).

1941, the Brooklyn Dodgers played a day game against the Reds in Crosley Field. During the usual ritual to discuss ground rules at home plate, neither manager Leo Durocher of the Dodgers nor Bill McKechnie of the Reds noticed that the shades, used only for night games, were in the down position. The shades, appearing as mere specks in the distance, managed to avoid even the umpires' usually discriminating eyes.

Came the last half of the ninth inning, with the score tied and no one out. Harry Craft, leading off for the Reds, hit a line drive that would have been a certain homer had it not ricocheted off the tiny shade in right center and caromed back onto the playing field. Craft was held to a triple. The Dodgers then retired the side and went on to win in extra innings.

In the Crosley Field press box, John McDonald, the Brooklyn traveling secretary, couldn't help asking anyone who would listen whether they thought Craft's hit could be referred to as a "shady" triple.

The building of modern baseball arenas also has removed an artistic element from the game, that of tailoring the field to the needs of one's team. When Hank Greenberg joined the Pittsburgh Pirates after World War II, Branch Rickey, who was then the club's general manager, greeted Henry with open arms and first rate accommodations in left field. Greenberg was a strong pull hitter, and most of his homers went over the left field wall. Rickey promptly moved the left field wall at Forbes Field a little closer to the plate by the simple expedient of erecting a temporary fence. The area was immediately christened "Greenberg Gardens." When Greenberg retired, Rickey removed the fence.

From the beginning, the umpire has been out there to be argued with. Nevertheless, a majority of former National Leaguers showed a genuine esteem for umpires.

"They've got a tough job," said Al Lopez, former catcher with the Dodgers, Pirates, and Braves. "They deserve what they make and shouldn't be treated like outcasts."

Billy Herman, a Hall of Famer who played second base for the Cubs, Braves, and Dodgers, agreed with Lopez but felt that today's umpires are too aloof. "When I was playing, back in the forties and fifties, we had fun with the umpires," he said. "You could talk back to them and they'd listen. I remember one particular incident involving Stan Hack.

"Stan wore a perpetual grin, but he was dead serious in uniform. Hack couldn't believe it one day when [Bill] Stewart, umpiring behind

the plate, yelled 'strike.' Hack turned to Stewart and asked if he had heard him correctly. Stewart repeated he had called the pitch a strike. Then Hack said, 'If you called that pitch a strike, Bill, I guess it'll have to be a strike. But always remember I've got great confidence in you.' A ballplayer would probably get thrown out for saying something like that today."

Joe McCarthy, a Cubs manager in the twenties and early thirties, had this to say on the subject of umpires: "They are part of the game, but a ball club that's always finding fault with the umpire is not a very good club. Umpires don't beat you. You beat yourself. Bill Klem was a honey, a great umpire. I remember one time when we were playing the Braves in Boston. Klem was umpiring at first. He wasn't having one of his better days. I went out to argue with him several times. Then he really missed one. Remember now, I had to run across the field to get to him. I went tearing over and, before I could say anything, he yelled, 'Joe, you've run at me twelve times today and you've been wrong every time.' It started me laughing.

"You remember, Klem used to say, 'I never missed one in my life.' What he meant was, he never missed one in his heart."

Times have certainly changed. Can you imagine an umpire playing by the rules of 1876? From the first official rule book:

"Should the umpire be unable to see whether a catch has been fairly made or not, he shall be at liberty to appeal to the bystanders, and to render his decision according to the fairest testimony at hand."

In the past, baseball writers, almost without exception, reported the game fairly and without bias. They were careful not to print a story that they didn't think belonged on the sports page. On one occasion, during spring training, a National League manager went on a four-day toot. The general manager of the team was informed of it by one of his subordinates.

"For heaven's sake," said the general manager, "don't tell the newspapermen."

"Don't worry yourself on that score," said the subordinate. "It was a newspaperman who told me."

Not a word of the incident ever appeared in the paper.

Thirty years ago and more, many a lasting friendship developed between baseball writers and big league ballplayers. Today's baseball writers say such associations are rare indeed.

Bobby Bragan was a friend of many writers, partly because he had a joyous sense of humor and was thus easy to write about. One year, when the Dodgers met the Yankees in a World Series, Bragan approached the club secretary, Harold Parrott. This same year a pitcher named Rex Barney was on the Dodgers' staff. Barney was a relief specialist, and that year a seldom used one. Bragan was primarily a bullpen catcher. Neither was expected to play in the Series.

"I'd like two good tickets for today's game," said Bragan to Parrott.

"Who are they for?"

"For me and Barney," answered Bragan. "We don't see so good from the bullpen."

A friendship between a writer and a ballplayer sometimes would lead to a delightful climax. Harry ("Cookie") Lavagetto became famous in 1947 when his pinch-hit double, off Bill Bevens in Ebbets Field, not only broke up a no-hit game, but drove in the tying and winning runs for Brooklyn. Throughout that summer, a *Herald Tribune* reporter had traveled with the Brooklyn ball club. Lavagetto's constant clutch hitting drove writers in the press box up the wall trying to think of new ways to describe his timely hitting. One day, in exasperation, the reporter wrote that Lavagetto was "as much at home at the plate as over a bowl of his native ravioli." He then showed the story to Cookie.

Months later, moments after Lavagetto hit his unforgettable two-bagger, he was being carried on Dodgers shoulders into the Brooklyn dressing room. He caught sight of the reporter across the jammed room, and yelled at the top of his lungs, "It was just like eatin' spaghetti!"

When Jackie Robinson broke baseball's color line in 1947, some National Leaguers were outspoken against the rookie just up from Montreal. These included a majority of the St. Louis Cardinals. If it hadn't been for Rud Rennie, an alert reporter on the old New York *Herald Tribune*, there is little doubt a Cardinals' strike would have been declared, and the National

Dodgers were taking no chances, for they knew the power of their club, and the future of the league depended on the contribution of black players. The coming of the black man to baseball may have had more impact on the game than any other change in baseball's history. It would be difficult for today's fan to think of his game without thinking of Willie Mays, Roberto Clemente, or Hank Aaron.

The changes that have taken place in the quarter century since Jackie Robinson made his major league debut have been made more off the playing field than on it. Although a majority of ballplayers may have been prejudiced in the late forties and fifties, only a minority voiced their opinions. Athletes then, as now, respect

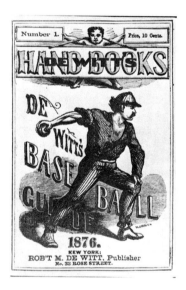 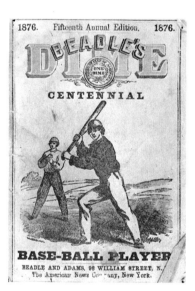 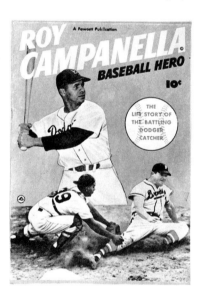

League would have been in a difficult position.

Rennie, a lifelong friend of Dr. Robert Hyland, the Cardinals' team physician, was told by the doctor of the impending insurrection. Before scooping the nation with the story, Rennie phoned the commissioner's office and told what he knew. The Cardinals in turn were instructed, in blunt terminology, that they would play against Robinson or face indefinite suspension.

There was no further talk of boycotts, insurrections, or rebellion. Before long, even though prejudice remained, Robinson gained the respect of everyone in the league—including that of Dixie Walker. Walker had been the most publicly vociferous of all the Dodgers against the appearance of Robinson, but at the end of the season apologized to Rickey. "I was wrong," he said.

52   It was too late. Walker was traded. The

another's athletic ability and if their respect is of a grudging nature, at least it is respect.

It was beyond the dugout where the black ballplayer met most of his trouble. Many states had laws that forbade the "mingling" of races. The Giants, who trained in Sanford, Florida, owned the town's respected hotel, The Mayflower. Even though the Giants' management would have welcomed black ballplayers into their hotel, state law would not permit them to do so. Black Giants would play a game in Daytona Beach and have to bus back to Sanford in soiled, soggy uniforms because at the ball park they were not permitted to use the shower facilities. Black ballplayers were not permitted in restaurants with whites, nor were they permitted access to decent hotels. They roomed instead with local families who were paid by the team. Even in major league cities such as Cincinnati, St. Louis, Philadelphia, and Chicago,

Although baseball publications might have cost the same in 1876 and 1956, the latter were far more sentimental (above right and opposite). Baseball publications today are more expensive and often void of sentimentality.

Shortly after World War I, Lieutenant Ralph Macklin Kiner returned to his home at Santa Rita, a mining town in New Mexico! There he met and married nurse Beatrice Grayson, who had served overseas with the AEF and on Oct. 27, 1922, their lusty young son, Ralph Jr., was born!

Mr. Kiner bought a bakery in Santa Rita! When Ralph was three...

CATCH THIS, RALPHIE!

I GOT IT, DAD!

Ralph helped his father deliver bread and rolls to Indians on a nearby reservation...

HERE'S YOUR BUNS, CHIEF!

ERY

R. KINER
LI-6715

But the two pals were separated when Ralph was four!

WHY ARE YOU CRYING, MAMA?

WE'RE ALONE, RALPH! YOUR DADDY IS DEAD!

DON'T WORRY, MOTHER -- I'LL TAKE CARE OF YOU ALWAYS!

I KNOW YOU WILL, RALPHIE!

The lonely mother and son moved to Alhambra, a suburb of Los Angeles! There Mrs. Kiner found work in a hospital!

I'LL BE NURSING ALL DAY, MRS. JONES! DON'T LET RALPH OUT IN THE RAIN!

I WON'T, MRS. KINER!

Even then young Ralph loved baseball!

SAFE AT SECOND!

YOU WON'T BE SAFE IF YOUR MOTHER CATCHES YOU!

LINDBERG WELCO

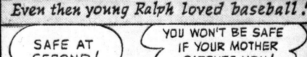

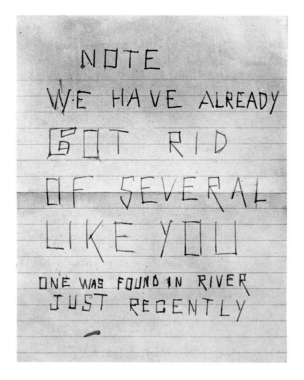

blacks were not given rooms in the same hotels as whites.

Next to travel, the most unsettling aspect of playing major league baseball for black men in the early fifties was the crowds. If there was any disappointment in making it to the big club, it was that the fans weren't any different than those in the small towns. Red-necks paid their admission and felt the price entitled them to insult the players. The black ballplayers quickly learned to either ignore the catcalls or, when that failed, to laugh at them. After all, two or three men can't take on a thousand antagonists.

Monte Irvin, a Hall of Fame player with the Giants who broke into the majors in 1949 at the age of thirty, remembers sitting in the visitors' dugout during a spring training game against Al Lopez's Indians. Cleveland's attempt at integration included a tryout at third for Minnie Minoso, and the awarding of first to big Luke Easter.

"Minoso missed an easy fly ball," Irvin recalls. "He was nervous. Some fan yelled down, 'Hey, Lopez, get that black son of a bitch outta here if you wanta win any games.' Well, an inning or two later, Minoso went behind the bag, made a nice play, and threw to first. Big Luke, he knew the play would be close, decided to make the biggest stretch of all time. He did, too. Caught the ball, the runner was out, and Luke laid on the ground in a split. He couldn't get up. Couldn't even move. Finally, they had to bring

out a stretcher and carry him away. Well, sure enough, this fan starts screaming again. 'Hey, Lopez,' he yells, 'I told you so. That's the way to get that big nigger off the field!' Know what we did in the dugout? We cracked up. We couldn't help it. Even big Luke, in spite of his pain, laughed."

A fan today would no more hurl a racial epithet from his grandstand seat than a manager would keep a black man out of the lineup. At one time, though, some teams, especially those in the American League, refused to hire blacks. If there is any single reason for the National League's superiority during the last twenty years, it is almost certainly the result of the American League's early resistance to the black player market.

Even after Jackie Robinson broke the color line, a quota system limited the number of blacks on a team. Irvin thinks the Giants could have won the pennant in 1950 had the team fielded one more black man. Irvin and Hank Thompson were already starters. The team's weakest position was third base. Ray Dandridge, an extraordinary ballplayer in his youth in the Negro leagues, was, at the age of forty, playing third base for the Giants' Triple-A farm club in Minneapolis. *Hank Thompson was the third baseman and set a record for double plays.*

"Sure, Dandridge was way past his prime," laments Irvin, "but even so, he was better than anyone the Giants had at third. He could still field, he could hit well, and he was hungry. He wanted to play in the major leagues. Hank and I pleaded with Leo [Durocher] to bring him up, but Leo said his hands were tied. I have to believe that, at that point in time, nobody wanted three black men on the field."

In today's game, prejudice, while it may exist in some quarters, is not a problem. Ironically, some concern has been voiced that perhaps not enough white ballplayers are making it to the majors. But such complaints are the result of fuzzy reasoning. Pittsburgh, in 1972, started an all-black nine. Nobody walked out of Three Rivers Stadium. In fact, the Pirates' management hadn't realized the fact until it was casually brought out a few days later.

Generally, a spirit of racial goodwill prevails throughout baseball. In 1952, Joe Black almost singlehandedly pitched the Dodgers to a pennant. Black was black. Quite naturally, he was eulogized by Brooklyn baseball writers. On the final day of the season, the writers were surprised and pleased to find a bottle of scotch next to each of their typewriters. Accompanying each bottle was a personal note from the pitcher, thanking the writers for the nice things they had

54

Above: *1951 letter threatening to kill Jackie Robinson if he were allowed to play against the Reds.*
Opposite: *George Magerkurth grapples with Brooklyn fan.*

been printing about him during the season. The brand of scotch: Black and White.

National League baseball had been played for 32 years before the memorable season of 1908, at which time two people—Jack Norworth and Albert Von Tilzer—went to work. You won't find them in the Hall of Fame, but you will find the fruits of their labor in Cooperstown. They set the game to music, composing baseball's own song, "Take Me Out to the Ball Game." The words, written by Norworth, are as true today as they were in 1908. The fans still "root, root, root for the home team." Indeed, the one facet of major league baseball that has remained constant over the years is the devotion of the fans.

In Brooklyn, when the Dodgers were the pride of Flatbush, being a Dodgers' fan was tantamount to having a second religion. The team frequently was made famous by its fans rather than by its ballplayers. Among the more illustrious citizens on the Ebbets Field fan roster was Hilda Chester, the so-called "cowbell" girl. Hilda would bring two large cowbells to the ball park. ring them incessantly, and then display a banner that proclaimed, "Hilda Is Here."

Ebbets Field also had its own musicians, in the form of the "Dodger Sym-Phoney," members of which would stroll through the stands and serenade the crowd between innings.

But perhaps the best example of dogged devotion occurred in 1938. The Dodgers, in early fall, deep in the second division, had just lost a meaningless game to the Braves. No sooner had the Braves retired the last weary Brooklyn player than an unidentified fan leaped to his feet, hurdled the guardrail near the first base box seats, and raced toward home plate. There he proceeded to rain blows on the frame of plate umpire George Magerkurth. Those who saw the "bout" still remember the ludicrous tableau of "Large Jarge," as Magerkurth was called, flat on his back as the fan punched him heavily around the head and body, obviously because he blamed Magerkurth's umpiring for the Dodgers' loss.

Magerkurth, having been rescued by Ebbets Field police, brought charges against his assailant a few days later in a Brooklyn court. The judge listened attentively to all the evidence, of which there was little on the side of the defendant, then announced his verdict.

"Six months in the workhouse."

Whereupon, to the utter consternation of the learned justice, the convicted assailant leaped three feet in the air, applauding the sentence. Unable to resist the temptation, the judge asked the accused what made him so happy about having to serve six months at hard labor.

"Your honor," explained the joyous fan, "the season's about over now. It's late September. With only six months to serve in the workhouse, I'll be out for opening game next year!"

55

The Teams

A Tale of Three Cities
The Braves

It has been the best of times and the worst of times. It's been the season of light and the season of darkness, the spring of hope and the winter of despair. That is the baseball Braves' tale of three cities, told in New England twang, Midwestern drone, and Southern drawl.

One of the best of times was 1914. In July of that year, just before World War I began, "the Miracle Braves" started their march from last to first place. Behind the pitching triumvirate of Tyler, James, and Rudolph, a trio as dear to Boston as Tinker, Evers, and Chance had been to Chicago, the Braves won 61 of their last 77 games and the National League pennant. Day in and day out for 60 straight games, George ("Lefty") Tyler, Dick Rudolph, and Bill James held the mound for the Braves.

After chasing, challenging, and, on September 8, finally passing McGraw's Giants, the Braves made it a romp, finishing on top by 10½ games. They were prodded and manipulated by manager George Stallings, a master of baseball strategy. Tyler, James, and Rudolph were the winning pitchers in 69 of the club's 94 victories. Johnny Evers, spark plug of the Cubs' famous double-play trio, anchored the Boston infield and won the Most Valuable Player award. Dashing young "Rabbit" Maranville, the Braves' all-time leader in triples, bounded after balls at shortstop and at the plate sent the opposition chasing his drives. Sturdy catcher Hank Gowdy

Boston's 1914 Miracle Braves. The prime miracle workers were three pitchers: George Tyler (second row, third from left), Bill James (third row, far left), and Dick Rudolph (first row, fourth from left).

led the team from his command post behind the plate.

In the 1914 World Series against the Philadelphia Athletics, the Miracle Braves were America's sentimental favorite—that is to say, big underdogs. Boston's Cinderella story did much to popularize and romanticize major league baseball and to excite staid New England. But few gave the Braves any chance to bring off another miracle against Connie Mack's powerful Athletics. The Braves entered the World Series with only one .300 hitter and a team batting average of .251. Philadelphia boasted its legendary $100,000 infield—Baker, Barry, McInnis, and Collins; a glittering pitching staff that included "Chief" Bender, Eddie Plank, Jack Coombs, and "Bullet Joe" Bush; and four pennants and three world championships in five years. Stallings was undaunted, even cocky. "Rudolph, James, and Tyler will stop them cold," he announced. "We are coming, and they are going."

And fast. Rudolph won the first game. James won the second game, and then the third in relief of Tyler. Rudolph won the fourth game. Thus, the underdog Braves became the first team in history to win a World Series in four straight games. And the favored Athletics lost not only a Series but a dynasty; it would be 15 years before Mack's men would again win a pennant.

Unfortunately, the Braves would do even worse. After the ecstasy of 1914 capped an era of the best of times (nine pennants in their first 39 years), it would be another 34 years, an interval of the worst of times, before the team from Boston would again finish first.

In the National League's first game, played on April 22, 1876, Boston defeated Philadelphia 6–5. Boston shortstop George Wright was the first man to bat, and his teammate Jim O'Rourke recorded the first hit. It was an auspicious debut for the Hub team, which was to experience great success before the turn of the century. Winning 39 and losing 31, the New Englanders finished fourth that first year, drew about sixty-five thousand fans, and made a profit. In 1877, Arthur H. Soden became president of the team. His name became a synonym for Boston baseball, and his cash grants to teams in financial distress helped the league survive.

With a mark of .358, James ("Deacon") White won the National League batting championship in 1877. His brother Harry steered Boston to pennants that year and the next. Pitcher Tommy Bond put together two of his three 40-victory seasons in 1877 and 1878. In 1883, there

was another pennant with a stretch drive that set the pattern of the future for Boston's pennant winners.

Three fifth-place finishes, 1885–87, and sagging attendance in Boston prompted Soden to reach for his checkbook. Michael ("King") Kelly was purchased for $10,000 from Chicago. The first time he played against his old team, the Boston team (now called "the Beaneaters") stood at attention, a band played, and this poem was read aloud:

Michael Kelly came to town.
To sing a little chanson,
He said, "I've come with Boston beans
To do up Baby Anson.
Oh, I've come high, but Yankee land
With its bright shekels bought me,
And though I didn't like to go
Ten thousand dollars caught me."

In 1888, another $10,000 caught another Chicago player, pitcher John Clarkson, forming what was called, logically enough, "the $20,000 Battery."

Frank Selee became Boston's manager in 1890. His 12-year reign would result in nine first-division finishes and five pennants. Such greats as King Kelly; base stealers Billy Hamilton and Harry Stovey; and Bobby Lowe, the first player to hit four home runs in a game, spurred the Boston offense. The team also had Hugh Duffy, whose .332 lifetime average is the highest in the club's history and whose .438 batting average in 1894 is the highest in baseball history.

Boston owed much of its success in the Gay Nineties to the speedball and sharp-breaking curve of Charlie ("Kid") Nichols. The Beaneaters finished first in 1891, 1892, 1893, 1897, and 1898; the Kid won 30 or more games a season during each of those years.

The beginning of the new century was a hopeful time for much of the rest of America, but the best the Boston National Leaguers could look forward to was change bred of failure. There were five eighth-place finishes from 1903 to 1912. The Dovey brothers came in as new owners of the team in 1906. The next season, the club had a new name, "the Doves." Four years later there was a new owner again, William Hepburn Russell, and the Doves became "the Rustlers."

In 1915, after the miracle of the year before, a season of darkness descended. The Braves dropped to second, then to third place, and then to oblivion. In Stallings' last four years, 1917–20, the team averaged a winning percentage of .429. Fred Mitchell brought the Braves in fourth in

1921. Plagued by player and owner upheavals, Boston would leave the second division of the National League only twice until after the Second World War.

In 1935, Babe Ruth signed as a free agent after the Yankees released him, played 28 games for Boston, and batted .181. The forty-year-old titan recaptured his lost youth for one day at least, on May 25 against Pittsburgh, when he blasted home runs 712, 713, and 714. The final homer was one of the very few that cleared the right field facade of the grandstand in Forbes Field. Paul Waner, playing right field, saw it go out and then watched the hobbling old man circle the bases. "Ruth could barely move about the field," Waner recalls. "When he hit the home run, he went around the bases in a fast walk."

The Yankees had Joe, the Red Sox had Dom, and Boston had the third DiMaggio, Vince. Playing for the Braves in 1938, Vince fanned 134 times, the Braves' all-time strikeout record. On the positive side, the team had its fifth batting champion in Ernie Lombardi, who batted .330 in 1942.

William ("Whitey") Wietelmann, now a coach for the San Diego Padres, played for Boston from 1939 to 1946. His time was a link between the season of darkness under manager Casey Stengel (who gave Wietelmann his nickname because of his white hair) and the age of light that would begin under manager Billy Southworth in 1946. Wietelmann remembers what it was like to be a wartime ballplayer for the hapless Braves against the scrappy Brooklyn Dodgers in their den at Ebbets Field: "Hugh Casey was pitching, and I come up to hit. The first ball was right behind my back. I don't say nothing. The second one went behind my shoulder. The next pitch hit me in the ribs. It hurt like a son of a gun. As I'm going down to first base, Leo Durocher hollered, 'How'd you like that Betty Grable?' . . . We got into some shoving. Later I couldn't get out of the stadium. I had tomatoes, eggs thrown at me. They had to take me in a cruiser to get me to the subway. But a man's never played baseball unless he's played in Brooklyn."

The end of the war brought the spring of hope to America and to the Boston Braves. Lou Perini and partners, who purchased the team in 1944, refurbished Braves Field and the team itself. Mort Cooper had come over in a trade with the Cardinals. Alvin Dark was signed off the campus of Louisiana State University for $40,000.

In 1947, Bob Elliott paced the team in RBIs and homers and became the first National

60

In 1917, Hank Gowdy, the catcher of the Miracle Braves, became the first major leaguer to enlist in the army to fight in World War I.

League third baseman to cop the Most Valuable Player award.

Recalling the prominence of Tyler, James, and Rudolph on the last Boston pennant winner, lefty Warren Spahn and righty Johnny Sain prompted the slogan "Spahn and Sain . . . and pray for rain." Their mound artistry accounted for 42 wins. "There was more than Spahn and Sain," says traveling secretary Don Davidson. "There were. a couple of guys named Bobby Hogue and Nelson Potter, but hardly anybody remembers them."

For the first time in history, the Boston National League team attracted more than a million fans to its home games, winning 86 games and finishing a highly respectable third. The next year brought the return of the best of times.

Bob Elliott's home run on September 27, 1948, clinched the team's first pennant since the miracle year of 1914. More than a million and a half Beantown rooters roared for Spahn and Sain, winners of 40 games between them; for Rookie of the Year Alvin Dark, who batted .322; for ferocious Eddie Stanky; and for the steady Tommy Holmes and Elliott.

The Cleveland Indians provided the competition in the Braves' second World Series, which was more exciting, perhaps, but ultimately far less satisfying than the first. Game one was a storybook duel between Sain and Cleveland fastball ace Bob Feller. After waiting 10 years to pitch a World Series game, Feller allowed only two hits in his first try, but lost on a play Cleveland fans still contest. With two out and two on in the bottom of the eighth, Feller apparently picked off Boston pinch runner Phil Masi at second base, but umpire Bill Stewart ruled Masi safe. "Everybody in the park saw it except the umpire," Feller lamented. Then Tommy Holmes singled, and Masi scored the game's only run.

When the Braves faced Feller again, in game five, they trailed the Indians 3–1 in games, having scored only two runs in three games off Bob Lemon, Gene Bearden, and Steve Gromek. This time, before a record-breaking crowd of 86,288 in Cleveland, they pounded the Cleveland ace, now destined never to be a winning pitcher in a World Series game. Bob Elliott smashed successive home runs off Feller, pacing Boston's 11–5 victory. However, the Braves could beat no one but Feller, and the Indians won the world championship the next day.

The Hub team slipped to fourth place in 1949, Del Crandall's rookie year, and Eddie Stanky's last in Boston. "As a young player, I was scared by him," Crandall remembers. "He used to tell me to stick the tag in the guy's ear. It was his way, not mine . . . but his attitude influenced my play in the majors."

On August 29, 1951, Johnny Sain was sent to the New York Yankees in return for $50,000 and Selva Lewis Burdette. At 5–13 after four 20-win seasons in five years for the Braves, Sain was a suddenly fallen star; Burdette was a slowly rising one who would shine his brightest against the Yankees.

Tommy Holmes replaced Southworth as manager during the season, and Boston recorded its third straight fourth-place finish. The fans sensed the good years were past. "We were playing to the grounds help," said Charlie Grimm, who replaced Holmes as manager in 1952. The Braves wound up in seventh place, their lowest finish in a decade, and lost a half million dollars. The Braves were ready to leave Boston.

A week before the start of the 1953 season, the announcement was made. In the first major league baseball franchise shift since 1900, the Braves, of Boston since 1876, became the Braves of Milwaukee. "It caught some of the players and their families in midstream," Crandall remembers. "Some of them were already headed to Boston."

They must have been further disconcerted by the passionate reception they received in Milwaukee. Thousands and thousands of exuberant and demonstrative rooters greeted their new team. They camped out on chilly spring nights to be able to purchase the coveted Opening Day tickets. They came three hours early to the games to watch batting practice, toting cowbells and picnic lunches. Through frigid football evening weather, they drank flasks of hot coffee and other drinks that warm the soul, and kept screaming for the Braves. Milwaukee County Stadium became a haven for the frenzied, and one wit was moved to call it "an insane asylum with bases."

After nine home games, the attendance of the Milwaukee Braves eclipsed that of the entire year of 1952 for the Boston Braves. By season's end, the turnstiles of modest, 35,911-seat County Stadium had clicked 1,826,397 times. Everything was up. The team batting average rose 33 points from 1952. The Braves produced 46 more home runs and 28 more victories. The team was up five places in the standings, to second place, 13 games behind the pennant-winning Dodgers. And the Braves were in the black again, by a half million dollars.

Former Milwaukee general manager John Quinn says, "I've been around for a couple of years [he began his baseball career in 1929], but I've never seen the loving way they received ballplayers there. In those first years the players paid for nothing. They were treated like royalty.... It was like a small town; some of the players lived five minutes from the ball park. Warren Spahn had his own car, but the fans wanted to do something for him so they gave him another car—for his family."

The Hall of Fame southpaw posted 23 wins that first season in Milwaukee, and a decade later recorded another 23 wins, the all-time high marks for a left-hander on the Braves. He lasted a record 21 years and accumulated more shutouts, innings pitched, and wins than any other National League left-hander. "If he lost a game," notes Davidson, "the next day he would be down early with the bullpen coach trying to find out why. He was a clown off the field, but he thrived on perfection on the field."

As the best of the arriving Braves, Spahn was a natural hero to the Milwaukee fans, but they idolized less talented ballplayers too. They cheered when Andy Pafko belly flopped after line drives. They applauded young Eddie Mathews in his awkward but unceasing efforts to master the complexities of third base, and they roared when the imperfect fielder unleashed his awesome power at the plate. They admired the speed,

grace, and daring of Billy Bruton, stolen base king from 1953 to 1955. When pitcher Max Surkont struck out eight consecutive batters, on May 25, 1953, they deluged him with more kielbasa than even big Max could consume.

Other local favorites were catcher Crandall, scrappy shortstop Johnny Logan, and slugger Joe Adcock. Crandall displayed the confidence and wisdom of a manager-to-be with an easy, graceful style of play. He seemed to lure foul pop-ups into his mitt. Logan supplemented his limited skills with fiery aggressiveness. "If you were in a fight, you'd want a guy like Logan on your side," observes Ernie Johnson, who was on Logan's side as a pitcher for the Braves in the fifties. Adcock, the first man ever to hit a ball into the center field bleachers at the Polo Grounds, continued the Braves' developing tradition of power men. On July 31, 1954, against the Dodgers, the Milwaukee strongman poled four homers and a double for 18 total bases, a major league record for a single game. "The next day he paid for it," Davidson remembers. "He was hit in the head by a Clem Labine pitch. The batting helmet saved Adcock's life."

In his decade with the Braves, Adcock was joined by numerous sluggers—Eddie Mathews (512 career homers), Joe Torre, Wes Covington, Mack Jones, Felipe Alou, Rico Carty, and out-

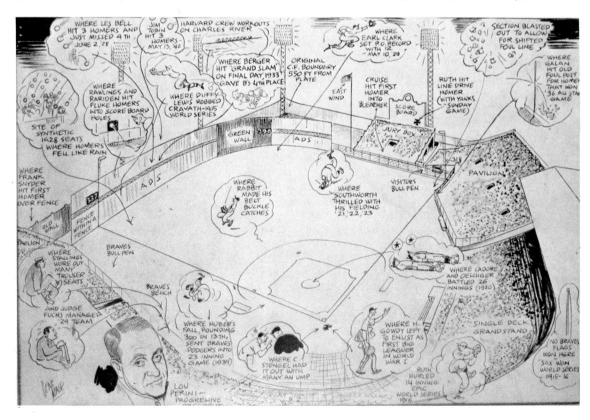

62

Above: *Shortly after Lou Perini bought the Braves, cartoonist Gene Mack cataloged the memorable moments of Braves Field.*
Opposite: *Spahn and Sain before the 1948 World Series.*

lasting most of them and transcending them all, Henry Aaron, the greatest home run hitter in baseball history.

At spring training in 1954, Aaron was a scared twenty-year-old kid with a moon face and two years of minor league experience. "He was such a shy kid that he was afraid to go to banquets," Davidson recalls. "He would go if he got a promise that he wouldn't have to talk." From the start, however, Hank Aaron had the thick wrists and sinewy body with which he produced a whiplash swing so consistent that it seemed to make him immune to slumps. Grimm says, "He was so good I knew we'd keep him, even though he was on the Toledo roster."

That first year Aaron batted .280 and knocked 13 home runs. His second year he was up to .314 and 106 RBIs. In 1956, he was the majors' only player to record 200 hits, winning the National League batting championship with a .328 average. "I just go up swinging," he said.

"His strike zone," Grimm said "is from the top of his cap to his shoes."

The Braves began the 1957 season by winning nine of their first ten games. In June,

with the Braves in the thick of a five-team pennant race, they acquired from the Giants the man who put them over the top, second baseman Red Schoendienst. "Some guys when they are traded are the ones you say played better against you than for you," Crandall observes. "Not Red—he was a real pro, and he was tremendously important in the spirit and success of the team."

As late as July 29, only two and a half games separated the top five clubs. Then Schoendienst put together a 23-game hitting streak, and the Braves began to pull away. In the first two weeks of August, the Braves won ten in a row, taking over first place for good on August 6. The challengers—St. Louis, Brooklyn, Cincinnati, Philadelphia—collapsed. For the season Schoendienst batted .309, getting his two hundredth hit, tops in the league, on the final day.

Wes Covington was another vital part in the Milwaukee pennant push. A broken leg sidelined Joe Adcock most of the year, and Covington was called up from the minors to supply power. He responded with 21 homers in only 328 at-bats. *63*

Billy Bruton injured his knee in the middle of the season and was lost for the rest of it, so "Hurricane" Bob Hazle took up the slack. In 41 games, the chunky, left-handed swinger batted .403 and seemed to have a knack for breaking open games with extra base hits.

Don McMahon joined the 1957 team for 32 games as a relief specialist. He remembers skipper Fred Haney, who replaced Grimm as manager in 1956 and guided the pennant charge the next year: "Haney just let you play. I came up to the Braves when I was twenty-seven, but he always called me kid. I'd come in and he'd say, 'Strike the guy out, kid.'"

McMahon struck out almost a batter an inning and posted a 1.53 ERA. Spahn, then thirty-six years old, completed his eighth year of 20 or more wins and received the Cy Young award. Bob Buhl was 18–7. Burdette was 17–9. "The competition of Spahn made Burdette a more effective and successful pitcher," Crandall believes. "Both men were really opposites. After a game, Spahn might have a lot of reporters around him and would freely talk about what he did. Burdette would say, 'Talk to the catcher. He's the one who caught the game.'"

Aaron, the National League's Most Valuable Player that year, hit 44 homers, the most in the majors, and drove in 132 runs.

The October opposition was Casey Stengel's New York Yankees, in their eighth World Series in nine years. "We all went to New York and looked at Yankee Stadium as if we were country bumpkins," recalls Ernie Johnson. It was easy to feel inferior to the Yankees. After six world championships in eight years, the New Yorkers had half-convinced the rest of the baseball world that they really were as bad as they were said to be—bloodlessly efficient sophisticates who disdainfully disposed of raunchy National Leaguers. It wasn't really true, of course, but the reputation was powerful enough, even if undeserved. When Milwaukee fans heard of New York's coolness to the Yanks, they must have thought New York viewed their wild enthusiasm for the Braves as some sort of Middle American vulgarity. Such sensitivities were further exposed when an anonymous critic labeled Milwaukee "Bush League."

Whitey Ford's five-hitter trimmed Spahn and the Braves in the opener at Yankee Stadium, 3–1. Then a fidgety country bumpkin from West Virginia, Lew Burdette, bested the New Yorkers 4–2 in game two, his first confrontation with the team that had traded him six years before. He was untouchable after the fourth inning, when the Braves broke a 2–2 tie.

Above: *Lew Burdette beat the Yanks three times and hurled 24 consecutive scoreless innings in the 1957 World Series.* Opposite: *Fred Haney managed the Braves' pennant winners in 1957 and 1958.*

The Series moved to Milwaukee, where two hundred thousand fans greeted the home team. Two home runs by Mickey Mantle and another by hometown boy Tony Kubek ignited a 12–3 New York rout. But good cheer returned in the fourth game when Milwaukee prevailed on Eddie Mathews' tenth-inning home run. The climactic moment followed the famous "shoe polish incident," in which pinch hitter "Nippy" Jones was awarded a base when shoe polish on the baseball substantiated his claim that he had been hit by a pitch. It was the end of an exhausting game for the Braves and Spahn, who had blown a three-run lead in the ninth and allowed the lead run in the tenth before a well-shined shoe and a homer saved the day.

Burdette continued his war against the Yankees in the fifth game, spinning a 1–0 seven-hitter and besting Whitey Ford. Wes Covington's crashing snare of Gil McDougald's extra base bid was the game's most spectacular play.

Back in New York, with the Braves only one win from the world championship, the Bombers rallied for a 3–2 win on Bob Turley's four-hitter. Aaron and Frank Torre hit solo home runs for the Braves, but these were offset by Yogi Berra's two-run blast for the Yanks. Then Hank Bauer's barely fair seventh-inning homer won the game.

Spahn was flu-ridden for the final game, so Burdette was called on, though he had had only two days rest. He pitched his third consecutive seven-hitter and second straight shutout, 5–0. That made 24 straight scoreless innings against the suddenly humbled Yankees. Beer flowed freely all over Milwaukee. Newspaper headlines announced, "BUSHVILLE WINS!" It was the season of light.

Winning 18 and losing 5 in a spurt that began on July 30, the Braves romped to the 1958 pennant by 8 games over runner-up Pittsburgh. With Bob Buhl out most of the season, the pitching staff consisted of a "big two"—Spahn and Burdette (42 wins between them)—and a "little four"—youngsters Joey Jay, Juan Pizarro, and Carlton Willey, plus veteran Bob Rush (32 triumphs collectively).

In the 1958 World Series, Milwaukee won three of the first four games against the Yankees. Spahn shut them out on two hits in the fourth game.

That was the Braves' last World Series triumph to date. For only the second time in Series history, a team leading 3–1 in games failed to take the world championship, and the Braves have never had another chance.

A third straight pennant beckoned in 1959, but Milwaukee lost the National League playoff to the Dodgers. Joe Torre joined the Braves in 1960. (His first major league appearance was as a pinch hitter for Warren Spahn.) Milwaukee finished in second place again.

The team turned its back on the fifties and moved into the winter of discontent of the sixties. Crandall hurt his arm and was relegated to the disabled list for most of 1961. Some of the older players were starting to wear down. "The crowds were there, and then they weren't," McMahon remembers. "It's an old town, Mil-

66

Above: *Atlanta Stadium.* Opposite bottom and top: *Hank Aaron belts his seven hundred fifteenth homer and passes in front of a celebrating scoreboard on his trip around the bases.*

waukee, and what hurt in the decline was getting rid of the older players all at once. They seemed to have traded everybody away in a year or so." On May 9, 1962, McMahon himself was shipped to Houston.

With three fifth- and one sixth-place finish in their last five years in Milwaukee, the Braves attracted fewer than a million fans a year. "It became a matter of geography," observes Torre. "Washington moved to Minnesota and this took away a lot of fans." Crandall blames the success of the Green Bay Packers and Vince Lombardi: "They were winning and we were not."

The last year of the Braves of Milwaukee was 1965. The power was still there: Aaron, Torre, Mathews, Mack Jones, Felipe Alou, Gene Oliver—they all hit 20 or more home runs, and the Braves led the National League in home runs. But the power was not enough. The team wound up in fifth place, drawing only 555,584 fans.

On April 12, 1966, 50,671 people came to see the South's first regular season major league baseball game. The tale of the third city, Atlanta, began. Joe Torre remembers, "There was a novelty about the whole thing. At a game against the Giants, there were forty-five thousand fans in the stands, and you could hear a pin drop. The fans did not know what to do at a ball game. It was quite a contrast to Milwaukee."

In popularity, if not success, the Braves had again gone from the season of darkness to the season of light. They finished fifth for the third straight year, but their attendance tripled that of their last season in Milwaukee. A million and a half fans came out to Atlanta Stadium (built in 52 weeks at a cost of $18 million).

Through the first decade of the Atlanta Braves, there were many fine individual achievements: Hoyt Wilhelm's one thousandth mound appearance; pitcher Tony Cloninger's two grand slams in one game ("He came up a third time and the shot he hit was caught right at the fence," remembers Davidson); Dave Johnson's 43 home runs, the all-time record for a second baseman; Phil Niekro's no-hitter; Felix Millan's six double plays in one game. The team flashed power, ripping four home runs in one inning in 1971 and scoring 13 runs in an inning the next year. Aaron, Darrell Evans, and Dave Johnson hit 40 or more home runs in 1973, the first time in history three players on the same team did so.

The first year of divisional play, 1969, the Braves won 93 games, racing down the September stretch at a .769 percentage. It was the season of hope once again. "That was the peak moment in the team's Atlanta history—beating the Reds and playing the Mets in the championship series," says Phil Niekro. In a reversal of form, New York power throttled the Braves. A five-run eighth made the New Yorkers victors in game one. Six Atlanta pitchers were pummeled in the Mets' 11–6 second-game win. And a two-run homer by Wayne Garrett climaxed the Mets' 7–4 final victory.

Through the reigns of managers Bobby Bragan, Billy Hitchcock, Ken Silvestri, Luman Harris, Eddie Mathews, and Clyde King, and through the dipping attendance figures from a million and a half in 1966 to 981,085 in 1974, the Braves had one constant highlight—Hank Aaron.

In 1968, he became the eighth player in history to record 500 career home runs. The next year he led the Braves to the divisional crown by ripping 44 homers (matching the number on his back), batting .300, and driving in 97 runs. He notched his three thousandth hit in 1970, and the next year recorded his six hundredth home run. On July 21, 1973, he hit home run

After years of having been known primarily for their power hitting, the Braves are attempting to win with speed and pitching too. Above: *Ralph Garr;* opposite: *Buzz Capra*

700 and on April 5, 1974, he hit home run 714.

"Hank Aaron is the same as when he came up," observes Del Crandall, later Aaron's manager with the Milwaukee Brewers. "He could have hit three-fifty or more for a career, but he made a decision early to go for the home run. Perhaps he was influenced by the sluggers on the Braves. Anyway, the rest is history."

On April 8, 1974, 39 years after Babe Ruth, wearing the uniform of the Boston Braves, hit his last homer, Hank Aaron, an Atlanta Brave, hammered number 715. The Atlanta Stadium scoreboard, in that moment of light for Aaron and the Braves, went ablaze: 7——1——5. The magic number was printed in six-foot neon. A national television audience and 53,775 spectators at Atlanta Stadium witnessed the historic moment. The home run that ended the quest jumped off the bat of the forty-year-old slugger at 9:07 P.M. It came in the rain of the fourth inning, on Aaron's first swing of the night, in his second time at bat against the Los Angeles Dodgers' pitcher, Al Downing. "When he first hit it," Downing said, "I didn't think it would be gone, but it kept carrying, carrying." The ball carried more than 400 feet and dropped over the left center field fence. The sky above Atlanta Stadium was set aglow with skyrockets. And "Bad Henry," head slightly bent, trotted around the bases into immortality.

In the post-Aaron era now in Atlanta, the Braves strive for a new identity, emphasizing speed and pitching. Ernie Johnson is optimistic: "This whole situation could be made into a great franchise with just a couple of winning years."

Phil Niekro, the Braves' only player to have played on the Milwaukee Braves, says, "When I signed with them in 1959, it was like signing with the Yankees. I've seen a lot of the guys here coming and a lot of the guys going. We've got to create our own dynasty here. We have to do our own thing."

The Braves and the Chicago Cubs are the only National League franchises that have been continuously in operation since 1876. For the Braves, the years since then have been the best of times and the worst of times, the season of light and the season of darkness, the spring of hope and the winter of despair. The South and Atlanta now await the Braves' new world.

Braves

Name of Park	Date 1st Game Played	Opponent & Score	Capacity
South End Grounds	April 29, 1876	Hartford 3, Boston 2	3,000
South End Grounds*	July 20, 1894	Boston 12, New York 1	7,000
Braves Field	August 18, 1915	Boston 3, St. Louis 1	44,500
Milwaukee County Stadium	April 14, 1953	Milwaukee 3, St. Louis 2	44,091
Atlanta Stadium	April 12, 1966	Pittsburgh 3, Atlanta 2	52,870

South End Grounds destroyed by fire May 16, 1894; rebuilt and reopened 1894.

Reach for the Stars
The Astros

Judge Roy M. Hofheinz and his associates had the vision of American ingenuity, but they were Texans and they dreamed bigger, bolder. They transformed a swamp into "the eighth wonder of the world"—a structure taller, greater in seating capacity, larger in overall size than the Roman Coliseum, and topped with a giant bubble that conquered nature. Where there had been air that was blast-oven hot, there was now a clean, fresh atmosphere free even of smoke and malodor, and always a perfect 72 degrees. There was no rain and no bugs. When natural grass wouldn't grow inside the man-made marvel, a new kind of grass was zipped together. Heat turned into cool, day into night.

Then the new mini-city expanded, and the Astrodome became just part of an Astrodomain that included a 57-acre family amusement center and a thousand-room hotel complex.

There was a magnificent control over all, except, alas, over things human that defied control—a baseball team. With the ball club there have been business mistakes, such as ill-advised trades. There have been tragedies, such as the deaths of players. And there has been communal misfortune in disputes between players and managers, managers and executives, executives and other executives. Perhaps the Houston club has had no more sorrow than other baseball teams, but it has not had success with which to soften the blows. True to their name, the Astros have reached for the stars, but on the field at least they have come up with only a paper moon.

It would be silly to deny the disappointment. Yet the extravaganza of National League baseball in Houston cannot be dismissed as a bust. The franchise that has been beset by human nature has overcome mother nature in a city where such feats have become a tradition. The Astros today pursue their quest for success in an atmosphere that continually reminds them of what can be done.

National League baseball began in Houston on October 17, 1961, with the Houston Colt 45's. At that time the Astrodome was just an idea in the mind of Judge Hofheinz, but it soon proved to be no idle dream. By the end of the year, the voters of Harris County approved an $18 million bond issue to finance a domed stadium. "I knew that with our heat, humidity, and rain the best chance for success was a weatherproof, all-purpose stadium," Hofheinz said. Buckminster Fuller, media ecologist and inventor of the geodesic dome, served as consultant to the project. Said Hofheinz, "Buckminster Fuller convinced me that it was possible to cover any size space so long as you didn't run out of money."

Approximately three years and $20 million later, Hofheinz's Houston Sports Association was still solvent, and the 208-foot-high pleasure dome was ready for its newly renamed tenants. the Astros. The Dome opened on April 9, 1965, with an exhibition game between the Astros and the New York Yankees, won by the home team, 2–1.

"There was a strangeness and a newness about the Dome for the first couple of years," notes Bill Giles, former publicity director for the team. "For the first couple of years, there was hardly any booing, not even of the opposing team. The Astrodome made baseball a different kind of game."

"When I first played there, it was a weird feeling; nothing ever changes in there," says Houston shortstop Roger Metzger. "But I got to like the Dome. When you leave your home, you know you're going to play."

Other players weren't so sure they enjoyed the ubiquitous control over nature. Dave Roberts, who came to Houston from San Diego in 1971, said, "It was going from air-conditioned house to air-conditioned car to air-conditioned stadium and never getting a day off."

The spectators were far more impressed by the stadium than by the game on the field. The fans—or patrons, as they are called in Houston—

rested in six tiers of plushly upholstered seats, each tier one of six different colors: lipstick red, burnt orange, terra-cotta, purple, gold, and, high up in the sky boxes, royal blue. Those lofty accommodations were reserved for the patrons who had reached the top of life's ladder. The sky boxes were actually luxury apartments, in which the beautiful people held lavish cocktail parties and occasionally peered down at the ant-like athletes below. It may have been a great ego boost, but it wasn't a good view of the ball game. Former Houston broadcaster Harry Kalas chuckles, "Those seats are actually the worst in the house. Judge Hofheinz made them the luxury boxes and sold them for a fine piece of change."

The mere mortals below spent much of their time looking up, not only at the sky boxes, but also at the magnificent translucent roof with its thousands of plastic skylights. Or they could watch the gigantic scoreboard, which stretches 474 feet across the center field wall, weighs 300 tons, contains twelve hundred feet of wiring, and best of all, produces a light show that makes conventional fireworks passé. Covering an area 360 feet by 36 feet on top of the scoreboard, the "home run spectacular" is an electronic fireworks display lasting 45 seconds that is ignited whenever an Astro hits a home run. The "astro-lite" is a ten-thousand-light screen in dead center field that projects animated or still pictures, or written messages.

Such impressive surroundings can be mesmerizing. "With the giant scoreboard, the fans

Opposite: *The splendor of the Astrodome has challenged the Houston ball club to live up to its surroundings.* Above: *Out at the plate.*

become automated," observes broadcaster Gene Elston. "A lot of people grow accustomed to doing what the scoreboard tells them to do. . . . If we get a couple of men on base, for example, it is very rare that the fans will react until they put a handclap on the board. Then they automatically do it."

In the opening years, the dazzle of the Astrodome made the fans want to shine too. Watching the Astros in the Dome "was like going to a social event instead of a sporting event," Kalas says. "You were almost afraid to drop peanut shells on the floor. Women dressed to kill—had their hair done, wore expensive furs."

"It's more like a theater," says pitcher Larry Dierker. "You don't see anything like a bleacher bum or a whole bunch of kids who come out on the subway by themselves, as they do in New York. It's more of a family thing—like going to the movies. And there are a lot of people here from out of town in to catch a major league baseball game. The Dome is a tourist attraction."

The Astrodome was as different as it was new, and not without its defects. In the first year, outfielders lost many fly balls in the glare of the sun shining through the roof, so the dome

had to be coated with a more opaque surface. Despite the problems, however, the initial effect of the extravagant new stadium was indisputable: the Judge had rescued his franchise from the blistering Houston sun, the torrential rains, and the suffocating humidity, and he had transplanted it in a greenhouse where it could not help but prosper. In the first year of the Astrodome, 2,151,470 patrons, still the greatest attendance in the history of the Houston franchise, came to ogle the world's eighth wonder and take in a ball game.

Since 1962, full page ads in *The Sporting News* had urged young baseball players to sign with the Texas team and "come play in the first domed, air-conditioned stadium." Now the much-heralded day had arrived. Houston baseball leapt from the nineteenth century, with the quaint Colt 45's six-gun emblem and makeshift ball park, to the twenty-first, with Astro mania so acute that the grounds crew was disguised as spacemen bounding about some lunar infield. Only the ball club itself failed to participate in this bold leap forward. The Astros, like the Colt 45's, were tail enders in the National League.

In 1962, their first year, the Colt 45's had won 64 games and, thanks to the Cubs and Mets, finished a relatively lofty eighth. The next year they won two more games but dropped to ninth, and in 1964 they again finished at 66–96 in ninth place.

The All-Star on the original Colt 45's was 20-game loser Dick Farrell. It has been said that one needs to be a good pitcher to lose 20 games, and Farrell proved the point. Toiling for the hapless Colt 45's, the veteran right-hander compiled a quite respectable 3.02 ERA over 242 innings. He began a Houston tradition, later strengthened in the Astrodome, of a team whose strength was pitching rather than hitting.

By the end of their third season, the Colt 45's had worn through their first manager, Harry Craft, and he was replaced by Luman Harris, part of the original coaching staff, with Jimmy Adair, Bobby Bragan, Jim Busby, and Cot Deal. Thus, the Colt 45's-Astros had a new manager when they moved into their new home in 1965. He lasted the season and no more.

For the third consecutive year, the Houston club finished in ninth place, losing six of every ten games. The year began with the first National League game in the Astrodome, on April 12, 1965. Powered by Richie Allen's homer, the Phils whitewashed the Astros, 2–0.

The brightest aspect of the dismal year was the rejuvenation of the old expansion team.

Rookie Joe Morgan replaced ancient Nellie Fox at second and led the team in runs scored, hits, and triples. Youngsters Rusty Staub and Jimmy Wynn became full-time outfielders. And eighteen-year-old fireballer Larry Dierker completed his first full year in the big leagues.

For 1966 there was a new manager, Grady Hatton, and a new artificial playing surface that inspired a new word in the English language, "AstroTurf." The bright green synthetic carpet, held together by eighty thousand feet of zippers, is removable and replaceable within a few hours. Judge Hofheinz hailed it as another of the Astros' major new advances. "Everything about the Astrodome is unparalleled and trailblazing," he glowed. "We feel the addition of this new playing surface will launch a new era in recreational engineering." As he had been about the feasibility of the Astrodome itself, the Judge was right about AstroTurf. Within the decade countless sports stadiums had adopted the artificial grass named for the site of its first installation.

Hatton, the new manager, launched something less than a new era, though the team did improve in 1966, moving up to 72 wins and eighth place. Staub and Wynn contributed solid years at the plate. Joe Morgan was selected to the All-Star team, and the new young shortstop, Roland ("Sonny") Jackson, stole 49 bases and stroked 160 singles. Screwballer Mike Cuellar led the pitching staff with a 2.22 ERA over 227 innings. Dave Giusti pitched a one-hitter.

In 1967, the team slipped to ninth again,

with 69 wins, and in June of 1968, with the Astros in last place, Hatton gave way to Harry Walker. The failure to improve in 1967 was particularly disheartening because many of the Astros had their best years yet. Staub and Wynn blossomed into the club's first true hitting stars, Staub hitting .333 with 44 doubles, Wynn hammering 37 homers and driving in 107 runs. All four marks set club records. Jackson slumped at the plate in his sophomore year but stole 45 bases; Morgan had another solid year at bat and had 29 swipes. To compensate for Dierker, gone most of the year for military service, the pitching staff had another strong young arm in Don Wilson, who at twenty-two became the youngest National Leaguer to hurl a no-hitter when he blanked the Braves 2–0. Cuellar led the staff with 16 wins.

In 1968, the Astros improved to 72 wins, tying their best mark for the previous six years, but compared to the performance of the league's other teams, such minuscule progress went unnoticed. The club fell to last, despite a respectable 49–52 record after the switch to Walker. The season's high point was a 24-inning, 1–0 victory over the Mets on April 15—the longest game in Houston history, in which Wilson pitched nine shutout innings. Later that year he struck out 18 Cincinnati batters in one game—8 of them in a row.

Under Walker in 1969, his first full year as manager, the Astros made their first dramatic improvement, winning 81 games and losing 81. It was the first time they won as many as they

73

Above: The Colt 45's won their first three games on the pitching of, left to right, Dean Stone, Bobby Shantz, and Hal Woodeschick.
Opposite: Cesar Cedeno has been billed as "the next Clemente."

Astros

Name of Park	Date 1st Game Played	Opponent & Score	Capacity
Colt Stadium	April 10, 1962	Houston 11, Chicago 2	25,000
Astrodome	April 12, 1965	Philadelphia 2, Houston 0	45,000

lost. Larry Dierker became Houston's first 20-game winner. Jimmy Wynn, a feared slugger now, drew more than a hundred walks and scored more than a hundred runs. Joe Morgan stole 49 bases.

In the winter of 1969, Rusty Staub was traded to Montreal for Jesus Alou and Donn Clendenon. "They felt they were at the stage where they could get two front-line ballplayers for Staub," Houston broadcaster Gene Elston explains. "The deal was completely aborted when Clendenon would not report here. The Commissioner stepped in, but we got the short end of the deal. We didn't get Clendenon [who wound up with the Mets], nor did we have Staub." Montreal substituted pitchers Jack Billingham and "Skip" Guinn and a sum of money for Clendenon.

There were two fourth-place ties and identical winning percentages of .488 in 1970 and 1971. Then one sultry August day in 1972, Walker went the way of Harry Craft, Luman Harris, and Grady Hatton. A new but familiar manager, Leo Durocher, directed the team for its remaining 31 games. Under the controversial manager, the Astros won more games than they lost and completed the season with an 84–69 mark and a second-place finish, best in their history. Suddenly, the Astros were no longer handicapping their pitchers with non-hitters. In 1972, the team paced the National League in offense, scoring 708 runs.

In 1973, the barrage continued with Lee May's 105 RBIs and 28 homers, Roger Metzger's .320 batting average (including the club record for triples in a season), Cesar Cedeno's .320 batting average, 25 home runs, and 56 stolen bases. However, the Astros slipped to fourth, two games over .500. Durocher retired at the end of the season.

The Astros won as many games as they lost in 1974 and finished fourth under new manager Preston Gomez, who had learned about hard times in San Diego but preferred to recall his happier days with the Dodgers. "I was a Dodger man for twelve seasons," he said. "You win pennants with the players you develop in your own organization . . . bringing them along; it's like raising children."

As any parent knows, there is sorrow as well as joy in child rearing. One of Gomez's most trying moments must have been the game in which he pinch hit for Don Wilson in the eighth inning, even though Wilson was pitching a no-hitter. The Astros were losing, and Gomez was more interested in getting the tying run than in preserving the individual feat. As manager of the Padres, he had done the same thing with Clay·

Top: *Colt 45's Opening Day tickets.* Above: *Greg Gross keeps his head down and hits for average if not power.* Opposite: *Ken Forsch, who wears Don Wilson's old number in memoriam on his sleeve, shared the load of the pitching staff after Wilson's death.*

75

Kirby, after which he said he would repeat the decision if the situation recurred. It did, and Gomez was true to his word. Unhappily, the Astros failed to rally and the relief pitcher in the ninth inning surrendered a hit. So they lost both the no-hitter and the game.

The Astros began the 1975 season optimistically. Larry Dierker said, "There is potential here; everyone knows it's here." Indeed, the 1975 Astros did have potential, which made it disastrous when they slumped miserably and finished dead last.

Jimmy Wynn had gone to the Dodgers after the 1973 season, but Cedeno was firmly established in his place in center field for the 1975 season. After his great year in 1973, Cedeno had fallen off in 1974, but his place as a superstar seemed assured. "He has as much ability or more than any other player in baseball," said manager Gomez. "He could be another Roberto Clemente."

Greg Gross had had an impressive rookie season in 1974, hitting .314 and setting the club record for hits with 185. After six years with Houston, Bob Watson was proving to be so reliable at bat that Grady Hatton predicted, "Someday he'll lead the league in hitting." Doug

("Rooster") Rader, the fiery third baseman, had become a fixture on the left side of the infield with rangy shortstop Roger Metzger. Huge catcher Cliff Johnson set a club record with five pinch-hit homers, just one short of the major league mark.

The Houston pitching staff boasted established stars in Dierker, Wilson, and left-hander Dave Roberts, a 17-game winner in 1973.

What then went wrong in 1975? The troubles began after the 1974 season, when Don Wilson died of carbon monoxide fumes in his automobile. He was not the first Houston player to die prematurely (a pitcher, Jim Umbricht, and a first baseman, Walter Bond, both died of cancer in the club's early years), but his loss, as well as a human tragedy, mortally wounded the club's chances. Pitching coach Roger Craig tells of the big plans he had for Wilson: "I was hoping to get three hundred innings out of him this year. He was big, and he was strong. I don't think Don ever reached his potential. He's a big loss to Houston and to baseball."

The eight-year veteran, who had yet to reach his thirtieth birthday, could have become the dominant pitcher in the history of the Houston club. He had followed his 1967 no-hitter with

another in 1969, perhaps the finest, certainly the most dramatic, pitching performance of his life. It came against Cincinnati, on May 1, the night after Jim Maloney of the Reds had beaten the Astros 10–0 on a no-hitter. Though the Maloney no-hitter provided an incentive to turn the tables, more important to Wilson was another Reds' thrashing of the Astros, 14–0, in the Dome the week before. "They weren't content to win that game," he explained bitterly. "They were laughing at us and wanted to make us look ridiculous."

Wilson and the Reds exchanged taunts in the early innings of the May 1 game. "They didn't have much to say in the late innings, though," Wilson remembered with grim satisfaction. "I was throwing the ball down their throats." As the no-hitter progressed, none of Wilson's teammates talked to him either. They were not about to interfere with what had become his obsession to humiliate the Reds. Firing away like a man possessed, the Houston hurler fanned 13 hitters that night en route to his no-hitter. His greatest obstacle was not the Reds, but his own hypertension. "I was thinking about a no-hitter from the first inning on," he said. "There were a couple of times when my

legs were shaking so much that I had to step off the mound. I never wanted anything so bad in my life as to pitch that no-hitter."

Doug Rader, who played with Wilson in the minors at Amarillo before both came to the Astros, remembers the fierce pitcher: "He was a kind of troubled person in many ways . . . but the good points outweighed the bad. He was a real good man. We miss him."

Without Wilson, the 1975 Astros relied heavily on Dierker and Roberts, neither of whom came through. Together they had barely 20 wins and an ERA over 4.00.

The hitters did somewhat better. Watson had another fine year, hitting well over .300 and leading the team in hits and RBIs. Gross beat the sophomore jinx with an average close to .300, and another youngster, outfielder Wilbur Howard, had a similarly high average in his first full year with the Astros. Cedeno and Johnson were reliable if not outstanding at the plate with averages in the two eighties. The biggest disappointment at the plate was Rader, who suffered through a year in which he hit well below his .254 lifetime mark.

In late season, with the Astros struggling to surpass the modest total of 64 wins they had achieved in their first year as the Colt 45's, general manager Spec Richardson and manager Gomez were both fired. As always in baseball, the manager was the victim more than the cause of the disaster. The Houston front office had continued the Astros' unenviable record of populating the rest of the majors with stars for relatively little in return. Many of the Houston club's great ballplayers—John Mayberry, Mike Cuellar, Lee May, Dave Giusti, Tommy Davis, Mike Marshall, Jerry Grote, Rusty Staub, Jimmy Wynn, Jerry Reuss, Jack Billingham, and most of all Joe Morgan—have had good years, usually their best, after leaving the Dome.

It has, of course, been discouraging to play for a club whose stadium has achieved far more notice than has the team itself. Says Rader, minimizing his personal achievements, which include many Gold Glove awards, "I've made some good plays, but they haven't really meant that much to me. We have not been in the playoffs or the World Series."

Most of all, the Astros show a determination to be worthy of the opulent Texas palace in which they perform. Dierker says, "I still have hopes that I'll be remembered in Houston history as the first player the team ever signed who lasted this long with the ball club . . . who led them to a pennant one year. Then it'll be come see the team, instead of come see the Dome."

Bob Watson seems to have caught the Giants' Von Joshua. In the last few years, Watson has become Houston's most consistent hitter.

77

Swashbuckling Bats
The Pirates

"O ur hitting has to be our story," says veteran Pirate Bob Robertson. In the Pirates' history, pitchers stand like unknown soldiers beside the great hitters. Phillippe, Camnitz, Aldridge, Kremer, Friend, Blass—without them there would have been no pennants. But the truly revered names are all those of hitters—Wagner, Cuyler, the Waners, Traynor, Kiner, Clemente, Stargell. The Pirates have won with great hitting and lost in spite of it; they have lived and died by the sword.

The first truly notable achievement of the Pittsburgh National League baseball club was to become Pirates, in name if not in fact. In 1889,

many major league ballplayers revolted against their bosses and formed their own league, the Players', or Brotherhood, League. The insurrection wounded the two established leagues, the National League and the American Association, but both proved more durable than the Players' League, which expired after just one season, 1890. The established leagues offered amnesty to the renegade players, and the feud between employers and employees subsided.

With the common enemy defeated, or at least subdued, the owners of the two leagues now engaged each other in battle. The Pittsburgh National League team, all but two of whose players had jumped, had finished a distant last in 1890, winning just 23 of 136 games.

Now only seven of the jumpers returned, so Pittsburgh began a hasty search for new recruits. It soon discovered that the American Association Philadelphia Athletics had failed to reclaim two of their expatriates, Louis Bierbauer and Harry Stovey. Boston snatched Stovey, and Pittsburgh signed Bierbauer.

Philadelphia asked politely for its players back—they had gone unclaimed only because of an oversight, the club explained. Finders keepers, Pittsburgh replied. "Pirates!" cried the Athletics.

An arbitration board upheld the National League, but the dispute had apparently escalated from a matter of equity to one of honor. The American Association declared war, and the two leagues sniped at each other for a year before they settled their differences and merged into a 12-team circuit in 1892.

Pittsburgh, still more plundered from the Brotherhood War than piratical in its aftermath, finished last again in 1891. Bierbauer, hardly a prize catch, hit .206 that year. So the only real spoils that Pittsburgh gained from the fracas was a richly undeserved nickname. No buccaneers ever rode the high seas of the Allegheny and Monongahela, and unless you count coal and iron ore, no treasures are buried on their banks.

In 1900, the more prosperous of the National League owners decided to pare down their league from twelve teams to eight. A streamlined circuit, it was thought, would produce greater profits for the remaining teams and thus strengthen the league's monopoly of major league baseball. However, these hard-headed businessmen grievously miscalculated, and to their dismay their planned venture in survival of the fittest became an embarrassing exercise of love thy neighbor. Ban Johnson made three of the disenfranchised teams—Baltimore, Cleveland, and Washington—cornerstones of his new rival American League, precisely the competition the National League owners were most eager to preclude. The fourth club they excised, Louisville, joined forces with the Pirates and promptly forged a dynasty.

The new recruits in Pittsburgh included player-manager Fred Clarke, third baseman Tommy Leach, and pitcher Charles ("Deacon") Phillippe—some of the finest players of the era—and one of the finest of any era, Honus Wagner. After his first game as a Pirate, "the Flying Dutchman" exclaimed, "I am going to be a Pirate all my life; this is where I belong." He was quite right. He played the rest of his 21-year career with Pittsburgh, winning eight

Pirates brandish their bats—Opposite: Al Oliver; top: Roberto Clemente. Bottom: Sanguillen salutes after 1971 Series win.

batting titles, stroking 3,430 hits, and establishing team records for most doubles, triples, and extra base hits.

A man who had built his body loading coal, Wagner stood only 5 feet 11 inches but weighed 200 pounds, most of it packed into his bull-like torso. Indeed he moved like a bull, loping after ground balls on heavily muscled bowed legs, shoveling the balls out of the dirt with his huge hands, then gracelessly flinging his throws to first amidst a shower of dirt and pebbles. In the early 1900s, he played every position but catcher, though he was best at shortstop. "The only way to get a ball past him is to hit it eight feet over his head," groused John McGraw.

At bat Wagner stood in the extreme far corner of the box, grasping the bat with his hands apart if he wanted to place a hit, with hands together if he was swinging away. As agile on the bases as he was in the field and at

National League in the first World Series, against the American League champion Boston Pilgrims. Two of the Pirates' best pitchers of 1902, Jack Chesbro and Jess Tannehill, had jumped to the American League, so the 1903 Pirates did not overwhelm their league. Nevertheless, they were prohibitive favorites to trounce the fledgling American Leaguers.

The record books show that Boston's Cy Young and Bill Dinneen outpitched Pittsburgh's Phillippe, who worked five times because the Pirates were short of starters. However, the Pirates might have won despite their pitching shortage if it had not been for Boston's rabid fans. They serenaded the Pirates with a popular song of the day, "Tessie," substituting their own unflattering remarks for the conventional lyrics. Eventually, the constant wailing got on the Pirates' nerves. "It was that damn song," grumbled Tommy Leach after .

the plate, he led the league in stolen bases five times and finished with 722 swipes overall, fifth most in baseball history.

Led by Wagner, who hit .381 and won the batting title in 1900, the Pirates climbed to second that year. For the next three years they won more than twice as many as they lost and took the pennant each season. Their spread of 21½ games over the second-place Brooklyn team is 1902 still stands as the greatest pennant-winning margin in baseball history. "That was some ball club," boasted Wagner. "Long about the middle of August nothing could stop us or slow us down. We could've won the pennant with each man holding a couple of bags of peanuts and his glove in his hip pocket."

The next year the Pirates represented the

Although the Pirates continued to win in succeeding years, first place eluded them. They were competing against the superb Giants and Cubs, and an average of 93 wins a year in the five-year period 1904–08 was not good enough. A defeat on the last day of the 1908 season cost them the pennant.

In 1909, the team abandoned Exposition Park, on the often-flooded north bank of the Allegheny River, and moved to new, 24,000-seat Forbes Field. Skeptics predicted that the big new park would never be filled, but they were proved wrong on Opening Day. The fans packed the new park.

Happily, the club produced a pennant, with 110 wins, including 16 in a row. The runner-up Cubs won 104. Wagner, one of only four men in the league to hit .300, won the batting title. Pitchers Howard Camnitz and Vic Willis each won more than 20 games.

In the World Series, Pittsburgh avenged its 1903 defeat by beating the Detroit Tigers of Hughie Jennings, Ty Cobb, Sam Crawford, and company. Young Babe Adams, who had had a 12–3 record in his first full year in the majors, became the Series hero by winning three games. Wagner hit .333 and prevailed in the field against the Tigers' ferocious baserunning. "That Goddamn Dutchman," Cobb was forced to admit, "is the only man in the game I can't scare."

In the years 1910–24, the Pirates fluctuated between second and last in the standings. The Flying Dutchman closed out his legendary career. Max Carey, a speedy baserunner and gifted outfielder, led the league in stolen bases 10 times. His 738 career stolen bases are fourth highest in major league history. On July 7, 1922, he reached base nine times with six hits and three walks. Southpaw Wilbur Cooper, four times a 20-game winner, had 202 victories in all, the all-time leader among Pittsburgh pitchers.

The Pirates also had the gentlemanly and courteous Pie Traynor, who arrived in 1920 and stayed for 18 seasons. Traynor played in 1,864 games. Five straight years he drove in more than 100 runs. In 1927–28, he struck out only 21 times. Unlike most players, who kept their own bats, Traynor borrowed bats. "There had to be some hits left in them," he explained.

Pittsburgh's bats forged another pennant in 1925. The team won 95 games, boasting eight .300 hitters and four players who each drove in more than 100 runs. Although the Pirates of that year finished last in fielding, the big bats and the speed of the club more than compensated for this deficiency. Kiki Cuyler personified the Pittsburgh batting prowess. He hit .354, scored 144 runs, and amassed 366 total bases.

Washington's Senators won three of the first four games from the Pirates in the 1925 World Series. But Pittsburgh's hitters produced 18 runs in the last three games, and the Bucs took their second world championship.

In the finale, the Senators' great Walter Johnson, who had won two Series games already, opposed Pittsburgh's Vic Aldridge. Glenn Wright, the Pirates' shortstop (whose unassisted triple play in May had been a highlight of the regular season), recalls the contest: "Washington jumped ahead with four runs in the first inning, but we came back with three in the third. . . . Johnson was having trouble with his footing on the mound because after the third inning it rained steadily. By the time we came to bat in the eighth, we were behind seven–six. Then Cuyler hit one with the bases loaded down the right field line. It lodged in the canvas they had been using to keep the field dry. Washington squawked like hell, but we got three runs. And [reliever] Red Oldham made them stand up, and we were champs."

In 1926, the Pirates slipped to third. Bill McKechnie, who had led them to the 1925 pennant and world championship, was dismissed. Donie Bush replaced him.

At about this time, two brothers from Oklahoma arrived in Pittsburgh, to reside there for 14 glorious years together. The older brother, Paul Waner, batted .336 in his rookie season of 1926, leading the league in triples. In one game he cracked six hits (using six different bats). In

Early heroes and early Forbes Field. Opposite: *left to right, Jack Chesbro, Deacon Phillippe, and Honus Wagner.* Above: *Dedication of Forbes Field, in 1909 against the Chicago Cubs.*

1927, his brother, Lloyd, joined him. At 5 feet 8 inches and 150 pounds, Paul was actually smaller than his little brother, but in deference to his seniority and slightly more prolific bat, the nick-namers tagged him "Big Poison" and Lloyd "Little Poison." The combined dose was usually deadly. Slashing, left-handed line-drive hitters, the Waners collected 5,611 major league hits between them. Paul had a lifetime batting average of .333 and won three batting titles. Lloyd recorded a career average of .316.

"They were hard to beat," says Glenn Wright. "Paul was the best left-handed hitter I ever saw. I remember one time after Dazzy Vance knocked him down Paul said, 'I'll knock *him* down next time.' Sure enough, next time up

Paul hit this wicked line drive right through Dazzy's legs. When Waner came back to the bench, he was madder than hell. He said, 'I got it a little too low.'

In 1927, nearly 900,000 fans paid their way into Forbes Field to see the Pirates' bat magicians. Even without Kiki Cuyler, who was out of the lineup much of the season because of a feud with manager Bush over where Cuyler should hit in the batting order, the Pirates batted .305, best in the league. MVP Paul Waner batted a league-leading .380, recording 237 hits and 131 RBIs. Lloyd chipped in 198 singles and a .355 average. Pittsburgh squeezed to the pennant by nine percentage points over St. Louis.

The New York Yankees of 1927, who had racked up 110 victories and taken the American League pennant by 19 games, wrecked the Pirates in four straight games in the World Series. Babe Ruth, who had blasted 60 homers in the regular season, added 2 more in the Series.

It has been said that the Yankees' record and an awesome batting practice display of power psyched out Pittsburgh. "I think they were the greatest team I ever saw," says Glenn

the plate in a high, lazy arc, tempting and frustrating overeager hitters. Sewell won 42 games in 1943–44. Bob Elliott drove in a hundred runs a season in the years 1942–46.

Ralph Kiner returned in 1946 and for the next seven years paced the league in homers and the team in RBIs. The Pirates' strongman cracked eight homers in four consecutive games in September 1947. On the Fourth of July, 1951, he exploded his own fireworks—a dazzling seven RBIs in two innings.

The fifties began with the Pirates finishing in last place and losing nearly 100 games. General manager Branch Rickey explained, "It was a young team."

After a season of maturing, it lost 112. Fred

Wright. "We were just outclassed, that's all."

It would be 33 years before the Pirates would again reach the World Series (when their opponents would again be the Yankees). Through the rest of the twenties and thirties, the Pirates still hit well and even produced some star pitchers, but the team did not have enough all-around talent. In Paul Waner's phrase, the Pirates were "all good boys, but we could never quite make it." They came close in September 1938, only to be deprived of a pennant by Gabby Hartnett's "homer in the gloaming."

Ralph Kiner remembers his introduction to the Pirates, in spring training 1940: "It was very impressive. Lloyd Waner, Mace Brown, and some of the other players that almost won the pennant in 1938 were there. . . . Before the war, a rookie just couldn't get batting practice. Bob Elliott gave me a bat and said, 'Why don't you get in there and hit some?' It was the first time I even had a chance to hit."

The war intervened, and it was not until 1946 that Kiner got another chance. Truett ("Rip") Sewell entertained the fans meanwhile with his "eephus ball," a pitch that sailed to

Opposite and above right: Max Carey and Pie Traynor, stars of the twenties. Above: Forbes Field for the 1960 World Series, the first in Pittsburgh since 1927.

83

Haney, summoned from Hollywood of the Pacific Coast League in 1953 to manage the Pirates, said, "We weren't going anywhere. We had to be patient." That year the Pirates lost 104 and finished last for the second of four consecutive years.

In 1952, Kiner's 37 homers led the National League. He asked Rickey for a raise. "He turned me down cold," Kiner recalls with a smile now. " 'I know you hit all those homers,' Rickey told me, 'but remember, we could have finished last without you.' " Kiner took a salary cut.

On November 1, 1955, Branch Rickey kicked himself upstairs to the board chairmanship. Joe L. Brown, son of the late Joe E. Brown, the famous comedian, succeeded Rickey. The youth movement Rickey had sponsored had, in Haney's words, "planted the seeds," but the harvest was still five years away.

Roberto Clemente was to make it a bumper crop. Those who called him a hypochondriac overlooked his torturous back spasms and the bone chips that rattled in the elbow of his throwing arm. Those who called him a loner ignored the dual prejudice he encountered because of his Spanish heritage and dark skin. And those who called him a showboat knew

nothing of his generosity, his dream to build a sports city for the poor of Puerto Rico. He was compared to Willie Mays—a slight to a genius who was above all else unique. "Everybody say I run like Willie, catch like Willie, throw like Willie, and hit line drives like Willie. I am not Willie," Clemente snapped. "I am Roberto Clemente!"

After Clemente's first year, 1955, Honus Wagner died. The Flying Dutchman had been coach emeritus and sometimes cheerleader to the youth movement of Rickey. In leaving at this moment, he seemed to be entrusting his legacy to the new outfielder. Clemente would surpass the Flying Dutchman as the leading Pirate in games played, at-bats, singles, total bases, and RBIs. He would win 12 Gold Glove awards and record a lifetime batting average of .317.

In 1956, the Pirates acquired Bill Virdon from the St. Louis Cardinals. He would patrol center field for the next nine years. "It was my first significant trade," recalls Brown. "Virdon was a compelling force in the makeup of our club." That same year, Dale Long, who had played for 15 different teams in 12 leagues over a dozen seasons, made his mark as a Pirate by

Above left: *Kiki Cuyler shined brightly but briefly.* Above right: *Pick your poison—"Little" Lloyd, left, or "Big" Paul.* Opposite: *Batting champ and star shortstop, Arky Vaughan.*

knocking eight homers in eight consecutive games, a major league record. He recorded 15 hits and 15 RBIs and hit .538 over that remarkable stretch. "It helped rekindle a lot of interest in Pittsburgh baseball," notes Brown.

Frank Thomas and Dick Stuart added to the Pirates' prowess at bat. Stuart could send the ball soaring over distant fences. Though he gave up as much in the field as he gained at the plate, the fans were used to such sacrifices on the Pirates' teams of the past. Thomas hit 30 homers in 1953, his rookie season, setting the club record for most homers by a rookie. In his six full seasons in Pittsburgh, he would contribute more than 160 round trippers.

In 1958, the Pirates won 84 games and finished over .500 for the first time in a decade. In Bob Friend, who won 22, the club had its first 20-game winner since 1951 and its biggest winner since Burleigh Grimes won 25 in 1928.

Two little men, Elroy Face and Harvey Haddix, closed the fifties with pitching feats. Face, a forkballer, won 18 and lost only 1 in 1959. Haddix, an inauspicious 12–12 that year, produced what manager Danny Murtaugh called "the most outstanding pitching performance I've seen in the history of Pirate baseball."

There were 19,194 fans in Milwaukee's County Stadium on May 26, a chilly spring night. Haddix faced the Braves of Hank Aaron and Eddie Mathews, Del Crandall and Joe Adcock—winners of two consecutive National League pennants. For 12⅓ innings he pitched a perfect game. "I threw good from the start," the slight left-hander said. "I had a fastball and a slider really working well, and perfect control." In the thirteenth inning, an error foiled the perfect game, and Joe Adcock's homer cost the no-hitter and the win.

From a fourth-place finish, barely over .500 in 1959, the Pirates were suddenly the class of the league in 1960. They set their all-time attendance record, 1,705,828, thrilling the city that hadn't had a pennant winner in 33 years. They won the pennant easily, specializing in a tenacious brand of baseball that made unlikely victories common, if not quite routine. "In all my years in baseball," says Brown, "I never saw so many games won with a team coming from behind in the late innings the way we did that year."

Clemente batted .314, drove in 94 runs, and scored 89. He gunned down baserunners 19 times, best among outfielders, and cracked 179 hits. Shortstop Dick Groat hit .325, leading the league. The consistent Vernon Law won 20 games. Then the Pirates looked up to find the

menacing Yankees waiting for them in the Series.

It was not that the Yankees were invincible. The Dodgers had shown that in 1955, the Braves in 1957, the White Sox in the pennant race in 1959. But it was hard to put the Pirates in that class. The Pirates? They had floundered through the fifties with only two winning teams. Now they were facing a club that had failed to win the pennant only twice in the last decade.

Perhaps in reality the Yankees weren't a better team than the Pirates, but they *looked* so much better. Their infielders—Boyer, Kubek, Richardson—were elegant; the Pirates'—Hoak, Groat, Mazeroski—were merely solid. At first base Bill ("Moose") Skowron radiated reliability. His counterpart, Dick Stuart, was erratic at best. Young, lean, powerful Elston Howard, the Yankees' catcher, moved like an athlete. The Pirates had stocky Smoky Burgess. The New Yorkers' outfield of Lopez, Mantle, and Maris may have yielded a trifle (but surely no more) in speed and polish to Skinner, Virdon, and

Clemente, but the New York trio was explosive, not just steady at bat, with 89 homers and 248 RBIs to the Pittsburgh outfield's 39 and 210. Pitching? The Pirates had the bigger winners, but the composite earned run averages of the two staffs were indistinguishable. Bench? Proven veterans versus faded journeymen: Yogi Berra and Gil McDougald compared to Gino Cimoli, Hal Smith, and Rocky Nelson.

The Yankees had the sheen of winners, the Pirates the style of runners-up. And so of course the Yanks were favorites, the Pirates underdogs. But baseball is not a contest of style. There is no bonus for impressive victory or respectable defeat. The Yankees would keep their royal raiments; the Pirates would just steal their crown.

In the first six games of the Series, the Yankees scored 46 runs to the Pirates' 17. The Yankees had 78 hits and eight homers, the Pirates 49 and one. No Pittsburgh pitcher came close to pitching a complete game.

After Pittsburgh had taken the opener, 6–4, Face relieving starter Vernon Law in the eighth and saving the victory, the Yankees erupted for 16–3 and 10–0 victories in games two and three. "We'll get the Yankees tomorrow," said first base coach Mickey Vernon. So they did. Face saved Law again, and the Pirates won 3–2. Then Face preserved a 5–2 win for Harvey Haddix.

As if insulted, the Yankees battered the upstart Pirates 12–0 in game six. This latest outburst seemed to shatter Pittsburgh fans' dreams of an upset.

The final round may have been the most exciting in World Series history. The Pirates opened with a four-run flurry in the first two innings off the Yanks' Bob Turley and Bill Stafford. New York got one back in the fifth when Skowron homered off Vernon Law. The next inning the Yanks erupted for four, knocking out Law. Once again the Pirates called on Face, but even he could not check the rampaging Yankees. Through seven and a half, it was 7–4 New York.

Suddenly, fate seemed to mock the supreme confidence of the Yankees. With none out and a man on first in the Pirates' eighth, Virdon slapped a double-play grounder to short. Kubek charged, set himself, but then, just as he was about to snatch the short hop and whip the ball to second, the ball bounced up sharply, striking him in the throat. He sank in pain to the ground, clutching his neck. The subsequent events seemed to explain the freak play better than the mundane fact that the ball had hit a pebble.

Above: *Ralph Kiner models his follow-through.* Opposite top and bottom: *Two of the most famous moments in the history of the Pirates—Haddix in despair after losing perfect game, Mazeroski exultant after knocking Series-winning homer in 1960.*

At this stage of a ball game—of a season—it is hard to resist the belief that accidents are planned.

The Pirates scored five runs that inning, three on Hal Smith's homer. They would have had none had the Yanks turned that grounder into a double play.

Still, the contest remained unresolved, as if the Yanks were defying fate and the Pirates tempting it. In the top of the ninth, New York scrounged—the once confident Yankees were reduced to scrounging now—for the tying runs.

Bill Mazeroski led off the bottom of the tenth for the Pirates against Ralph Terry. The chunky second baseman took ball one, then crashed a high slider just over the left-center field wall.

Mazeroski was the perfect man to break the stalemate. He bounded around the bases with the exuberance of a man who knew that he carried the fulfillment of a third of a century of Pittsburgh hopes. The celebration could not be contained. "Maz had a tough time finding home plate to tag it," recalls Mickey Vernon.

During the rest of the sixties, the Pirates were a sporadic contender with three third-place finishes. It was mainly a transitional period, during which the dominant force of the Pirates of the seventies was emerging: many of

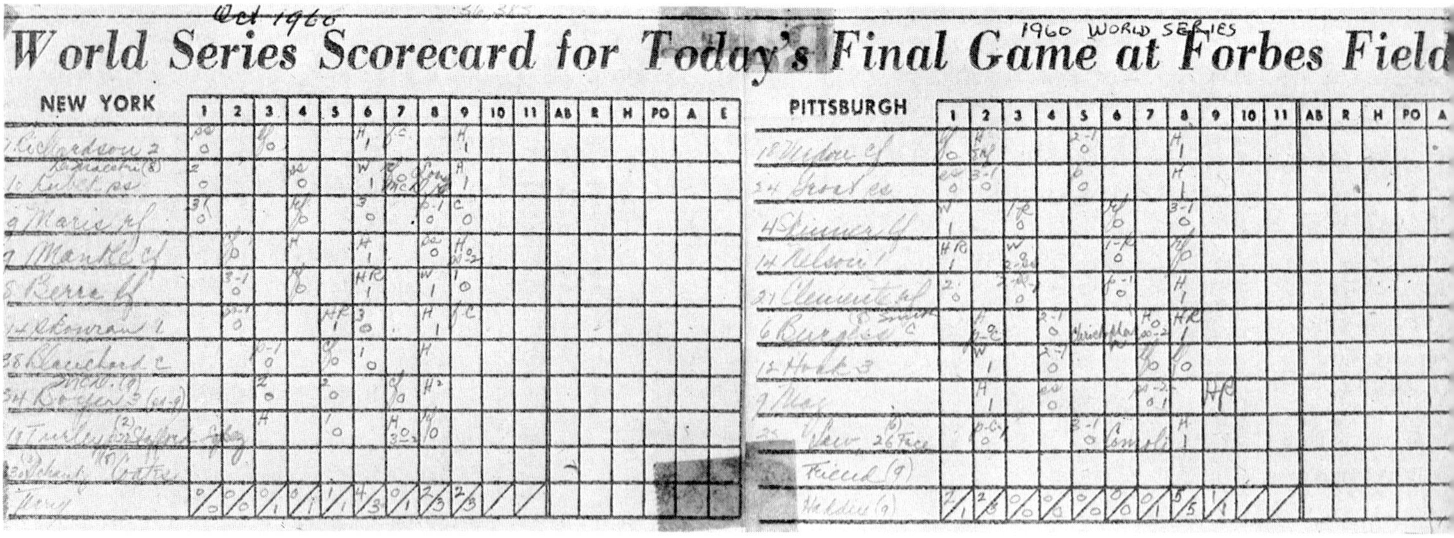
Oct 1960

1960 WORLD SERIES

World Series Scorecard for Today's Final Game at Forbes Field

NEW YORK	1	2	3	4	5	6	7	8	9	10	11	AB	R	H	PO	A	E

PITTSBURGH	1	2	3	4	5	6	7	8	9	10	11	AB	R	H	PO	A

Pirates

Name of Park	Date 1st Game Played	Opponent & Score	Capacity
Recreation Park	April 30, 1887	Pittsburgh 6, Chicago 2	9,000*
Exposition Park	April 22, 1889	Chicago 7, Pittsburgh 6	6,500*
Forbes Field	June 30, 1909	Chicago 3, Pittsburgh 2	24,000 35,000**
Three Rivers Stadium	July 16, 1970	Cincinnati 3, Pittsburgh 2	50,235

** Estimated attendance that day.*
*** Capacity expanded.*

Top: *Scorecard of 1960 Series finale.* Above: *Three Rivers Stadium, Pirates' home since 1970.* Opposite: *Dean of the current sluggers, Willie Stargell.*

the new Pirates were blacks and Latins. "We were one of the early clubs in Latin America," says Brown. "Some people feel that at times we've had too many blacks and Latins on the team. You look at the Motas, Clementes, Sanguillens, Alous, Olivers, Pagans, Stennetts, McBeans, Stargells—they've been a big part of our story. If they can play the game, that's all we're interested in, and we've got a lot more down the line."

In 1971. Pittsburgh batted its way to the World Series against the Baltimore Orioles. Joe Brown has a special affection for those 1971 Pirates: "Most of the players were ones I had brought to the team; it was my baby." Willie Stargell smashed a league-leading 48 homers and drove in 154 runs. Clemente hit .354.

Against Baltimore in the World Series, Clemente was an acrobat, a dancer, a warrior. He fielded with consummate skill and his arm ruled the basepaths. But if he was formidable in the field, he was sublime at bat.

Clemente was not a scientific hitter; any one of a number of pitches could badly fool him. But a pitcher didn't dare repeat that pitch. The low outside curve he had just waved at would wind up in the right field corner if it came in again. Clemente's greatness lay in his ability to foil any consistent pitching strategy.

In the Series he continued to hit intuitively but with such astounding reactions that nothing seemed to fool him. The body rocked, leaned, lunged, as always, but the bat remained cocked in readiness until the last moment, until the pitch revealed itself. Only then did he attack it.

Clemente made out in that Series, but almost every time up he hit the ball hard. While his teammates hit barely .200 against the Orioles' pitching, Clemente hit .414, and with power. He had two doubles, a triple, and two homers, including the game and Series winner in the seventh game.

There was a third straight Eastern Division title in 1972. In September of that year, Clemente recorded the three thousandth, and last, hit of his career. On New Year's Eve he was killed in a plane crash en route to Managua, Nicaragua, to aid earthquake victims. The complex man, never fully understood or appreciated, left behind mourners still struggling to realize just what he had meant to the Pirates and to baseball. "He was the Pirates," offers a Pittsburgh fan, Mary Anne Connolly, "and they were different without him."

In 1973, Clemente became the first Latin American ballplayer to be inducted into the Hall of Fame. That year, without him for the first

time in 18 years, the Pirates lost more games than they won and wound up third, though Stargell led the league in homers and RBIs. The next year, a late-season drive powered once again by hitting gave the team its fourth divisional title in five years, but the Pirates lost in four games to the Dodgers in the playoffs.

In 1975, Pittsburgh again rose to the top of the Eastern Division, this time with some of the best pitching in the league as well as with the usual potent attack. However, the Reds proved too powerful in the playoffs, and for the fourth time in five tries the Pirates lost the pennant after winning their division.

There was cause for frustration but hardly for alarm. With the Al Olivers, Rennie Stennetts, and Dave Parkers leading the parade of farm system-bred talent to the big club, the Pirates show no sign of stopping their hitting. And when the Pirates are hitting, they are usually healthy.   89

Spirit of St. Louis
The Cardinals

O verall, the St. Louis Cardinals have been a flourishing flock. They have done a bit less feasting than some, but a lot less starving than most. They have not been the richest team, but they are among the most vigorous and deeply rooted. The squawking that has erupted in St. Louis in good times as well as in bad has kept the nest from becoming too cozy. The franchise has rarely been tranquil, but it has never been stagnant. And as for roots, well shortly after the American League Browns changed to Birds themselves and left St. Louis to this species, the nickname and the city showed such an affinity for one another that the football Cardinals flew down from Chicago.

Now the Redbird resides in St. Louis from April through December (the interlude filled with basketball Spirits and hockey Blues). There is no thought of leaving; after all, it has been a good life.

National League baseball did not begin prosperously in St. Louis. During the Gay Nineties, the St. Louis ball club was a drag. First called "the Browns" ("Grays" might have been more appropriate), then even more incongruously, "the Perfectos," the team left the National League twice, then returned by finishing twelfth three times, eleventh three times, tenth once, ninth once, and once as high as eighth in the years 1892–99. Owner, president, and manager

Ted Simmons is the most accomplished of the Cardinals' current batch of youngsters. Bake McBride, waiting on deck was, through 1975, promising.

Chris Von Der Ahe, unaccustomed from his American Association days to failure, watched St. Louis frolic as his team floundered, and decided to embrace the spirit of the times. To attract customers to Robison Field, he arranged promotions that make today's seem like Cracker Jack box give-aways. Von Der Ahe transformed the ball park into an amusement park—"the Coney Island of the West," he called it—with chute-the-chutes (tubs that plunged with their riders into a pool), night horseracing, a Wild West show, and later, boating. To play the top tunes of the day, he hired the Silver Cornet Band, an all-female contingent spiffed up in long striped skirts, elegant blouses with leg of mutton sleeves, and broad white sailor hats. Somewhere in the midst of all this activity there was a ball game, which itself deserved glamorizing, so in 1899, the home team was decked out in flashy new uniforms featuring red trim and red-striped stockings. Thus, the ball club became "Cardinals," or "Redbirds."

The improvement was strictly in appearance. In the first 15 years of the new century, there were 13 second-division finishes.

In 1917, a brainy, 36-year-old executive with a passion for record keeping and a reputation for new-fangled ideas became president of the Cardinals. Wesley Branch Rickey, whose major league career had lasted 119 games, in which he compiled a .239 batting average, knew mediocrity when he saw it, and the Cardinals assaulted him with it. In 1916, with the worst pitching in the league and six of the eight regulars batting less than .250, St. Louis had finished tied for last. The only bright spot was a twenty-year-old Texan named Rogers Hornsby, purchased by the Cards for $400. Under the tutelage of manager Miller Huggins, Hornsby hit .313 in 1916, and the next year raised it to .327. Apparently, some of "the Rajah's" prowess rubbed off on his teammates, who also improved their averages in 1917. The Redbirds shocked the league by finishing third, winning the most games to that point in their history: 82.

The next year Huggins was gone to New York, and the Cards "returned to normalcy," in the words of a popular political sentiment of the next few years, plummeting to last place. Rickey realized that the Cards couldn't match other teams in the riches they offered players. So he convinced new owner "Lucky Sam" Breadon to spend money more thriftily and fruitfully in the acquisition of minor league teams, which would, by the Rickey plan, hatch a flock of good young Redbirds. In short, Rickey formulated the first modern farm system. "What

Rickey's trying to do can't be done," snapped John McGraw, who was doing just fine under the old system. "It's the stupidest idea."

Undeterred, "Farmer" Rickey got $200,000 in seed money from the sale of Robison Field, and began planting. The Cardinals purchased Houston in the Texas League and then Fort Smith in the American Association. The parent club moved up to third in 1921 and 1922 mostly on the strength of Rickey's shrewd scouting and trading, but thereafter the harvest from the farm began to roll in.

One of the first really good pickings was "Sunny Jim" Bottomley, a good-natured fellow whose cap rested permanently askew on the side of his head, perhaps to accentuate his powerful left-handed swing. After moving through Houston and Syracuse to the big club, he hit .371 as a rookie in 1923, second only to Hornsby. On September 16, 1924, he set a modern league record with six hits in one game and tied a major league record by driving in 12 runs.

Chick Hafey was another find. He came to the Cardinals as a pitcher, but Rickey instantly changed him to an outfielder when he saw him hit the line drives that gained him the nickname, "Chain Lightning." He reached the big club in 1924 and was a regular the next year.

At about this time the pitching staff acquired two mainstays in Jesse ("Pop") Haines, an overpowering fastballer with a wicked curve, and "Flint" Rhem, a drawling South Carolinian with a tan the color of the soil in his home state. Both would be 20-game winners for the Cardinals, and Haines pitched a no-hitter in 1924.

Despite the improvement in capability, the Cards were in last place on Memorial Day, 1925. Breadon became impatient. Rickey, who had managed the club since 1919, was kicked upstairs, and Hornsby succeeded him as manager. "I just couldn't stand it," the owner groused. "We had too much talent to stay here."

The Cardinals' play under Hornsby—particularly the play of Hornsby himself—proved Breadon right. The new manager led by example, winning the triple crown with a .403 batting average, 39 homers, and 143 RBIs. He also led the league in total bases with 381 and slugging percentage at .756. The Cards climbed to fourth by season's end.

The Rajah was a prickly boss, who remained aloof from the rest of the squad. "He never hung around much with his players," recalls Haines, "even before he became manager."

The 1926 Cardinals won the pennant, though their leading hitter "slumped" to .317 and 93 RBIs. Bottomley took up some of the slack with 120 RBIs, and a couple of midseason additions put the Cards over the top. One was aging outfielder Billy Southworth, who batted .317. The other was ancient Grover Cleveland Alexander, thirty-nine years old and often an excessive drinker but still with something left. He won nine games, saved two, and compiled a 2.92 ERA, the best on the staff.

His greatest moment of glory came in the World Series against the Yankees—not in games two or six, both of which he won, but in the finale, in which he was not supposed to pitch. After winning game six and celebrating that night, Pete was sleeping it off in the bull pen during the seventh game when starting pitcher Jesse Haines developed a blister on a finger of his pitching hand and had to come out. Alexander was awakened to pitch to Tony Lazzeri with two outs in the seventh inning, the bases loaded, and the Cardinals clinging to a 3–2 lead.

"Don't worry," the old reliever told Hornsby as he arrived on the mound. "I guess there's nothing to do but give Lazzeri a lot of trouble."

Alexander conferred with battery mate Bob O'Farrell and agreed to pitch Lazzeri low and away. Then he wound up and fired an inside fastball. "Lazzeri creamed it," Haines remembers. "Yup, it started out fair; we thought it was going to get out. Then it hooked foul at the last moment. We all had our hearts in our mouths as we watched it."

The imperturbable Alexander threw two more pitches, curves low and away this time, and Lazzeri struck out. "Pete was a silent drinker and he'd probably had a little more than he should have," Haines concedes. "But I'll tell you, he was dead sober when he faced Lazzeri."

After the hangover lifted, the Yanks couldn't touch the old master in the last two innings. He allowed Babe Ruth to reach in the ninth, but the Babe was gunned down stealing for the final out of the Series. "We don't know why he came," said Hornsby in his moment of triumph, "but we were ready for him." Alexander had saved the Redbirds' first World Series win. "There will never be a thrill like that one for any of the 1926 Cardinals," gushed Hornsby.

At the end of his eleventh full season with the Cards, Hornsby should have been at the height of his popularity. The greatest right-handed hitter in the history of the game had won six consecutive batting titles and as manager had brought the team not only to its first pennant but also its first world championship, over the mighty "Murderers' Row" Yankees. The fans loved the Rajah, but neither Rickey

nor owner Sam did. That winter, Hornsby was sent to New York (where he would last a year before moving on to Boston) in exchange for "the Fordham Flash," Frankie Frisch, and Jimmy Ring. The St. Louis fans were stunned and furious. They hung black crepe around Breadon's home in mourning for Hornsby, or, as others said, as a threat to the owner.

The defiant fans made it trying for new second baseman Frisch and new manager Bob O'Farrell, the MVP the year before, but despite the pressure, each man performed admirably, and the Redbirds almost won the pennant again.

In 1928, the Cards switched pilots again, Bill McKechnie replacing O'Farrell. The new face in training camp that year was the grimy, grizzled mug of one John Martin, who true to his appearance, had ridden the rails to get to camp. Not yet good enough to stick with the club, the disreputable-looking fellow spent the 1928 sea-

son shuttling between the Cardinals and their farm teams, playing 39 games for the parent club. He stayed in readiness by prospecting for hairpins, which he said brought him luck. The peculiar fellow disappeared back to the minors for the 1929 season, but Pepper Martin would be back soon, to be the leader of a spirited pack called the Gashouse Gang.

Meanwhile, the Cards hummed along at a .617 clip in 1928, the best winning percentage in their history—and squeaked past McGraw's men for the flag. Firing like a siege gun, Sunny Jim hit .325, with 31 homers and 136 RBIs, and won the Most Valuable Player award. Pop Haines won 20 again, ageless Alexander 16, and Bill Sherdel 21. The Cards drew 778,147 fans, more than they ever had drawn, and ever would until 1946.

The Yankees of Ruth (.625 average, three homers, all in one game) and Gehrig (four homers and .545 average) battered the Cards' best three pitchers in the Series, and the Redbirds expired in four straight. Miffed, Breadon switched managers for the third time in three years—not unusual in the Russian roulette world of managers but for the fact that this club had won two pennants and a Series in three years. McKechnie was exiled to Rochester and replaced by the Rochester manager, Billy Southworth. By July they switched back, Southworth leaving as managers traditionally do—as a loser. Lucky Sam had shuffled his managerial Cards once too often; the club finished fourth.

As usual, the skippers had little to do with it. Pitching was the problem. In a year when hitters owned the league—the lowest *team* batting average was .280—the St. Louis pitchers fared worse than most. Alexander and Sherdel were all but through, and Haines had the worst ERA of his career, 5.71, though he won 13 games.

Opposite: *In 1926, player-manager Rogers Hornsby led the Cards to their first pennant and world championship.* Above: *The final out of the 1926 Series—Babe Ruth caught stealing by Tommy Thevenow.*

BILL HALLAHAN

Fortunately, in 1930, "Wild Bill" Hallahan, who had been up briefly in the mid-twenties, finally arrived as a solid starter, winning 15 games. "Old Stubblebeard," Burleigh Grimes, was picked up in a trade with Boston in June and contributed 13 wins. And on the last day of the season, young Jay Hanna Dean made his major league debut with a three-hitter.

On August 17, 1930, the Cardinals were 10 games out of first, but their winning stretch drive had already begun. Winning 39 of 49 starting on August 9, they swept to the pennant by two games over the Cubs. All eight starters hit better than .300.

The new man in charge of the 1930 team was a World War I veteran, "Ole Sarge," Gabby Street. He would last longer than his three predecessors put together. In the 1930 Series, unlike the Cards' 1928 meeting with the Yankees, it was not hitting but pitching that doomed St. Louis—Philadelphia's George Earnshaw and Lefty Grove each won two games. The Cards fell in six.

"You play me here or you trade me," the pugnacious Martin told Branch Rickey before the 1931 season. Pepper played—in center field —hit .300, and became one of two new major contributors to the Cards' second consecutive pennant. The other was big Paul Derringer, who won 18 games in his first year in the majors. The Cards of Frisch, Hafey, Bottomley, Hallahan, etc. needed no more help. Indeed, they may not have needed even that much. They romped home by 13 games over the pack. Frisch was the MVP, Hafey the batting king (by less than a point over Bill Terry and Bottomley), and Hallahan the strikeout leader. (He also tied for most wins, with 19.)

"You know that Cardinal team in thirty-one was really something," remembers Grimes. "It

94

could do everything: run bases, field, hit—the whole works. And you know, that was some team we beat in the Series, those A's of thirty-one."

They weren't as good as the Philadelphia team that had beaten the Cards the year before; they were better. The 1930 Athletics had won 102 games; the 1931 club won 107, for a .704 winning percentage, the second best in the history of the American League. The 1930 staff had two 20-game winners; the 1931 staff did too, and a 30-game winner in Lefty Grove, by far the best pitcher in the majors, with a 31–4 record and a 2.06 ERA. (This in a year when the average American League club hit .278.)

The Athletics' Grove and Earnshaw pitched well in this Series, as they had in the last one, but this time they had to contend with the frenetic Pepper Martin. "The Wild Hoss of the Osage" (so-called for his origins in Oklahoma, where the Osage Indians lived) had 12 hits in the first five games, and to the chagrin of the great Philadelphia catcher, Mickey Cochrane, five stolen bases.

"The thirty-one World Series was a pip," Jesse Haines recollects. "And my Lord, Pepper was really something. . . . He really had Mickey going crazy. He'd go up to the plate and say, 'Mickey, you'd better not let me get on because

Above right: *The frolicsome crew on its way to 1936 preseason fun and games in Cuba.* Top left and right, and opposite: *Some of the most frolicsome—Pepper Martin, Wild Bill Hallahan, and Leo Durocher.*

if I do, I'm a-going!' And he'd go. Poor Cochrane —he drove him crazy."

A thorn but not quite a dagger in the side of the Athletics, Martin subsided in games six and seven, and the Cards almost let Philadelphia off the hook. Grove's 8–1 victory in the sixth game tied the Series. Then, down by 4–0 in the finale, the American Leaguers rallied against the tiring thirty-eight-year-old Grimes in the bottom of the ninth. Enter Bill Hallahan, with the sterling Series record of 2–0, 0.49 ERA, to notch the final out in the 4–2 victory.

"My gallbladder was in awful shape," Grimes remembers. "I had it taken out later on. It would hurt even more when I'd look at Simmons, Foxx, and some of those guys."

It might have been expected that in victory there would be unity, but the Cardinals continued to be a fractious flock. The next year, though manager Street stayed, Grimes and Hafey were gone in trades.

In 1932, the Cardinals slipped to sixth, and the next year, with the team mired in fifth place in July, Frisch replaced Street as manager. Happily, this move more or less coincided with the spiraling career of Dizzy Dean, and the general resurgence of the Cards.

Jay Hanna Dean, born in a rickety shack to destitute Arkansas sharecroppers, realized the American dream at a time when most Americans had abandoned it. The country wanted entertainment more than inspiration, and he filled the need. He ingenuously boasted that he had perfected his pitching at Oklahoma State Teachers College, though in fact his formal schooling had ended in second grade. "I never bothered with what those guys could and couldn't hit," he drawled. "All I knowed is that they weren't gonna get a-holt of that ball ol' Diz was throwin'." Armed with that simple philosophy and the tools to accomplish it, the boy who had picked cotton for 50¢ a day became the highest paid and best pitcher in the National League. He led the league in strikeouts four times, and in 1934 was its Most Valuable Player. He and his brother Paul won 49 games for the Cards that year—30 for Dizzy, 19 for Daffy. Before a doubleheader against the lowly Dodgers, Diz predicted, "I doubt the Brooks gets a hit off'n me an' Paul today." If the Dodgers are given the benefit of Dean's doubt, he was quite right. The brothers allowed the Bums one hit in the doubleheader, Paul pitching a no-hitter in the nightcap.

That 1934 team was in all but name the legendary "Gashouse Gang." (The nickname was first applied a year later.) Jim ("Ripper") Collins

Detroit third baseman Marv Owen while sliding into third on a triple in the sixth. The next inning the fans pelted Medwick with all the refuse at their disposal when he took his position in left. Amidst the hail of rotten fruit, eggs, and glass bottles (where, one wonders, did it all come from if the Detroit fans hadn't planned the bombardment before the incident), Medwick stood his ground resolutely, his jaw jutting out in defiance. Finally, Commissioner Landis ordered Medwick removed from the game "to protect the player from injury and allow the game to proceed." No soldier ever left the firing line as reluctantly.

Though they came close, the Cardinals didn't win again until 1942, by which time most

had replaced Bottomley at first. Frisch continued to hold down second. The shortstop was screechy young Leo Durocher, who came from Cincinnati in exchange for Paul Derringer. Pepper Martin had been moved from center to third. Virgil ("Spud") Davis was the catcher. The outfield consisted of Jack Rothrock in right; Ernie Orsatti, Martin's sidekick in fun and games, in center; and Joe ("Ducky") Medwick in left.

This was a team as free spirited on the field as off. Medwick, nicknamed "the Hungarian Rhapsody" for the ardor with which he played, could tomahawk a head-high fastball or golf a curve at his feet. As an infielder, Martin disdained use of his glove in stopping ground balls and used his chest instead. Medwick and Martin led the team in romping around the basepaths and belly flopping into bases. If ever any team did, the 1934 Cardinals charged to the pennant.

St. Louis first entered first place in the last series of the year. Dizzy Dean, pitching with only two days of rest, blanked the Reds 4–0. Paul won the second game 6–1. Then Dizzy returned, with only one day of rest, and mowed down the Reds 9–0 for the pennant clincher and his thirtieth win.

In the 1934 Series, "the Dazzling Deans," as they were known, pitched St. Louis to the world championship over the Detroit Tigers. With the Cards trailing 3–2 in games, Paul Dean beat the Tigers' Schoolboy Rowe 4–3, evening the Series. Then Dizzy clinched it with his second win of the Series, a six-hit 11–0 shutout at Detroit.

Medwick sent the Detroit fans into a frenzy during the final romp when he allegedly spiked

of the Gashousers had gone. Dean was traded to Chicago in 1938, after a line drive off Earl Averill's bat in the 1937 All-Star Game cracked his toe, hobbling him for the rest of the season. He left the Cards having won an average of 22 games a year in his six years. He would never win as many as 10 in a season again.

In 1942, the Cardinals did better than any other Cardinals' team, winning 106 games, and introduced the player who on the whole would do better than any Cardinals' player. Nicknames tend to distort a ballplayer's importance as they glorify him, but in the case of "Stan the Man" Musial, the nickname perfectly describes his stature. For two decades he was the preeminent hitter in the National League. At twenty-one he

The greatest of the Gashousers: Dizzy Dean, above left; Frankie Frisch, above right; and Joe Medwick, opposite, sliding into Detroit's Marv Owen on the play that provoked 1934 Series rhubarb.

hit .315; at forty-one he hit .330, one point under his lifetime mark. Today, he remains the Cardinals' Man with most games played, runs, hits, doubles, triples, homers, and total bases.

Musial twisted himself so tightly in his batting stance that he seemed frozen when in fact he was poised for the kill. Only the bat somehow remained loose, hovering in readiness. Uncoiling like a striking rattler, he sprayed his venomous line drives wherever the defense was exposed. He could pull the ball down the right field line or lash it into the power alleys. He hit with power (475 career homers) but not at the expense of control. He struck out only once in about fifteen at-bats, compared to Snider's and Mantle's once in six, Kiner's once in seven, Mays's once in eight, Aaron's once in ten. Musial came as close as any hitter to finding that ideal balance between power and consistency.

The 1942 Cardinals won the pennant by defeating the third team in the twentieth century to win more than 100 games and not win the pennant, Leo Durocher's Dodgers. Then the Cards crushed the DiMaggio-led Yankees in the Series four games to one.

It was difficult to choose which achievement was the more impressive. In winning the pennant, the Cardinals came from 10 games back in August. They caught up with the Dodgers in a late September two-game series in Ebbets Field, winning the second game 2–0 behind Mort Cooper. Rookie Whitey Kurowski accounted for the runs with a two-run homer off Whitlow Wyatt, who had beaten Cooper and the Cardinals 1–0 at Sportsman's Park a year before in the pivotal battle in that pennant race. This year the Dodgers won their last eight straight, but the Cardinals never faltered and the pennant was theirs.

There were not many who said the Yankees were beatable in the Series, certainly not in five games. Like many of the Yankees' great teams of the era, this one depended on no one man.

The Cardinals beat this beautifully well-balanced team not with overpowering pitching, nor with fine consistent hitting, nor even with particularly good fielding. They allowed the Yanks 18 runs in five games, batted only .239, and committed an average of two errors per game. They beat the Yankees at their game—balance, winning four consecutive cliff-hangers with the clutch plays that distinguish a truly great team. The Yankees were as resilient in adversity as the Dodgers had been during the pennant race, but the Cards were again indomitable. The baseball axiom that championship teams show their greatness in tight games was never more convincingly proved.

After Red Ruffing beat Mort Cooper 7–4 in the opener, the Cardinals led 3–0 in the second game behind their rookie 21-game winner, Johnny Beazley. Then in the top of the eighth, Joe DiMaggio scored Roy Cullenbine with a base hit and Charley Keller followed with a game-tying homer. But Enos Slaughter's double and Musial's single regained the lead for St. Louis in the bottom of the inning, and in the ninth Slaughter preserved the victory by gunning down pinch runner Tuck Stainback at third.

In game three Ernie White shut out the Yanks on six hits. The Cards had only five, but they got a run on a scratch single in the third,

97

The youth movement and the elder statesman.
Clockwise from above: *Al Hrabosky, Ken Reitz,*
Bake McBride, and thirty-six-year-old Lou Brock.

HOME CLUB PLAYERS	Pos.	A.R.	Runs	Hits	T.B.	2B.	1B.	H.R.							P.O.	A.	E. D.P.
Schoendienst	2b	5		2	2								1		1	7	2
Moore	cf	5	1	3	3										1		
Musial	1b	4	2	3	3	1		1							10		3
Slaughter	rf	4		2	2								4		1		
Kurowski	3b	2	1					2	1				1		2		
Garagiola	c	4		3	3				2	1			2				
H. Walker	lf	3		1	1			1	1				3				
Marion	ss	4											5	4	3		
Pollet	p	4											1		2	1	1
		35	4	12	14	1		4	4				27	16	1	3	

Passed Balls:

Double Plays (Names): Pollet-Marion-Musial; Schoendienst-Marion-Musial, two.

Grounded Into Double Plays (Names):

VISITING CLUB PLAYERS	Pos.	A.R.	Runs	Hits	T.B.	2B.	1B.	H.R.							P.O.	A.	E. D.P.
Stanky	2b	3	1	1					1	2			3	2			
Lavagetto	3b	3			1								1	2			
Medwick	lf	4	1	1									1				
1-Tepsic	--	0															
Whitman	lf	0											1				
F. Walker	rf	4															
Furillo	cf	4											5				
Reese	ss	4	1	2	2								2	2			
Edwards	c	4		2	2								5	1			
Schultz	1b	3	1	2	5	1	1			2			6				
Branca	p	1											1				
Higbe	p	0															
s-Rojek	--	0					1										
Gregg	p	0															
t-Ramazzotti	--	1															
Lombardi	p	0															
Melton	p	0															
		31	2	8	11	1	1	3	2				24	7			

Passed Balls:

Batted for Higbe 5 inning   Batted for Gregg 7 inning

Batted for inning   Ran for Medwick 8 inning

Double Plays (Names):

Grounded Into Double Plays (Names): Lavagetto, Stanky, F. Walker.

Score by Innings	1	2	3	4	5	6	7	8	9	10	11	12	13	14	15	16	17	18	19	Totals
St. Louis	1		2			1		x												4
Brooklyn	1			1			1													2

PITCHER'S SUMMARY

PITCHER	CLUB	Lost	Innings Pitched	Runs	Hits								
Pollet	St. Louis	9	35	2	8	1	2	1	3	2			x
Branca	Brooklyn	x	2-2/3	16	3	6	3	2	3		x		
Higbe	"		1-1/3	5	1								
Gregg	"		2	8	1			1	1				
Lombardi	"		1/3	2	1	1	1						
Melton	"		1-2/3	8	3		1					x	

PLAYS FILL IN
Men on bases when   Branca   was relieved in   inning   No. out   2
    Lombardi   "   7   1

Weather Conditions: Wind from N. E. and S. E. Fair; 63 degrees game time. Ground Conditions: Dry. Time: 2 hr. 48

Umpires: Beardon, plate; Pinelli, first base; Goetz, second base; Boggess, third base.

Martin J. Haley
St. Louis Globe-Democrat

REMARKS: First game of the first post-season play-off series ever played to decide a major League pennant. St. Louis and Brooklyn tied for first place at end of the regular 1946 season with 96 victories and 58 defeats each. ATTENDANCE, 26,012 paid; 320 military personnel.

added another in the ninth, and won, 2–0. The next day, St. Louis erupted for six runs and a 6–1 lead in the fourth, only to blow it in the Yankees' five-run sixth. Once again, however, the Redbirds prevailed, on Walker Cooper's base hit and Marty Marion's fly ball in the seventh. Then they clinched it in a thrilling finale, beating Ruffing for Beazley 4–2, on Kurowski's two-run homer in the ninth. Quickly and convincingly, if not easily, the St. Louis Cardinals had proved themselves the best in baseball.

The next year the Yanks got their revenge, but in 1944, the Cards were world champs again, beating the Browns in the first and only all-St. Louis World Series.

In 1946, the Cardinals and Dodgers resumed their bitterly contested pennant races after the interruption of four years of wartime baseball. For the last time, the Cardinals beat their arch-rivals, this time in two straight games in a best-of-three playoff after the regular season ended in a tie.

The seven-game Series against the Red Sox turned on one of the most famous plays in baseball history: Enos Slaughter scoring from first on Harry Walker's double to left center after shortstop Johnny Pesky allegedly hesitated in relaying the throw from the outfield. Films of the play revealed that Pesky hardly hesitated at all, and that in any case Slaughter could not have been caught. He simply ran the bases with the speed and daring of a baserunner who knows when and how to gamble.

This was the Series in which Ted Williams was supposed to continue the decimation of the National League that he had begun in the All-Star Game. Whatever he didn't deliver, his teammates in run production, Rudy York and Bobby Doerr, surely would. The three had accumulated 358 RBIs during the season. Tex Hughson and Boo Ferriss were to stifle the Redbirds' bats. In short, the scenario was similar to the one the experts had envisioned for the 1942 Series with the supposedly unbeatable Yankees—particularly similar in its inaccuracy.

No one, it seems, anticipated the moment of glory of Harry Brecheen, the slender left-hander from Broken Bow, Oklahoma. After the Sox beat Pollet in 10 innings in the opener, Brecheen whitewashed them 4–0 on just four singles. Then Boston won two of the next three (4–0 and 6–3 sandwiched around a 12–3 St. Louis rout) before Brecheen evened the Series with a seven-hitter in game six.

And so it was to be settled in seven—the Cards' little Murry Dickson against the Sox' big Boo Ferriss. At first it looked like a mis

Above: *The official scorecard of Cards' win in the first game of 1946 playoff. St. Louis won the next day too, for the pennant.* Opposite right and left: *Busch Stadium and its most illustrious resident.*

match. With one out, one on, and one run already in for the Sox in the first, Williams blasted a high drive off Dickson to deep center, well to the right of center fielder Terry Moore, who was positioned in right center for the pull hitting slugger. Had the drive fallen, the Red Sox would have had at least one more run and likely been rid of Dickson before Brecheen could rescue him. But Moore, still agile at thirty-four, raced after the drive and stabbed it backhanded. The next inning the Cards tied the score, and then preserved the tie with two more great catches—Harry Walker on Williams again, Terry Moore again on Pinky Higgins. Then, in the fifth, St. Louis knocked out Ferriss with two runs and led 3–1 in the eighth. Here Dickson finally tired, and in came the hero. "I knew he'd had only one day's rest," said manager Eddie Dyer of Brecheen, "but I figured I could still get two good innings out of him."

Actually, Brecheen surrendered a game-tying double to Dom DiMaggio before retiring the side, but thanks to Slaughter he had a second chance to nail down the win in the ninth. "It was a two-out situation; I was running all the way," said Country. All the way to the world championship.

And so the Cardinals ended a 20-year period that had been one of the most productive in modern National League history—nine pennants, five world championships, and an average of 91 wins a year. They were destined to go downhill from here.

In 1947, Breadon sold out for $4 million to Fred Saigh and Robert Hannegan. In 1953, August A. Busch, Jr., the Anheuser-Busch mogul, bought the club, refurbished old Sportsman's Park (where the Cards had played ever since Rickey sold Robison Field), renamed the park Busch Stadium, and in all, saved baseball in St. Louis. For by the early fifties, the Cards were a .500 ball club and sinking.

Fortunately, the farm system had been grooming executives as well as ballplayers. Vaughan P. ("Bing") Devine began climbing the ladder at the lowest rung, at Johnson City, Tennessee, of the Class D Appalachian League in 1941. Today, he is executive vice-president and general manager of the big club, or in a word, its architect. It was Devine who built the world championship team of 1964 with shrewd trades to supplement the homegrown talent. Curt Simmons, Curt Flood, Bill White, and Dick Groat all found new lives in St. Louis and cost the Cardinals virtually nothing in return. And it could only have been Devine inspiration that procured Lou Brock from the Cubs for Ernie Broglio.

"He came running when he was traded to St. Louis," says Schoendienst, "and he's been running ever since." Brock arrived in St. Louis in mid-June 1964. That year, in 103 games for the Cardinals, he hit .348 and stole 33 bases. "Coming to St. Louis," he remembers, "they asked me if I could steal bases. I didn't know anything about stealing bases."

If 33 steals is ignorance, what, one could justifiably ask, is the point of learning? Ten years later, at the tenderfooted age of thirty-five, Brock framed the final answer to that question with 118 swipes, handily breaking Maury Wills's record of 104. Like Wills, Brock at many times appeared to know before the pitcher did whether the ball was going to the plate or first base. When he broke for second, it was not so much a race between baserunner and throw

101

as a contest of calculations—the precise computations of Brock matched against the rough estimates of pitcher and catcher. Science consistently defeated intuition.

As the slightly built Brock dominated the basepaths for a decade, the towering Bob Gibson loomed invincible on the pitching mound. After Sandy Koufax retired in 1966, Gibson, already a superstar, became the undisputed king of the hill. In 17 seasons he was a 20-game winner five times, an All-Star six, and a 200-strikeout man nine (a record). No Cardinal has won more games; no National League right-hander has more strikeouts.

The Gibson style was overpoweringly direct: bust 'em with the hard one, break 'em with the curve, blow 'em down before they get settled.

He took almost as little time between pitches as his pitches took to reach the plate. A batter who took practice cuts was made to feel he was wasting time. Gibson was the quintessential man in a hurry.

By 1964, Gibson had established himself as the ace of the St. Louis pitching staff, not the strongest in the league but adequate to support the Cardinals' balanced attack. In addition to Brock, who filled the hole in the outfield left when Musial retired, the Cards had a .300 hitter in first baseman White and 100-RBI men in both White and third baseman Ken Boyer. Flood hit .311, Boyer .295, Groat .292, and catcher Tim McCarver .288. In 1963, essentially the same team won 93 games and failed to catch the Dodgers. The 1964 team again won 93 games, but

this time it was enough. The Dodgers were in eclipse, and the Phillies, after they folded in the stretch, recovered to knock the Reds out of first place with two wins in the last two games. When the smoke had cleared, the Cardinals, panting but still breathing after salvaging the one game they needed of the season-closing set with the Mets, had the pennant.

They had barely caught their breath from this most exhausting pennant chase when they moved on to the Yankees, themselves in the unaccustomed position this year of having been pressed for the pennant. If not for the September heroics of young Mel Stottlemyre, the Bronx Bombers would have surrendered their place in the October follies to the hitless wondrous Chicago White Sox.

In short, neither the Cards nor the Yankees won the pennant on great pitching. Nor would the Series be won that way, as quickly became clear in game one when the Yankees cuffed 20-game winner Ray Sadecki and the Cards treated Whitey Ford even more rudely. St. Louis prevailed 9–5, and Ford retired sore-armed from the shooting gallery for the remainder of the Series. Except for a fine pitching duel between Jim Bouton and Curt Simmons in game three, the hitters continued to predominate the rest of the way.

By game seven each team was averaging better than four runs per contest. The style of the Series had been set, and it held through the rubber match. With six runs in the first five innings, the Cardinals provided a cushion just

Cardinals

Name of Park	Date 1st Game Played	Opponent & Score	Capacity
Grand Avenue Grounds	May 5, 1876	St. Louis 1, Chicago 0	3,000*
Robison Field	June 6, 1885	Chicago 9, St. Louis 2	10,300
Sportsman's Park	July 1, 1920	Pittsburgh 6, St. Louis 2	17,600
Busch Stadium**			30,500
Busch Memorial Stadium	May 12, 1966	St. Louis 4, Atlanta 3	50,100

Estimated attendance that day.
**Sportsman's Park renamed Busch Stadium and capacity expanded.*

big enough for Gibson, who struggled to his second win of the Series, 7–5.

Thus the Cardinals beat the Yankees for the third time in a World Series, more often than any other team has. However, as the Cardinals had discovered before, all was not well that ended well. Manager Johnny Keane, shaken when Busch had fired Devine in midseason, now jumped before he was pushed, and for the third time in their history the Cardinals changed managers after winning the pennant.

Three years later St. Louis returned to the Series with a better team and more stable leadership. Under the guidance of Red Schoendienst, who was to become the longest tenured manager in the team's history, the 1967 Cardinals romped to the pennant by 10 games, even though they lost Gibson for seven weeks with a broken leg. Dick Hughes, Steve Carlton, and Nelson Briles stepped ably into the breach, supported by Joe Hoerner in relief. Strong-armed Mike Shannon had moved from right field in 1964 to third base in 1967 in order to make room for New York refugee Roger Maris. At first base Orlando Cepeda (cost: Ray Sadecki) had replaced Bill White, and led the league in RBIs with 111. The other major change from 1964 was light- but clutch-hitting Dal Maxvill for Dick Groat at short.

Without Gibson the Cardinals might have won the pennant, but they depended on him dearly in the Series against the Red Sox. Hughes was hit hard in two starts, and Carlton failed to win another. Only Briles, with a 5–2 victory in game three, supported the indomitable Gibson.

Bob pitched 27 innings—three complete games. He struck out an average of a batter an inning and allowed an average of a run a game. Thus, he single-handedly shattered the Red Sox' "Impossible Dream." Boston could survive the rapacious baserunning of Brock, the hot streaks at bat of Maris and Javier. But the Red Sox were helpless before Gibson's assault from the mound. The Series lasted seven games, perhaps longer than it should have, but ended decisively, with the Cardinals battering an exhausted Jim Lonborg and Gibson cracking a homer, as if his pitching wasn't enough.

Until the last game, the 1968 season was virtually a repeat. The lineup was identical. The hitting fell off, but the pitching picked up. And this time Gibson pitched the entire season— probably the most brilliant of his career (and

104

Preceding pages: Busch Memorial Stadium has the famous Gateway Arch among its neighbors in downtown St. Louis. Clockwise from above: Willie Davis, Lynn McGlothen, and Reggie Smith.

possibly anyone else's). He won 22 games, including 15 in a row and 13 'shutouts. His ERA, 1.12, was the lowest in National League history for a pitcher who worked more than 300 innings. He finished 28 of his 34 starts. He won the Cy Young Award and the MVP. "The entire year stands out in my mind," he says now. "You don't think about a year like that while it's going on. You just go out and you pitch, and you can't wait to go out there the next time. But it's a thing you think about seriously later."

Neither 31-game winner Denny McLain nor any of the other Detroit Tigers could cope with Bob Gibson in the Series opener. Gibson whiffed 17 batters, a World Series record, and shut out Detroit on five hits, 4–0. In game four he thrashed McLain again, 10–1, and again allowed only five hits.

Through the first six games, the Series followed the pattern of 1967. The Cardinals won the first, third, and fourth but failed to clinch it in the fifth or sixth. Once again it came down to the seventh game, but this time the Cards faced a still-strong Mickey Lolich in the finale instead of an overworked Jim Lonborg.

For those St. Louis fans who believe in omens, the sixth inning was ominous. Lolich picked off Brock, who had stolen seven bases in this Series (as in the previous year's), and then Curt Flood. Even so the Cardinals might have prevailed behind Gibson if not for a fateful fly ball in the seventh. With two on and two outs, Jim Northrup lifted one to the usually impeccably fielding Flood in center. Flood started in, then realizing that he had misjudged the ball, began to scramble back, only to slip and fall as the ball carried over his head for a two-run triple. Down 3–0 before the inning was over, the mighty Cardinals (big favorites before the Series to trounce the Tigers) had slipped and fallen too.

St. Louis has yet to return to the World Series, or even to win a divisional title. Gibson is gone now and Brock slowing down, so the team that was close to the Mets in 1973 and even closer to the Pirates in 1974 will depend on a new generation to win. As usual, the promise is there, in pitchers Lynn McGlothen, Bob Forsch, and bull pen king Al Hrabosky, "the Mad Hungarian"; outfielders Reggie Smith and Bake McBride; infielders Mike Tyson, Ted Sizemore, and Ken Reitz; and most talented of all, catcher Ted Simmons. Devine is back as GM, Schoendienst seems secure as manager, and the Cardinals are solid contenders. If their past indicates their future, it won't be long before they're on top again.

Amazin'!
The Mets

n spirit they were from the beginning the replacement for the lowbrow but often successful Brooklyn Dodgers. The form took a little longer. The first run they ever scored came home on a balk. They lost the first nine games they played. They finished last their first four seasons. Once, they were losing a game 12–1, and there were two outs in the bottom of the ninth inning. A fan held up a sign that said "PRAY!" There was a walk. Ever hopeful, thousands of fans responded to that minuscule rally with their irrepressible chant, "Let's go Mets!"

They were 100–1 underdogs to win the pennant in 1969 and, incredibly, finished the year as world champions. They obtained the man who was to become their best pitcher by picking his name out of a hat on April Fool's Day. In good times and bad, they have been truly Amazin' Mets.

The team was born on October 17, 1960, when the National League awarded a New York franchise to a group headed by Mrs. Joan Payson. Thus were rewarded the efforts of Mayor Robert F. Wagner, attorney William Shea, and a special committee appointed by Wagner and headed by Shea to return National League baseball to New York. M. Donald Grant, who had been the only board member of the New York Giants to vote against their move to San Francisco, was—and still is—chairman of the board. "They are moving away from the greatest

The Mets play in Shea Stadium (opposite) *before some of the most demonstrative fans in baseball.* Above: *Fans celebrate 1969 Series win.*

baseball town in the world," he said of the Giants, and put his money where his mouth was. George Weiss and Casey Stengel, both released by the New York Yankees, were signed by the Mets, Stengel to handle the team on the field, Weiss to build a ball club. "They are professionals," Grant explained. The team was christened "Mets" after a batch of other names were rejected, among them "Burros," "Skyscrapers," "Skyliners," "Bees," "Rebels," "Avengers," and even "Jets."

Grant remembers that in the National League expansion draft, the Mets' approach "was to intentionally choose players who had been favorites of New York, and young pitchers. . . . Our aim was to give people a good time, develop a team, and provide nostalgia."

The Mets' first official lineup, of April 11, 1962, was instant nostalgia:

Richie Ashburn	cf
Felix Mantilla	ss
Charlie Neal	2b
Frank Thomas	lf
Gus Bell	rf
Gil Hodges	1b
Don Zimmer	3b
Hobie Landrith	c
Roger Craig	p

And for those who wanted to wander even more misty-eyed into the past (the better to obscure the sorry state of present affairs), there were backup old-timers: Clem Labine, Gene Woodling, and Wilmer ("Vinegar Bend") Mizell, among others.

In the opening game, Gus Bell got the Mets' first hit. Gil Hodges delivered the first home run. And the Mets started a string of nine straight Opening Day losses, bowing 11–4 to St. Louis.

The Mets finished 60½ games out of first that initial season, losing more games than any other team in the twentieth century. Richie Ashburn was selected to the National League All-Star team, batted .306 for the season, and retired. He explained, "It was the only time I went to a ball park in the major leagues and nobody expected you to win. . . . I couldn't see going out there again and losing a hundred games. I enjoyed the Mets' players though, and the fans were good to us."

The fans were more than good. Playing in the aged Polo Grounds (Shea Stadium was being constructed at a cost of approximately $28 million near the site of the 1939 World's Fair, and would not be ready until 1964), the Mets drew almost a million fans. In their second year, they attracted more than a million rooters, won eleven more games, and played in a carnival-like

atmosphere before bed sheets and banners bearing messages of blind devotion. Such bumblers as Marvin Eugene Throneberry, whose initials, personality, and limited skills symbolized the club, melted the hearts of cynical New York sophisticates while winning the hearts of the impressionable kids who had never warmed to the Yankees. And of course, there were all those old fans of the Dodgers and Giants, who could be as patient with the new club as they had been through many a long season in Ebbets Field and the Polo Grounds.

"Throneberry looked like Mickey Mantle hitting, but he didn't get the same results," Ashburn says gently. "Marvelous Marv" was harder on himself. Once he yelled at a teammate who dropped an easy pop fly, "What are you trying to do, steal my fans?"

The other Mets, even the good ones, surrendered to the aura of incompetence. Duke Snider, his glorious days as a Dodger behind him, hit 14 home runs, made the All-Star team, was traded at the end of the 1963 season to the Giants, and labeled the Mets "a bunch of clowns." Clarence ("Choo-Choo") Coleman was Casey Stengel's favorite low-ball catcher. (Unfortunately, the Mets had few, if any, low-ball pitchers.) Jay Hook, possessor of a master's degree in engineering, could explain in scientific detail what made a baseball curve, but was usually frustrated in his attempts to put the theory into practice. Al Jackson was a gritty left-handed pitcher who in one epic demonstration of pure Metsian pathos hurled 15 innings of three-hit ball only to lose on two errors committed by not-so-marvelous Marv.

With characters such as these on the ball field and Casey Stengel in the dugout, the Mets became a box office success, each year increasing attendance, though on the field they did little to inspire devotion. No matter. Their manic fans supplied inspiration and devotion themselves. There were standing ovations for routine catches and loud fouls.

However, behind the fun and games of the losing early years, there remained the inescapable reality that the Mets could not be happy-go-lucky losers for much longer if they hoped to prosper. "The Mets and their management were determined to improve themselves and kept making efforts towards that end," Grant recalls. "Complacency is the greatest sin a ball club can have."

By 1965, "the youth of America," as Casey Stengel had dubbed his newly developing home-grown ballplayers, were transforming the Mets. Just four of the original expansion Mets re-

Casey Stengel was both the oldest and youngest of Mets—their parent and their biggest kid. Cartoonist Bruce Stark captured the dualism.

Clockwise from left: *Staub follows a foul; Kingman in the batting cage; Milner swipes at Oakland's Campaneris; the sign man disapproves.*

mained: Al Jackson, Chris Cannizzaro, Jim Hickman, and Joe Christopher. On the farm teams there were such promising players as a young left-hander at Greenville, South Carolina, Jerry Koosman, whom an usher had brought to the attention of management. Tug McGraw, Cleon Jones, Bud Harrelson, and Ron Swoboda were already arriving in New York.

Like children growing up—which many of them were—the Mets' fans said good-bye to some of the lovable relics of more innocent times, Rod Kanehl, for example. An escapee from eight years in the New York Yankees' farm system, Kanehl played seven positions for the Mets with more zest than skill. Gil Hodges left the Mets to manage Washington, and in return, Jimmy Piersall arrived. He smashed his one hundredth career home run, ran backward around the bases in jubilation, and was released by Casey Stengel. "Casey had a funny image," Ed Kranepool says, "but he was all business on the field."

From a series of front-office maneuvers around the majors, the Mets gained two of the men who would help produce their 1969 world championship team: Bing Devine and Yogi Berra. Devine, released as general manager of the St. Louis Cardinals in 1964, joined the Mets as assistant to Weiss. Berra was fired by the Yankees after losing the 1964 World Series to Johnny Keane's Cardinals. The Yankees replaced Berra with Keane, who had resigned as manager of the Cardinals, and Berra became a player-coach for the Mets in a public relations coup for the team over the seemingly heartless Yankees.

Devine shaped a good part of the Mets' future, stocking the farm teams with young ballplayers. "It was a challenge to help build a ball club from scratch," the affable executive remembers. By 1967, 54 different players, among them 27 different pitchers, played for the Mets. It seemed to be a practical demonstration of Stengel's boast: "This here team won't win anything until we spread enough of our players around the league and make the other teams horse—— too."

Stengel joined the list of former Mets in 1965 when he broke his hip in a fall and retired. There were those who had long before concluded that Stengel had outlived his usefulness to the team, but he was missed. "I really enjoyed playing for him," Kranepool recalls. "He was a book of knowledge. He could talk for hours. We didn't have enough talent for him. He kept a lot of guys from going crazy." Swoboda called Stengel "the star of the early Mets."

Stengel's successor was Wes Westrum, as quiet as the "Ole Perfesser" was loquacious, and thus with no sideshow to divert attention from the failures of the team. Westrum finished the 1965 season and remained until September 21, 1967, when his letter of resignation was accepted. The club's attendance had dropped for the first time. The improvement to a ninth-place finish in 1966 was forgotten when ineptitude and lassitude produced a cellar finish in 1967.

In 1968, Gil Hodges returned to the Mets and led the club to a ninth-place finish and a record 73 wins. In Kranepool's view, "Hodges was the turning point. He changed the attitude from clownishness to playing baseball."

For the first time. the Mets had the nucleus of a good ball club. Koosman won 19 games, Tom Seaver 16. ("Tom Terrific" came to the Mets after he was ruled a free agent because the Braves had signed him after his college baseball season had begun. The Mets were the lucky team that picked his name out of a hat.) Left fielder Cleon Jones, who batted .297; fellow Mobile, Alabama, native Tommie Agee in center; and Ron Swoboda and Art Shamsky platooning in right gave the Mets a solid outfield. Kranepool, Bud Harrelson, Ken Boswell, and Ed Charles formed the Mets' best infield yet.

Hindsight uncovers the roots of the 1969 success, but the drive to the world championship will never cease to be one of baseball's greatest upsets. More than two million fans pushed through the turnstiles at Shea to witness the miracle—a 100–1 pennant longshot winning 100 of 162 games, 38 of 49 after being 9½ games out of first on August 13. McGraw recalls that magnificent feeling of invincibility that grips a pennant winner: "We were making plays that we didn't even expect ourselves to make. We were playing a kind of reckless ball, and it was working. We'd hit a ground ball at them, and it would take a bad hop and we'd get a base hit. They'd hit a ball that was going through, and we'd turn it into a double play. Those kinds of things were happening every game, *every* game."

The New York newspapers told of the war in Vietnam that divided America and the mayoral campaign that divided New York. But millions were united by the Miracle Mets. To hippies and hard hats alike, the Mets provided a unifying respite from partisan politics. New York City gave the Mets a ticker tape parade to celebrate their three-game sweep of the National League playoff against Atlanta and the start of the World Series with Baltimore.

Just before the Series began, Baltimore's Brooks Robinson sniped, "We are here to prove there is no Santa Claus." After game one,

Robinson's words seemed prophetic. The score was Baltimore 4, Mets 1. New York ace Tom Seaver was the losing pitcher.

Unimpressed, Jerry Koosman promptly evened the Series in game two, beating the Orioles 2–1 with relief help from Ron Taylor. The Series now moved to New York, where the Orioles would be no match for the Metsian magic.

The third game was perhaps Tommie Agee's finest as a professional, and it proved to be the turning point of the Series. The Mets won 5–0 behind the combined four-hit pitching of Gary Gentry and Nolan Ryan. Agee led off the game with a home run. Later, as if guided by radar, he streaked first to his right and then to his left to snare two deep drives that would have accounted for five Baltimore runs had they dropped. The first catch came on a fling that carried Agee to the base of the wall in left center. The second was a diving, skidding effort to the glove side. After witnessing these miraculous contortions, Baltimore manager Earl Weaver groused, "I've never seen two such catches by the same player in the same game."

The Mets won the fourth game 2–1 in 10 innings behind Seaver, who in one superlative stretch retired 19 of 20 batters. If Weaver had some unpleasant feelings over Agee's theatrics, Ron Swoboda left him speechless—or at least not quotable—this day. With one out in the ninth, the Mets ahead 1–0, and Orioles on first and third, Brooks Robinson hit a sinking liner to right field. Swoboda raced in, stretched the full length of his body in midair, and speared the ball backhanded just before it hit the ground. The Orioles scored only one run where they might have scored more, and then surrendered in extra innings.

Tug McGraw: "That catch by Swoboda typified the entire second half of the year. If Swoboda were still playing, he would know more about himself, more about baseball. He wouldn't try to make that play. He just felt that he saw the ball and had a chance to catch it.

The fifth and final game attracted 57,397 screamers—an all-time Shea Stadium record—to root the miracle home. The Orioles took the lead early, 3–0 on Frank Robinson's home run, but by the seventh inning they had blown it. In the sixth, Donn Clendenon, who was to be voted the most valuable player in the Series, smashed one into the left field stands, his third Series home run, bringing the Mets within a run. In the seventh, Al Weis tied the score with a 375-foot blast into the temporary left field stands—his first home run at Shea Stadium in two years as a Met. By the eighth, "the greatest fans in the world," in Donald Grant's phrase, had become hysterical, and the Orioles were shaken.

Left fielder Don Buford misplayed Swoboda's soft line drive into a double, and the go-ahead run scored. A Jerry Grote grounder was fumbled, scoring Swoboda. The Mets led, 5–3.

The Orioles went quickly in the ninth, and so did the Mets' fans—onto the field, streaking, scratching, strutting, screaming. Huge globs of turf were ripped from the field. The bases were stolen. People danced and hugged and kissed. And the Miracle Mets, now world champions, were succinctly characterized by Casey Stengel: "They did it slow, but fast."

No longer did the Mets have to pretend to enjoy their improbable defeats; this triumph outshone every one of them. They could forget the longest doubleheader in history, on May 31, 1964, when they had played the Giants for 32 innings, made a triple play, and lost both games. Or the six hour and six minute, 24-inning 1–0 loss to the Astros in 1968. Ed Kranepool, with the Mets since 1962 and therefore the Met with the longest service, recalls 1969: "We never anticipated getting to the World Series."

And Ron Swoboda reminisces about 1969, which he calls "the birth of the Mets as a baseball team": "It's still magic to me, a fairy tale. But if you look at the record, it was no fluke. We had hitting when we needed it, fielding, and we were up to our tails in pitching. We were fortunate to blend together."

The blend was a team that hit .327 and compiled a 1.80 earned run average in the Series. That fail-safe combination easily stifled the vaunted Baltimore Orioles, who had finished 19 games in front in the American League East but could muster only a .146 team batting average against the Mets' aces in the Series.

A snowstorm of ticker tape and torn paper, blaring auto horns, and jubilant school children dismissed early from classes welcomed the Mets as their victory parade danced its way down Broadway. The miracle of the New York Mets had charmed a contentious city and taken it on a summer joy-ride that was ending in a final spurt of celebration. That special time is preserved on a baseball that Donald Grant keeps on his office desk. Embossed on the ball are Grant's words that became Quotation of the Day in the New York *Times*: "Our team finally caught up with our fans."

Number 14, manager Gil Hodges, whom Ron Swoboda described as a "man into winning, into success," had done the job. Hodges had planned and improvised brilliantly until it   *113*

seemed that the Mets could not fail to win. "He had all the moves to make the Mets a winner," states Kranepool. "You played his way or you didn't play. He molded young players. He was the turning point."

Under new manager Yogi Berra, the Mets were a little older in 1973, and seemed more brittle. Since their miracle of 1969, they had produced only three third-place finishes. In mid-August, with 44 games to play, they were in last place. Harrelson and Jones had missed nearly half the team's games. Jon Matlack and Jerry Grote had also been on the disabled list. Willie Mays had returned victoriously to New York as a Met on May 14, 1972, smashing a game-winning home run. But now he was old and worn.

Then the injured regulars returned and hit their stride. The Mets moved out of last place. "Nothing can ever be like 1969 was," Bud Harrelson said, "but in a lot of ways this was better." Harrelson anchored the Mets' infield. Jerry Grote batted .280. Cleon Jones made acrobatic catches and hit better than .300 in the stretch drive. Wayne Garrett blasted timely

home runs. Tug McGraw reeled off 12 saves and five wins, starting on August 22. "You gotta believe," the slogan McGraw introduced, became the battle cry. The Mets clinched the Eastern Division title on the season's last day. They had won without a 20-game winner, without a .300 hitter, without a 100-RBI man.

Next, the Mets dismantled Cincinnati's Big Red Machine in the National League playoffs, taking the final game, 7–2, behind Seaver with relief help from the omnipresent McGraw. Two fights enlivened the baseball action—a fistfight between Bud Harrelson and Pete Rose, and a "throwing contest" in which bottles and other missiles ping-ponged between Rose and irate fans in the left field stands. Peacemakers Tom Seaver, Cleon Jones, Yogi Berra, Rusty Staub (bat in hand), and Willie Mays (in his first public appearance since announcing his retirement two weeks before) rambled out to left field to calm the screaming, debris-throwing mob.

Oakland's mustached marvels were the Mets' opposition in the seventieth World Series, the first official meeting between the teams.

In Oakland in the opener the home team

The agony and the ecstasy. Opposite: *Mets lost this call and the*
1973 Series, though they had Mays pleading their case. Above:
Charles, Koosman, and Grote celebrate the final out in 1969.

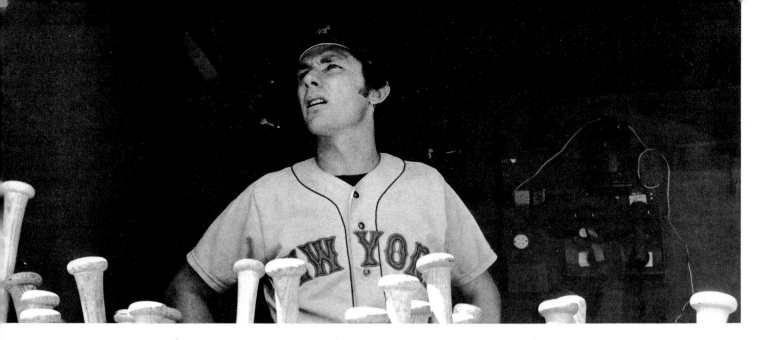

Mets			
Name of Park	**Date 1st Game Played**	**Opponent & Score**	**Capacity**
Polo Grounds	April 13, 1962	Pittsburgh 4, New York 3	55,000
Shea Stadium	April 17, 1964	Pittsburgh 4, New York 3	55,300

delighted the crowd of 46,021 with a 2–1 victory. The American League's designated hitter rule had restricted Oakland pitcher Ken Holtzman to one official batting appearance in 1973, but Holtzman's double in the third inning set up the A's two unearned runs. "They have fabulous pitching," Oakland manager Dick Williams observed of the Mets, "but we'll scrounge for all the runs we can."

The second game was a festival of scrounging. Before the Mets prevailed, 10–7 on the strength of a four-run twelfth inning, the usually neat-and-clean A's and Mets had played four hours and 13 minutes (the longest World Series game), committed six errors (five by the A's), and used eleven pitchers.

Ed Kranepool observes that "1973 was nothing like the first time—we'd been there before." But the Mets' fans, no less enthusiastic or reserved than they had been four years earlier, wanted 1969 all over again. A reinforced security force patrolled Shea Stadium for game three to deter any repetition of the frenzied fan reaction during the Cincinnati series. The weather, too, diminished the fans' exuberance. For this, the first nighttime World Series game in New York, temperatures hovered ominously close to freezing, and the crowd was too busy trying to keep warm to attempt any mischief. On the field the ballyhooed classic match between Tom Seaver and "Catfish" Hunter ended in a draw. Seaver pitched eight innings, Hunter six. Each allowed two runs and seven hits. Bert Campaneris singled home the winning run in the twelfth off

New York reliever Harry Parker, and the chilled spectators trundled home in their blankets, casting about for ways to light a fire under their Mets and perhaps themselves as well.

The pregame temperature was a relatively balmy 53 degrees for game four. The Mets won, 6–1, squaring the Series at two games apiece. Jon Matlack yielded but three singles through eight innings. Rusty Staub supplied the power— four hits and five RBIs.

Oakland coach Irv Noren: "I thought they had fifteen guys out there. I kept counting to make sure they hadn't slipped in any extra."

The Mets' exceptional pitching, and even more exceptional fielding, won game five, 2–0, for a 3–2 lead in games. Koosman pitched six and one-third innings, and McGraw, as usual, finished up. New York's Mayor Lindsay jubilantly flapped a huge "YOU GOTTA BELIEVE" sign from his box seat next to the Mets' dugout. Then the Series returned to Oakland with the Mets needing only to repeat their split of the first two games there to clinch the Series. Underdogs all year, they had finally become favorites but, sure enough, would to the very end confound the experts.

Oakland's Reggie Jackson had two doubles and a single and drove in two runs while Hunter, Darold Knowles, and Rollie Fingers limited the Mets to six hits in a 3–1 Oakland win in game six. The Mets' starter in the final game at Oakland was Jon Matlack, who had come as near to being the hero of this Series as any player. Blowing his fastball past the A's, Matlack had

In 1975, Tom Terrific, opposite top, *may have been the best pitcher in baseball, but the rest of the Mets were far less impressive.* Above: *Harrelson in repose.* Opposite bottom: *Phillips at work.*

allowed just one earned run in a string of 14 innings. Then disaster. In the third inning, Reggie Jackson and Bert Campaneris blasted two-run homers. After that the A's were never headed. Matlack said, "The first two innings I was getting away with mistakes, but in the third, they didn't miss any mistakes."

The Mets had come from last place on August 30 to game seven of the World Series, but no further.

The next year, the team plunged to fifth place and, inevitably, mass alterations were made for 1975. Tug McGraw, Ken Boswell, and Duffy Dyer, among others, were gone. Dave Kingman was purchased from the San Francisco Giants for $150,000. Gene Clines, Joe Torre, and Del Unser came in trades with the Pirates, Cardinals, and Phillies, respectively.

The 1975 Mets, and Berra in particular, were victims of rising expectations. Seaver regained his 20-win form, but the pitching staff as a whole, the core of previous pennant winners, was a disappointment. Matlack and Koosman were erratic winners, and only Bob Apodaca was a reliable reliever. Kingman hit dozens of homers and Kranepool batted well over .300, but there was little speed and often shoddy defense. The talented Mets, having outgrown their reputation as underdogs, seemed uncomfortable as contenders. In August, after an aborted run at the division-leading Pirates, Berra was sacked and coach Roy McMillan replaced him as interim manager.

There was sadness when Berra, as close as possible to a sacrosanct New York hero, got the axe. But the Mets' fans, like the team they nurtured, are full grown now, and they can accept, whether or not they agree with the firing of a manager when the team is not playing as well as it should.

Today, in place of the early infatuation and exaltation is love and marriage, in the long run a good deal more reliable. There will be squabbles between the fans and the club, as there must be between spouses, but neither partner is about to desert the other. In 1975, despite the disappointing play of the Mets, more than one and a half million New Yorkers came to see them. The Mets have won the loyalty of millions of New York National League fans, and it is this—more than the pennants and world championship—that has been their greatest accomplishment. Says Grant, "We worked hard to see that the old Dodger and Giant fans came back. We have developed the most ardent fan relationship in baseball. They are truly the greatest."

117

On the North Side of Chicago
The Cubs

The present preserves the past on Chicago's North Side at Wrigley Field, where the Cubs have played baseball since 1916. All the games are played in daylight on grass that is real and green. The fans are close to the action. Ivy vines climb the red brick outfield walls. Tall buildings crowd close to the little ball park, serving as penthouse seats for Cubs' rooters. There is no electric message board, no advertising. And through the many decades, almost mocking mass media, a flag with a "W" or "L" has been hoisted atop the scoreboard after each game to inform passersby whether the home team has won or lost.

The Cubs have specialized in stability and tradition. This is the only National League charter team with an uninterrupted life in the city of its birth. It has been owned for an unbroken line of 55 years by the Wrigley family. The Cubs haven't won a pennant since 1945, but if ever any club has proved that winning isn't everything, it has been the denizens of Chicago's North Side.

Of course, they haven't always been losers. As America took a fancy to baseball in the late nineteenth century, one of her first objects of affection, indeed of adoration, was the Chicago team led by baseball's first superstar, Adrian C. ("Cap") Anson. As player and manager, the powerfully built Anson led the club to six National League pennants between 1876 and 1886. It was Chicago's first great era in baseball and

Above: *North Side landmark.* Opposite top: *Early World Series ticket stub.* Opposite bottom: *The popular first baseman-manager, Frank Chance, who led the Cubs to four pennants.*

the first real dynasty in the history of the sport.

While the Cubs ruled the National League, Anson established something of a personal dynasty. He hit .300 or more for twenty years, won four batting championships, and was the first player to record 3,000 hits. An innovator too, he was credited with originating spring training when he took his team to Hot Springs, Arkansas, in 1886. And finally, he was a National League chauvinist. When asked to manage in the junior American League, Anson archly replied, "I will not insult my twenty-two year record by affiliating myself with minor league ball."

In 1890, many players abandoned the team for the Brotherhood League, so Anson recruited young players to replace them. The youthful team was called "Colts" and "Orphans," names that officially gave way to "Cubs" in 1900, by which time Anson was no longer a player and could concentrate fully on his role as mother bear to the pack.

The next great era for the Cubs was 1906–10, when a collection of now-legendary players brought Chicago four pennants and two world championships. The 1906 club, regarded as one of the greatest of baseball teams, won 116 games, setting the all-time major league record for victories in a season, and for winning percentage.

In the World Series, the Cubs faced their crosstown rivals, the Chicago White Sox, who had won the American League pennant with a .230 batting average. Their anemic hitting brought them the nickname "the Hitless Wonders," but it was no wonder how they won—pitching. The Sox' pitching staff recorded shutouts in 32 of the team's 93 victories. The pitching mastery continued in the Series, and the Cubs lost in six games.

Frank ("Husk") Chance, a performer in the tradition of Cap Anson, epitomized the Chicago Cubs of the time. Chance joined the team in 1898 and survived some brutal turn-of-the-century baseball. In 1904, for example, he received five well-deserved passes to first base in one game after being hit by five pitched balls. Apparently, the shelling didn't slow him down; he recorded 404 stolen bases in his career—a club record.

For his base stealing, clutch hitting, and generally spirited play, player-manager Chance was aptly nicknamed "the Peerless Leader." His troops were easily led. As first baseman, Chance anchored a peerless infield of Johnny Evers at second, Joe Tinker at shortstop, and Harry Steinfeldt at third. The underrated Steinfeldt tied for the league RBI title, and led all third basemen in fielding in 1906.

119

Johnny ("the Crab") Evers was a grouchy, combative fellow whose baseball training included repeated readings of the rule book. There might have been no 1908 pennant for the Cubs—no Fred Merkle play—had Evers not had a passionate interest in the nuances of the game. It was Evers who convinced umpire Hank O'Day that Merkle had not touched second and was out on a force play in the bottom of the ninth, nullifying what would have been the game-winning run. A victory in that late-season game would have given the Giants the pennant. Instead, the game ended in a tie and was replayed after the regular season ended with the Cubs and Giants deadlocked for the league lead. A 4–3 victory in the playoff gave the Cubs the title.

"Evers was a great ballplayer," Joe Tinker remarked, "but how he could ride you!" Chance often expressed the wish that Evers played the outfield, where his barbed tongue and frenetic personality wouldn't annoy the more easygoing Cubs. There were even a couple of years during which Tinker and Evers went without speaking to each other off the field. On the field, when Evers was his garrulous self, Tinker just didn't answer.

Tinker, Evers, and Chance made the double play into an art form of body language and instinctive understanding of each other's moves on the baseball diamond. With an assist from Franklin P. Adams, the trio became a legend, though their meager total of 54 double plays in their heyday (the 1906–09 period) hardly qualified them for such status. Wrote Adams, a newspaperman of the time, and a poet of sorts:

> These are the saddest of possible words—
>   "Tinker to Evers to Chance"
> Trio of Bear Cubs and fleeter than birds—
>   "Tinker to Evers to Chance"
> Ruthlessly pricking our gonfalon bubble,
> Making a Giant hit into a double,
> Words that are weighty with nothing but
>   trouble—
>   "Tinker to Evers to Chance."

Though the double-play combination of the Cubs received the bulk of the plaudits, the pitching staff was the hub of the team. The ace was Mordecai Peter Centennial ("Three Finger") Brown—"Centennial" for the year of his birth, 1876; "Three Finger" for his right hand, mangled in a childhood accident. "It gives my pitches a bigger dip," he said of the injured pitching hand, and his contention was difficult to dispute. Brown averaged nearly 24 wins a year in the 1906–11 period, allowing barely a run per game in the 1906 and 1909 seasons. He finished his

career with 56 shutouts. Others on the great pitching staff were Ed Reulbach, who pitched a double shutout in a doubleheader against Brooklyn in 1908 and won 14 games in a row the next year; Orval Overall, with 23 victories, 9 of them shutouts, in 1907; Carl Lundgren; and Jack Pfeister.

By 1912, the great years had passed. Many of the players of the era had already left. Next, two managers would go, and then the owner. Frank Chance, who began as manager in 1906, ended his reign in 1912 with a third-place finish, lowest in his term. Evers brought the team in third in 1913 and was released.

The back-to-back firings of Chance and Evers created a furor, and the Cubs' owner, Charles Webb Murphy, left soon after. He was bought out, and the Cubs were held in absentee ownership by Charles F. Taft of Cincinnati. Joe Tinker, the only part of the legendary double-play trio who hadn't yet managed the team, got his chance in 1916, the first year at the new ball park at Clark and Addison—then called "Cubs' Park." He too lasted only a year, leaving after a mediocre, fifth-place finish. However, the Cubs did gain some stability in 1916, when William Wrigley, Jr., joined with a group of wealthy Chicagoans to purchase the club from the Taft family. In 1921, Wrigley assumed the majority ownership of the team. He ruled the club until his death in 1934, when his son, Philip, succeeded him. Today, Phil Wrigley continues as president, with his son, William, ready to continue the family reign.

Jim ("Hippo") Vaughn, a pitcher who recorded 155 victories in a 13-year career, was one of the better Cubs of the teens. He deserves a historical note for his activities at Cubs' Park on May 2, 1917, when he pitched a nine-inning no-hitter and lost. Other pitchers have lost no-hitters, of nine innings and longer, but thanks to Fred Toney, of Cincinnati, Vaughn's failed no-hitter was particularly noteworthy. Toney, the game's winning pitcher, also pitched a no-hitter—for ten innings. Thus, Toney and Vaughn produced the only double no-hitter in a single game in major league history. The Reds scored the game's only run on a tenth-inning bunt by the fabled Jim Thorpe. Said Vaughn, no doubt stunned to insensitivity, "Well, it's just another game."

The next year brought happier times for the bovine left-hander and his teammates. In 1918, Vaughn's 22 triumphs and league-leading 1.74 ERA led the Cubs to the pennant.

In 1929, the stock market crashed and the country plunged into depression, but the Cubs of

The abrasive Johnny ("the Crab") Evers played 12 years for the Cubs despite often strained relations with his teammates. As a manager, he had three different terms, none lasting over a year.

Chicago had already had their slump and were well on the way to recovery. A last-place finish in 1925, the instability of three different managers, and declining attendance prompted massive changes that would result in perhaps the greatest era in the history of the team. The Cubs would win the National League pennant in 1929 and every third year thereafter through the thirties.

Marse Joe McCarthy took over as manager of the Cubs in 1926, and promptly sold the star of the team, Grover Cleveland Alexander. It was a symbolic as well as a practical gesture, for "Ol' Pete" (15–11 and fading in 1925) had called the new manager, who had never played or managed in the majors, a bush leaguer. Axing Alexander proved a most effective way for McCarthy to demonstrate his authority.

In the overhauling of the Cubs, two minor league acquisitions had an especially dramatic impact. The first came from Toledo of the American Association—a short, red-faced gorilla-shaped man whose physique prompted many derisive jokes. "Let 'em yowl," he said. "I used to be a boilermaker, and noise doesn't bother me." The imperturbable strongman was Lewis Robert Wilson, dubbed "Hackenschmidt" after a wrestler folk hero of the time. "Hackenschmidt" was shortened to "Hack," and thus the squat slugger acquired a suitably compact name. Hack Wilson would lead the league in home runs four of the next five years. He would draw a salary second only to Babe Ruth's and drive in more runs in the next six years than any other player in baseball except Ruth and Lou Gehrig.

The other minor leaguer, Riggs Stephenson, from Indianapolis of the American Association, was as reserved as Wilson was boisterous, until he got to bat. The clutch-hitting outfielder would be a Cub until 1934, when he would retire with a .336 career batting average, the highest in the history of the Cubs.

As the ball club was renovated, so too was the ball park—double-decked to accommodate 37,741 fans and freshly painted. And the old ball park got a new name: Wrigley Field, in honor of its owner.

With Joe McCarthy in charge, the Cubs moved up to fourth in 1926 and 1927. They obtained Kiki Cuyler in 1928 and climbed to third place. "They tell me we don't look good on paper," McCarthy snapped at the critics. "Well, we don't play on paper."

Despite the progress under McCarthy, the Cubs still felt they lacked a pennant winner as the 1929 season approached. As McCarthy remembers, "I told Mr. Wrigley that if he could get

one more big hitter we could win it in twenty-nine." The clincher turned out to be Rogers Hornsby, whose petulant personality had made him persona non grata in St. Louis, New York, and now Boston. The Cubs stepped in with ready cash ($250,000), expendable talent (five ballplayers) and goodwill, and "the Rajah" became a Cub.

"We spent a lot for Rogers, but he gave us that extra punch that won the pennant for us in twenty-nine," McCarthy notes. "He was a great hitter, one of the best who ever lived." With Hornsby as the final component, McCarthy's "Murderers' Row" was assembled: Hornsby, Wilson, Cuyler, Stephenson, and Charlie Grimm.

123

Opposite top and bottom: Two early-century VIPs—Mordecai Brown, a five-time 20-game winner, and William Wrigley, Jr., the first of the Cubs' Wrigleys. Above: Heinie Zimmerman, batting champ in 1912.

Scoring nearly a thousand runs, winning 24 of 33 games in July, the Cubs romped to the 1929 National League pennant by 10½ lengths. Pat Malone won 22 of 32 decisions, and Charlie Root recorded 19 of his 201 career victories. McCarthy's acquisitions batted a collective .361, driving in more than half the team's runs. Hornsby smashed 40 home runs, batted .380, and drove in 149 runs. His 229 hits and 156 runs scored that year are all-time club records. Cuyler batted .360, led the league with 43 steals, and had 102 RBIs. Stephenson drove in 110 runs, slugged 17 homers, and batted .362. Wilson led the league with 159 RBIs, hit 39 home runs, and batted .345, foreshadowing the 1930 season, when he would blast 56 home runs, still a National League record, and drive in 190 runs, still a major league record. "That team we had in 1929," McCarthy exclaims, "was as good as any of them."

For the World Series in 1929, against Connie Mack's Philadelphia Athletics, the seating capacity at Wrigley Field was expanded to fifty thousand with the addition of wooden bleachers. Unhappily for the huge crowds, who expected to see the Cubs dismember the Athletics' shaky pitching, slow baller Howard Ehmke, George Earnshaw, and Lefty Grove easily handled the Chicago hitters. Some of the wind in the Windy City came from the flailing bats of the 26 Cubs who struck out in those first two games, 3–1 and 9–3 Philadelphia victories.

Kiki Cuyler's two-run single gave the Cubs a 3–1 win at Philadelphia in the third game, setting the stage for the biggest blowup in World Series history, a baseball legend impossible for an old Chicago manager to forget but still painful to recall. "We got some rough breaks in that Series against Connie," McCarthy observes quietly, four and a half decades after the game that shaped his managerial career and very likely the destiny of the Cubs for the next decade.

The Cubs led 8–0 after six innings. In the seventh, the Athletics had already scored four times when Mule Haas came up with two men on base. His drive to center was lost in the sun by Hack ("Sunny Boy") Wilson. Before the devastating inning was over, the score was 10–8. "We just couldn't get them out," McCarthy mourns. "Connie had a great team, but everything was going against us. . . .

"The next day, one of my coaches, Jimmy Burke, said to me, 'Goddamn that Brick Owens.' Well, Owens was an umpire then, but he wasn't working the Series, see, and I said to Jimmy, 'What's the matter with Brick?'

" 'Well,' says Burke, 'the son of a gun came

125

Above: *The 1906 Cubs marched through the National League to the tune of 116 wins, inspiring this tribute.* Top: *The next dynasty began with the 1929 team.* Opposite: *A Cub for only six years, Hack Wilson had more than 700 RBIs over five of them.*

to my hotel room looking for some tickets, and he threw his hat on the bed. I yelled, "Get that Goddamn hat off the bed—you know it's bad luck." Brick was sorry, but see what happened to us?' "

Among salesmen of the time, a hat on a hotel bed was said to insure no sales the next day. Apparently, the Cubs borrowed the unhappy superstition with a vengeance, for the next day the spell still hadn't worn off. With President Herbert Hoover in the stands, the Cubs performed a replay of the fourth game debacle, blowing a 2–0 lead in the bottom of the ninth and losing the deciding game 3–2.

The Athletics were world champions and recriminations gripped the Cubs. Joe McCarthy had lived by the powerhouse he had created. When it faltered, owner William Wrigley held him responsible. "I want a manager who will win a world championship for me," the owner said testily.

With four games left in the 1930 season, and the Cubs heading for a second-place finish behind the Cardinals, Wrigley replaced McCarthy with Hornsby, no doubt reasoning that the man who led the team to a pennant in 1929 ought to be able to produce the world championship the owner craved. Unfortunately, Hornsby did not bring Wrigley a world championship, or even a pennant. On August 4, 1932, the tyrannical Rajah was dumped in favor of a man of the people, loose and lively Charlie Grimm. This time, the switching in midstream seemed to help. The Cubs tore through the stretch by winning 37 of 57 contests, and took the flag.

An old colleague, Joe McCarthy, who had joined the New York Yankees as manager in 1931, sought and gained revenge in the World Series. Babe Ruth, Lou Gehrig, et al, helped him get it, in four straight games. Gehrig batted .529, leading the Yanks' attack, but it was the aging Ruth who provided the Series' most memorable moment. Like so much else about the Babe, in this case it is difficult to separate fact from legend.

In the third game's third inning, Ruth smashed a three-run homer. When he came to bat in the fifth inning, the Cubs' bench taunted him, as it had throughout the Series. Pitcher Charlie Root picked up two quick strikes on Ruth. Before Root delivered the next pitch, Ruth waved his hand. Some said it was to indicate that he had one strike left. Others said Ruth called his shot. In any case, Ruth sent the next pitch sailing into the center field bleachers—his last World Series home run, and one of his most memorable. He circled the bases and, shoving the dagger of revenge in to the hilt, bowed sarcastically to his hecklers.

In 1935, the Cubs did it again: they acquired some talented ballplayers, raced to the pennant with a torrid stretch drive, and then wilted in the Series. The new recruits in the 1935 pennant race were Babe Herman, acquired in 1933, Fred Lindstrom and Chuck Klein, who arrived in 1934, and Phil Cavarretta, who began playing full time in 1935. The stretch drive included a 21-game winning streak, fostered by Grimm, who celebrated each victory by driving a tack into his shoe afterward. "He was probably the only man ever to run around with twenty-one tacks in his shoe," Chicago author Jim Enright chuckles. The Cubs won the flag by four games over the world champion "Gashouse Gang" Cardinals.

Phil Cavarretta, born and raised in Chicago, made an auspicious debut in September, 1934, when he slammed a home run in his first major league game, giving the Cubs a 1–0 victory. A year later, he hit another homer, for another 1–0 Chicago victory, under even more impressive circumstances. This one beat the Cardinals, clinched a tie for the pennant, and extended the Cubs' winning streak to 19 games. Thus, Cavarretta justified the faith of manager Grimm, who had replaced himself at first base with the eighteen-year-old kid at the start of the season.

"One of the best drives in history," Cavarretta contends. "Going down the stretch we had to win just about every game to go to the pennant. . . . For an eighteen-year-old boy, it was quite a way to break in. . . .

"For some reason we could win the pennant but not the Series." The Cubs lost the 1935 World Series to the Detroit Tigers in six games. The final game symbolized Chicago's frustrations. With the score tied 3–3 in the ninth inning, Stan Hack tripled with no outs, but the Cubs could not bring him the final 90 feet. Grimm incurred the wrath of the second-guessers when he allowed pitcher Larry French to bat with Hack on third and one out. Like Billy Jurges before him, and Augie Galan after, French failed to knock in the run. Then he gave up the winner in the bottom of the ninth.

The finish to the 1938 campaign was the most thrilling yet of the team's triennial slam-bang pennant victories. Charlie Grimm ended the first of his three managerial stints with the Cubs when he resigned in midseason with the team 6½ games out of first. Gabby Hartnett, regarded by many as the greatest all-around catcher in history, became player-manager, and "Ol' Tomato Face" guided the club home. Again

there was a winning streak—this time 10 in a row—and the Cubs started moving up. By the time they faced the first-place Pirates, in a crucial three-game series in late September, they trailed the leaders by only a game and a half.

Phil Wrigley singles out the second game of the series, on September 28, 1938, as his most memorable. The Cubs had won the opener, shaving the Pirates' first-place margin to one-half game. In the second game, the score was tied 2–2 in the bottom of the ninth inning. Darkness, dampness, and cold enveloped Wrigley Field. The umpires informed both teams that if the contest were not decided quickly it would be called and replayed as part of a doubleheader the next day.

Gabby Hartnett came to bat. Mace Brown of the Pirates got two strikes on him, and then Hartnett smacked a "homer in the gloamin'" that lit up Chicago. Years later, when the catcher was inducted into the Hall of Fame, he said, "I

now have two souvenirs all the money in the world won't buy—my Hall of Fame plaque and my home run ball of 1938." The Cubs pounded Pittsburgh 10–1 the next day and moved into the World Series against Joe McCarthy's Yankees again.

There is a poignant memory of that World Series: Dizzy Dean, his arm ruined, pitching gamely against the Yankees, only to be abandoned by his fielders as he had been by his fastball. "I never worked for a finer man than Mr. Wrigley," said Dean. "He paid me as much money in three years as the Cards did in seven." In addition Dean cost Wrigley $185,000 and the three players he sent to St. Louis to get him. Yet the owner commented, "I am satisfied—we got Dizzy's spirit, courage, and enthusiasm, in addition to his arm."

Unfortunately, there was not much left of the arm. For eight and two thirds innings in the second game of the 1938 Series, Dean held off

127

Above left: *In his brief and stormy career as a Cub, Rogers Hornsby led the Cubs' pennant winner in 1929 but failed as a manager to repeat.* Above right: *Poor little butter Cubs.*

the bats of the Yankees seemingly with nothing more potent than the memory of his great years. He wore a Chicago uniform, but there are those who saw the ghost of a Redbird on the mound.

With the Cubs leading 3–2, there was a collision in the Chicago infield and a Crosetti home run. Suddenly, Dean and the Cubs were undone. "I wish I could call back one year. You wouldn't get a loud foul off'n me!" yelled a still-defiant Dean at Crosetti.

"Diz, you're sure right," the gracious winner concurred.

After the 1938 World Series, the Cubs dropped out of contention. Grimm left. Hartnett managed the team for two more years and then yielded to Jimmie Wilson. Chicago finished no better than fourth. In 1944, Grimm returned, and in 1945, the Cubs led the league in batting, fielding, pitching, and the standings. Grimm was ecstatic. "At the Cub victory party," Enright recalls, "he had a pair of shears. Everybody who had a necktie on contributed. He had a quilt made. It's probably the oddest pennant souvenir in the history of the game."

The 1945 team featured Phil Cavarretta, in his tenth season as a player (the midpoint of his career) leading the league with a .355 average; Hank Wyse, a 22-game winner; Stan Hack, whose quick wrists produced a .323 average; Andy Pafko, top RBI man with 110; Bill ("Swish") Nicholson, riding balls out of Wrigley Field on the wind stream; and Hank Borowy,

purchased for $100,000 on July 27 from the New York Yankees in what Grimm called "the best deal the Cubs ever made." Borowy had already won 10 games with the Yankees when he came to Chicago. With the Cubs he added 11 more, and a sparkling 2.13 ERA.

The Cubs lost the World Series to the Detroit Tigers, in seven games this time. It was to be their last pennant and last World Series to date. The Cubs finished third in 1946, dropped to sixth in 1947, and in 1948 finished last. The fate of their superstar of the twenties and thirties, Hack Wilson, seemed to symbolize the plight of the team. The old slugger died of pneumonia in 1948 at age forty-eight, and only a $350 grant from the National League kept his body from being buried in a pauper's grave.

Grimm would leave in 1949 and Frankie Frisch would manage, then Phil Cavarretta, then Stan Hack, then Bob Scheffing. Grimm would return again in 1960 for 17 games and then trade places with one of the Cubs' radio announcers, Lou Boudreau.

When the managerial switches did not improve the Cubs on the field, owner Wrigley decided he could do without the pretense of a permanent headman. The grand experiment called "the College of Coaches" was launched, whereby a staff of coaches would share in the managing, coaching, and player development. The new system was anointed by the hiring of that inveterate Cub, Charlie Grimm, as one of the original staff of eight coaches. "I seem to have been caught in a revolving door," Grimm jokes, "that always brought me back to Chicago." His colleagues were Bobby Adams, Ripper Collins, Harry Craft, Vedie Himsl, Goldie Holt, Elvin Tappe, and Verlon Walker. The College of Coaches brought 205 years of combined baseball experience, but in the 5 years of its existence (1961–65), the Cubs never finished higher than seventh. The innovation was scrapped—costly, confusing, and chaotic was the postmortem.

Nevertheless, the system did have some positive results. Most importantly, it helped nurture some of the players who would bring the Cubs back into contention. Ernie Banks, now organizational instructor for Chicago, says, "Each of those coaches gave personal attention to us. Billy Williams, myself . . . the others were brought close together. We got counsel in every area of the game from a specialist. They really helped in the total team effort."

The lithe Banks played 19 years with the Cubs, beginning in 1953. He and Billy Williams, who wore the Cubs' uniform for 14 seasons, dominate the team's all-time statistical records.

They are one-two in games played, at-bats, doubles, home runs, runs scored, runs batted in, and extra base hits.

Banks was voted the all-time favorite Chicago Cubs player. "He is Mr. Cub," Grimm notes. "He's a baseball poet." The steady shortstop recorded 512 career home runs, made the National League All-Star team a dozen times, and won the Most Valuable Player award twice.

A fine outfielder and slugger, Williams was also the most durable of the Cubs. From September 22, 1963, to September 2, 1970, he played 1,117 straight games, then asked that his name be omitted from the lineup card, thus ending his streak. "If I had it to do all over again," he said, "I wouldn't go for the consecutive game record. It just isn't worth it. It hurts you and the club."

Leo Durocher became manager of the Chicago Cubs on October 25, 1966. The College of Coaches had lasted for five years; Leo would survive for a little more than six. When his stormy reign was over, his record showed a marked improvement over the college—three third- and two second-place finishes. Yet Durocher's time with the Cubs is remembered as an era of unfulfilled promise, of a set lineup of stars that in shortstop Don Kessinger's words had "ample opportunity to win," but never quite made it. Shortstop for the Cubs through 1975, Kessinger was the last link to that team. "When you don't win, changes are made," he notes with a ballplayer's resignation.

Although Durocher did not bring the Cubs a pennant, he did bring great excitement. In 1969, the year Chicago led most of the way only to be overtaken by the miracle New York Mets, the Cubs sported a "tenth man on our team," as Banks put it. The extra help was "the Bleacher Bums," those yellow-hard-hatted, beer-swizzling zealots who taunted opposing players at Wrigley Field. They were the most ostentatious but not the only sign of the baseball revival on the North Side. More than a million and a half fans crammed Wrigley Field to witness the pennant chase.

Most of the ball parks in the major leagues are now pastel and plastic. Most of the grass is artificial. Most of the superstadia were built for other spectacles as well as baseball. All have lights. All have commercial promotion. But in Chicago, some things never change.

Ernie Banks, "baseball poet," flashes back over the years: "Being a Chicago Cub, I think I got more out of it than I gave. It was just great, even getting up in the morning. We got to the park around nine in the morning, and we didn't

Opposite top and bottom: *Through the sixties, two infield stalwarts—Ernie Banks and Ron Santo. Banks is all-time team leader in homers, total bases, and extra base hits.*

leave until five in the afternoon. We lived there.

"For the fans, coming to Wrigley Field is like a habit, and as a player, you could almost set your clock for the time when the fans would be there. On Sunday, there were families; Fridays were Ladies' Days; Tuesday was Senior Citizens' Day. . . . We got to be part of their lives, of themselves. You got to know people there as if they were brothers and sisters."

The atmosphere now in that revered antique of a ball park, Wrigley Field, is paradoxical. Amidst the ghosts of the past—Hack Wilson, Rogers Hornsby, Gabby Hartnett, Three Finger Brown, Hippo Vaughn, Cap Anson, Joe Tinker, Johnny Evers, Joe McCarthy, Charlie Grimm, even Ernie Banks and Ron Santo—manager Jim Marshall tries to build a future "forgetting the past." But the past is hard to escape, and much of it is pleasant, despite all the lean years.

The Bleacher Bums are gone, but in their place are kids who string pencils and scorecards down the old bleacher walls, fishing for autographs. "People remember their days at Wrigley Field," Ernie Banks muses. "It's the same there; it never changes. And when you leave . . . you're still there."

Cubs

Name of Park	Date 1st Game Played	Opponent & Score	Capacity
23rd Street Park	May 10, 1876	Chicago 6, Cincinnati 0	2,500
Lake Park	May 14, 1878	Indianapolis 5, Chicago 3	3,000*
Loomis Street Park	June 6, 1885	Chicago 9, St. Louis 2	10,300*
West Side Park	May 13, 1893	Cincinnati 10, Chicago 8	13,000
Cubs' Park	April 20, 1916	Chicago 7, Cincinnati 6	14,000
Wrigley Field**			37,741

Estimated attendance that day.
** *Cubs' Park renamed Wrigley Field and capacity expanded.*

While rebuilding from within, the Cubs have traded for players who could contribute immediately. Above: Steve Stone; opposite: Rick Monday *fouling one off.*

Mission in the Valley
The Padres

The Padres play baseball where California began, at the edge of Mission Valley, in San Diego. It is a distinctly Western setting. The desert, the mountains, the beaches are all within a fifty-mile radius. And the beautiful, circular California stadium has an open and clean atmosphere.

In the stands, a collegiate-looking crowd watches the games while the Laguna Mountains and the hills of the valley turn blue in the twilight, as day turns to night in San Diego. McNamara's Band, led by "the Tuba Man"—United States Marine Jim Eakle—goes oom-pah-pahing up and down the aisles between innings. The drum man, the flute lady, the sign man, the tambourine lady, and the pompon girls eagerly trail Eakle as if he were some new Pied Piper. The crowd cheerfully responds to the tunes, "Happy Days Are Here Again," and "California, Here I Come"—suitable theme songs for the newest team in the West. The atmosphere is festive, exuberant, hopeful.

The optimism seems justified now. Like latter-day frontiersmen, the Padres began shakily out West, and almost expired. But after five years or so of deprivation and desperation, they are almost respectable and secure now. If they haven't quite yet struck it rich, surely prosperity is not too far away. "The history of the Padres is being written now," observes San Diego broadcaster Jerry Coleman, looking to the future to minimize the struggles of the past.

132

San Diego Stadium. Sunny San Diego's miles of beaches and dozens of golf courses have given the ball park and its Padres stiff competition for the recreation dollar.

"Every time you blink your eyes there's a new record."

The San Diego Padres were born in 1969 at the cost of a $10 million franchise fee to owner C. Arnholt Smith. With former Dodger Buzzie Bavasi as president, his son Peter as farm-system head, and another former Dodger, Preston Gomez, directing the team on the field, the investment seemed well protected. "Buzzie and Peter make an excellent team," says Coleman. "Buzzie is bright, with a lot of moxie. He put the Dodgers together and kept them together. Peter is the new breed of executive. There's not a rule in the Blue Book he doesn't know cold."

Unfortunately, from the start there wasn't enough money. "In the expansion draft we went for young players, figuring to build the future around them," Peter Bavasi explains. "Instead of promoting the San Diego Padres, who were mainly twenty-five unknowns, we geared our promotional efforts to the name National League players who were coming to beat our brains out. We used to promote the Brocks, Aarons, Roses, with whom the fans were more familiar. If we had it to do all over again, we might not have gone so heavily for youth. But at that time we couldn't afford the salaries of name players."

Of the Padres' first spring training, in Yuma, Arizona, veteran California baseball writer Phil Collier recalls, "We had a pitching staff that had won a combined total of twenty-two games the year before. There was no player who had ever caught a game in the majors. There was a shortage in just about every department. Near the end of spring training, we got [catcher] Chris Cannizzaro. You'd have thought we got Johnny Bench."

Such unrestrained—and unwarranted— enthusiasm increased when the Padres defeated the Houston Astros, 2–1, on Opening Day. "The first game in the National League was like the last game of a World Series for us," recalls Fred Kendall, the only Padre left from the original expansion team. Kendall was right, in the sense that the win in the opener was the highpoint of San Diego's first season. The Padres won their first three major league games, but after that it was a dreary first year.

If nothing else, the Padres produced at least one hero that initial season. Nate Colbert drove in 66 runs and smashed 24 homers, giving every indication of a star in the making. Ollie Brown contributed 20 homers, and Clay Kirby pitched 216 innings, losing 20 games.

In 1970, the Padres won 11 more games and produced more offensive power. Colbert drove in 86 runs and hit 38 homers, still a single-season record for the club. Cito Gaston, the Padres' thirtieth and final pick in the expansion draft, hit 29 home runs and produced 93 RBIs. But the team finished last again, and attendance improved only marginally, to 633,439.

"At the outset, when we traded our players, we used to get four or five in return," says Peter Bavasi. "We tried to build our farm system through trades. It was a holding action." In 1969, the Padres got three players for Joe Niekro and three for Dick Selma; in 1970, four for Pat Dobson and Tom Dukes; in 1971, three for Dave Roberts. Again, the problem was money.

Collier remembers Bavasi musing, " 'If I had a hundred thousand dollars, I could get four good minor league ballplayers.' Imagine! They paid ten million for the franchise and they didn't even have a hundred thousand to get four ballplayers."

On the field there were some better moments in the Padres' third year, but at the box office and in the standings the results were discouragingly familiar. Clay Kirby and Dave Roberts anchored the pitching staff, combining for 29 wins, 366 strikeouts, and 537 innings pitched.

After 11 games in the 1972 season, Don Zimmer replaced Preston Gomez as manager. Departing with Gomez was the patient Roger Craig, characterized by Jerry Coleman as "the only man to live through the tragedy of the New York Mets and come back here and do it again."

Under Zimmer in 1972, the Padres again finished last. "There are ballplayers and managers, and then there are the Zimmers, who play harder than they know how to play," Coleman notes. "Of all the things that epitomized the Padres in the early years, it was Zimmer, with his lion heart and his association with winners, not being able to win and aching to have a winner."

The spirited manager and the Padres did have the satisfaction, on August 1, 1972, of witnessing the greatest hitting exhibition in the history of the team. In a doubleheader against the Braves in Atlanta, Colbert slugged five home runs, drove in 13 runs, scored seven, and recorded 22 total bases on seven hits in nine trips to the plate. Kendall recalls, "I think the whole team, and even Nate, were in a daze just watching him do it."

Colbert's clouting tied the record for home runs in a doubleheader and broke the marks for RBIs and total bases in a twin bill. The previous total-base mark, 21, was set by Stan Musial in the presence of eight-year-old Nate Colbert. "I

133

Above: *Danny Frisella, former Met and Brave.* Opposite left:
Dave Winfield, the brightest star on the San Diego horizon. Opposite
right: *Tito Fuentes provides infield experience and a quick bat.*

was in Busch Stadium that afternoon when he did it," Colbert remembers. "I never thought that anyone would equal that record, certainly not me."

Colbert was a bona fide star, but not a franchise. In 1972, attendance fell below the previous year's mark as the Padres again finished last. Once again, the seventy miles of beaches in the San Diego area, the sixty golf courses, Tijuana, and Mission Bay proved greater attractions than major league baseball. When matters failed to improve in 1973, a crisis loomed. The half million or so fans that the Padres attracted were not enough, said owner Smith, to keep the franchise in San Diego. He made it clear that the team was going to be sold and moved to another city. Thus, 1973 became a year of frenzied City Hall meetings, frantic press releases, and more than one panic-inspired rumor. The most reliable of these held that the Padres were bound for Washington, D.C., to fill the void in the nation's capital left by the departure of the Senators.

"Mayor Pete Wilson [of San Diego] was very instrumental in the San Diego Padres being the San Diego Padres and not the Washington Padres," Peter Bavasi notes. "It was not a politi-

cal issue; it was a personal issue. He felt that on behalf of some million spectators of Padre baseball, he had to speak up.

Wilson and his city attorney, John Witt, went to court to keep the team in the city. "They gave the National League pause to move the club," Bavasi continues, "at a time when if the city had turned its back on the plight of the Padres, the club might very well have been moved."

Meanwhile, the front office was working overtime to bolster the team's image, making a number of pivotal trades that Peter Bavasi terms the most significant in the club's history. Willie McCovey came over from the San Francisco Giants, and Glenn Beckert, a former All-Star, from the Cubs. Bobby Tolan and Dave Tomlin were acquired from Cincinnati for Clay Kirby, whose total victories, innings pitched, and strikeouts had paced the Padres in their first four years. Matty Alou was picked up from St. Louis. "At the time we made the trades, we were doing our best to dress the roster up, as any homeowner would do prior to selling his house," Peter Bavasi explained.

The problem with this attempt at instant   *135*

franchise building was the same one that had gripped the club from the start—money. In the midst of the dealing, Buzzie Bavasi recalls, "Our skeleton staff was rattling. We were out of options, and our bank account showed a balance of two thousand dollars."

Then in January, 1974, a phone call changed everything. "A guy calls me and says he represents someone named Kroc who is interested in buying the San Diego franchise, and he'd like a meeting to discuss it," Bavasi recollects. " 'Sure,' I say, 'has he got his group together?' 'Oh, yes,' he says, 'Mr. Kroc is the group.' " A few days later there was a luncheon meeting. "It took exactly half of that luncheon meeting

to close the deal," Bavasi says. "Mr. Kroc shook hands with Mr. Smith, and the rest is history."

Kroc, the head of McDonald's Corporation, had read in his morning newspaper that the Padres were for sale, and decided to buy them. After trying for eight years to purchase the Cubs, Kroc got the Padres in a few days.

The energetic owner proclaimed, "A winning team, a fighting team, a personality team—just like a great show—will be a success."

Kroc's enthusiasm was catchy. The city approved a new lease on the stadium for the team. Mayor Wilson called the new owner "outspoken, fresh, colorful, a superb merchandiser who intends to aggressively promote the team.

136

. . . Now I hope I can spend at least one-tenth of the time in the ball park that I spent trying to keep the team here."

According to Bavasi, the first time Kroc walked into Bavasi's office after the sale, "he looked around at the office staff and before he said anything else to me, he said, 'Give everyone in this room a raise.' Nobody had had a raise in five years. A gesture like that had to be felt throughout the organization.

In 1974, a new optimism gripped the Padres' organization. The failures of the past—the selling of good ballplayers just to keep the franchise going—were no longer self-perpetuating legacies but painful lessons that had been learned. "With the sale of the club to Ray Kroc, the whole thing changed," Coleman contends. "The fans realized they might have lost the ball club. Now it was saved. They came out."

More than a million fans came to San Diego Stadium in 1974 to see the team they thought they had lost. "For the first time, you could see young adults bringing their dates, notes Coleman. "And the middle ground of twenty-five- to forty-five-year-olds came to the ball park." More than just the reprieve, the new look of the Padres lured them. The McCoveys and Tolans, initially intended only as window dressing to make the team more palatable to a potential buyer, proved to be blessings in disguise. Tolan added defense and aggressiveness, McCovey power and run production (22 homers, 63 RBIs). And the team finally had a core of home-grown talent to supplement the aging stars. Center fielder John Grubb, who hit .311 as a rookie in 1973, produced a respectable .286 in his sophomore year. Outfielder Dave Winfield, who came to the Padres in 1973 directly from the University of Minnesota, with no minor league experience, smashed 20 homers and paced the team in game-winning hits and RBIs. Enzo Hernandez, a fine defensive shortstop, stole 37 bases.

Presiding over the renovated Padres was a new manager, John McNamara. Like McCovey and Tolan, he had been chosen to put the veneer

Left: *Cito Gaston and the ball slip past Johnny Bench.* Above: *In 1975, Randy Jones became the first 20-game winner in the Padres' history.*

Padres

Name of Park	Date 1st Game Played	Opponent & Score	Capacity
San Diego Stadium	April 8, 1969	San Diego 2, Houston 1	47,634
58,000*

Expanded capacity.

138

of healthy change on a sickly Washington transplant. Instead, he wound up leading a revitalized San Diego club. "The team lost a hundred and two games," he acknowledges, "but these young people gained experience. We felt the first thing we had to do was set our pitching staff in the right direction. We gave our pitchers the ball every fourth day—Randy Jones, Bill Greif, Dan Spillner, Dave Freisleben—and they came a long way in less than a year's time, even though we're still in the apprenticeship stage."

The young ballplayers seemed satisfied with their new mentor. Says Grubb, "He's consistent all the time, able to get his points across. . . . Everybody likes to play ball for this man; we're a bunch of guys happy to play together."

In 1975, happiness was finally translated into at least modest success. Drawing nearly a million and a half fans at home, the team broke the pattern of its perennial last-place finishes. The Padres won more games (71) than in any other year in their history and climbed to fourth place.

The year began with an even heavier emphasis on youth, with the departures of Cito Gaston and Nate Colbert. "They were both nearing thirty, and it was time to make a move," explains Coleman.

Three of the young pitchers McNamara "gave the ball to" won a total of 32 games in 1975. Lefty Randy Jones became the first 20-game winner in the history of the Padres, compiling a 20–12 record and a league leading 2.24 ERA. A tribute to the development of the Padres as a team, and to Jones as a pitcher, came in the All-Star Game when National League manager Walter Alston chose Jones over such established relief aces as Mike Marshall and Tug McGraw to pitch the ninth inning and hold the National League lead.

McCovey, the venerable old Giant, spends his waning days standing beside the batting cage in balmy San Diego Stadium, wishing he could be a bigger part of the resurrection of the Padres. "I had my days hitting in the batting order with Willie Mays, Orlando Cepeda, and Jim Ray Hart," McCovey reflects, as he tightens the batting glove in preparation for his cuts. "The way Winfield and some of the others are going, I wish I was having those days again. We'd be something."

At McCovey's side, Winfield adds, "In the years to come, people will give this expansion club the respect it deserves. We're beginning to open eyes of people in the National League. We're beginning to open eyes all over the country."

The new confidence flows from the top down. Ray Kroc, the man who is reversing the fortunes of the Padres, is a veteran of the can-do world, and he exudes enthusiasm for baseball and his Padres.

Roy Campanella once said, "You've got to have a lot of little boy in you to be a good player," and Kroc is showing that perhaps the formula applies to owners as well. A self-confessed "red-hot, proud fan who'll never be calloused enough to just sit there coolly—I have to scream and holler," Kroc is busily transforming San Diego Stadium into a mecca for kids of all ages. "We promote more than any other baseball club," Buzzie Bavasi notes. "Of the seventy-six playing dates, we have promotions on about sixty of them."

Like hamburger servers at the local McDonald's, the Padres' players are encouraged to befriend the customers, through the media, speaking engagements, autograph signings, whatever. All this unprecedented wooing of the baseball fan leads Buzzie Bavasi, whose Dodgers teams finished first in 10 of 16 years, to reflect, "Somebody once said, 'There are three ways to play baseball—the right way, the wrong way, and the Dodger way.' We're young, we're learning, and someday they'll add '—the Padre way.' "

139

Opposite top: *Taking the sun.* Opposite bottom: *Willie McCovey brought his awesome size and stature to the Padres in 1974.*
Above: *Mike Ivie is one of a bevy of promising young players.*

Pride in Philadelphia
The Phillies

"IT'S EASY TO BE A FAN WHEN YOUR TEAM IS IN FIRST PLACE."
—message on the back of old Phillies' yearbook

The Phillies haven't coddled their fans. While other teams developed, or at least tried to develop, winners, the Phillies of the twenties and thirties stayed in business by helping the competition. Assisted by the other seven clubs, the Phillies were a halfway house to the majors for youngsters, to unconditional release for fading veterans. If there is merit in being ahead of the times, credit the old Phillies for fielding teams that anticipated wartime baseball.

Then came the Carpenters, not the richest owners in baseball perhaps but, at the time they bought the club, probably the spendingest. Within five years they had a winner, only to learn in subsequent seasons that spending money is helpful, even necessary, but not sufficient. The Phils dropped to the cellar, surfaced again as a strong contender in the mid-sixties, then plummeted again. Now they've risen for the third time in thirty years.

These days the farm system is well established and producing bountifully. The team plays in a ball park, not a tinderbox, before impressively large and enthusiastic crowds, not clusters of jaundiced spectators and captive newspapermen. Success has been fleeting, but failure is no longer endemic. The Phillies have

After years in antiquated stadiums that more often than not symbolized the condition of the team, the Phils today are as impressively up to date as their new Veterans Stadium.

left the cellar, in spirit at least never to return.

The Philadelphia National League team began as a loser. In the first game in National League history, played in Philadelphia on April 22, 1876, a Philadelphia team called the "Quakers," or "Athletics," lost to Boston 6–5. The historic occasion rated a few lines of fine print in a Philadelphia newspaper:

"On Saturday afternoon about 3,000 persons assembled upon the grounds of 25th and Jefferson to witness the first championship game of baseball between the Boston and Athletic clubs. Boston won the game 6–5." Within a few months, the Philadelphia club had already provoked the beginning of a century of criticism. One newspaper complained:

"The Athletics are doing so poorly that nobody takes stock in them anymore. They rank today among the poorest of the league clubs, when they should be in the front ranks. The material is good enough . . . but the trouble is bad management. The players . . . collectively don't play worth a cent."

A few days later, the team left the league, suspended because it had refused to make a Western trip. There was simply no money to pay for it.

It was not until 1883 that Philadelphia returned to the National League. Alfred J. Reach purchased the Worcester, Massachusetts, baseball team, moved it to Philadelphia, and adopted the nickname "Phillies." On May 1, the Phillies played their first game, losing 4–3 to the Providence Grays before twelve hundred spectators at Recreation Park, Twenty-third Street and Ridge Pike.

Those first Phillies were by far the most futile. They won just 17 of 98 games (a .173 percentage) and finished a distant last. John Coleman, one of the club's two regular pitchers, entered 65 games and lost 48 of them. From the beginning the Phillies have been looking up.

The early club improved rapidly. In the decade 1885–95, it placed no worse than fourth and as high as second, though it never really came close to a pennant. Harry Wright, the old original Redstocking and manager of the Boston and Providence National League teams, managed the Phillies for most of these years.

In 1899, after Wright had departed, the Phillies boasted the league's batting leader in almost every category, the great Ed Delahanty. He topped the league in batting average, .410; slugging percentage, .582; total bases, 338; RBIs, 137; hits, 238; and doubles, 55. The second baseman on that team was young Napoleon

Lajoie, despite a knee injury a .378 hitter that year. Lajoie would win four batting titles, but not for the Phillies. Both Delahanty and Lajoie jumped to the new American League shortly after it began—the first of many ballplayers who would experience their best years as former Phillies.

The Phillies dropped to seventh in 1902 and last two years later before beginning a slow recovery. It got a boost in 1911, when a twenty-four-year-old rookie, Grover Cleveland Alexander, arrived and won 28 games. Four years later he won 31 (more than a third of the team's total), and the Phils made it to their first World Series. Alexander led the league not only in wins but in winning percentage, .756; ERA, 1.22; strikeouts, 241; shutouts, 12; complete games, 36; and innings pitched, 376. If ever any man did, Alexander pitched his team to the pennant.

The lesson was not lost on the Boston Red Sox, who faced the Phils in the 1915 World Series. At a clubhouse meeting before the Series began, Bill ("Rough") Carrigan, the Boston manager, told his players, "We'll have to win this thing early or we'll have to face Alexander three times." Heeding their manager's advice, the Red Sox won the Series in five and had to cope with the Phils' ace only twice. The Red Sox' pitchers allowed Philadelphia an average of fewer than six hits per game, and manager Carrigan used his hot young 18-game winner, Babe Ruth, only as a pinch hitter.

It was a quick Series but a close one. In the opener, Alexander bested Ernie Shore 3–1, saddling Shore with the dubious distinction of being the only pitcher to lose a World Series game to the Phillies. The next day Rube Foster permitted the Phillies only three hits and knocked in the winning run in the ninth inning of a 2–1 Boston victory.

The Series moved to Boston for game three, which Boston owner Joe Lannin staged in Braves Field, the new ball park of his National League competition. When the Braves were in the Series the year before, Braves Field had not yet been finished, so the Series was played in the Red Sox' Fenway Park (only a couple years old itself). Lannin was doing more than returning the favor. Braves Field offered a few thousand more seats, every one of which, to the owner's delight, was filled for game three.

The more spacious left field in Braves Field handicapped Philadelphia's big hitter, Gavvy Cravath, who led the National League in homers (24) and RBIs (115). In both games three and four, he powered long drives that would have cleared the wall in Fenway, but in the new park

*Leaders of the Phillies' latest resurgence
include,* clockwise from opposite, *Steve Carlton,
Mike Schmidt, Dave Cash, and Dick Allen.*

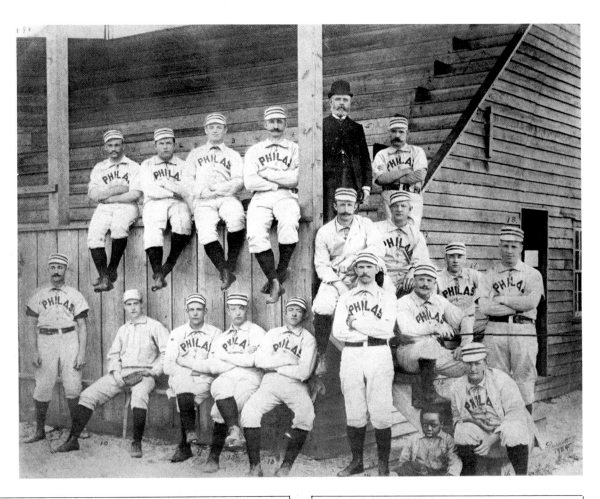

Above: *An elegant invitation to an early
all-star game.* Top: *Posing at new Baker
Bowl.* Right: *Early superstar, Ed Delahanty.*

144

the Red Sox' nimble left fielder, Duffy Lewis, hauled them down. Lewis also had the game-winning hits in Boston's 2–1 victories in both games.

When the Series returned to Philadelphia for the fifth game, the Phillies' owner, Bill Baker, decided that his Baker Bowl too would accommodate more fans. He erected bleachers in center field so that "more of our fans would see the game." Then Boston's Harry Hooper reached the temporary stands with two home runs, the margin of victory in Boston's 5–4 final triumph, and the press discerned a different reason for Baker's new bleachers. "You did it to get more money, you Midas you!" the papers cried.

"Midas" was quite the right term, for the Phillies were entering an era in which everything they touched turned to quite unprofitable gold. In 1918, Baker sold his star battery, Alexander and Bill Killefer, to the Cubs for $60,000 and a couple of nonentities. (The Cubs won the pennant that year, though Alexander spent most of the season in the service.) In 1920, Baker peddled the best shortstop the Phils ever had, Dave ("Beauty") Bancroft, to the Giants. And the next year Emil ("Irish") Meusel left for New York, shortly to knock in 100 runs or more in four straight seasons and finish an 11-year career with a .310 batting average. (From 1921 through 1923, the Giants won the pennant, with Bancroft and Meusel in key roles.)

Alexander, Bancroft, and Meusel were no sleepers; everyone knew how good they were. Baker simply sold them to the highest bidder. When manager Pat Moran complained about the sale of Alexander, Baker fired him. Moran left for Cincinnati, where he won a pennant and a World Series in 1919.

This unhappy state of mismanagement, which produced eight last place finishes in 12 years, continued until 1930, when Mr. Baker died and a new, equally inept leadership succeeded him. Old Mr. Baker left much of his stock in the Phillies to his trusted secretary, Mae Catherine DeSalles Mallen, of Kincraigie, Conshohoken (Pennsylvania). Other than her mellifluous name, a natural for newspapermen desperate to Phil space, Miss Mallen had little to recommend her as a major league club owner. But then neither did Mr. Baker. When Mrs. Baker died, in 1932, Miss Mallen gained a controlling share in the Phillies.

Though Miss Mallen used her maiden name (or the newspapers used it for her), she was married, to a Mr. Gerry Nugent, who, as his wife acquired more stock, climbed higher in the Phillies' hierarchy. By 1930, he was business manager, and three years later president.

It was Nugent's contention that Mr. Baker hadn't been misguided so much as inefficient. And so a new era of more efficient mismanagement evolved.

Instead of trying to make a profit by building a winner, Nugent ran a talent bazaar, buying young ballplayers cheap, showcasing them for a few years, and then selling them off at a profit just as they reached their peak of prowess. Of course, most Philadelphia baseball fans were not to be persuaded to come out and watch the Phillies' fruit ripening on the vine when somebody else was going to pick it. That, supposedly, was how the minor leagues worked. So the fans stayed away from Mr. Nugent's modest talent orchard at the Baker Bowl, and he had to swing some profitable deals indeed in order to come out ahead.

Take the case of the Phils' best player of the era, Chuck Klein, who led the league in runs scored three years in a row. It so happened that Klein had his best years for the Phillies, but not for want of Mr. Nugent's urgent desire to trade him. In fact Nugent unloaded him twice, both times at a handsome profit, and the owner had enough left after expenses to acquire Klein a third time.

Klein came to the Phillies in 1928 from Fort Wayne of the Central League for $10,000. In 1934, when he was thirty and had just won the triple crown with 28 homers, 120 RBIs, and a .368 average, Nugent sold him to the Cubs for $100,000 and some small trade bait. In 1936, Nugent got him back plus $50,000 for pitcher Curt ("Coonskin") Davis. Klein stayed for 29 games in Philadelphia the second time around before Nugent closed another deal for him, this one with the Pirates. Then Klein finished his career in Philadelphia, but by this time he was a .200 hitter and apparently Nugent could find no more takers. The benefit that accrued to the team on the field from these transactions was purely coincidental. To salvage the franchise Nugent was willing to destroy the team, but he didn't insist on it.

Like any merchandiser, Nugent depended on his suppliers. Other teams had farm systems, but rather than invest in one for his franchise, which was in effect a high-priced farm system already, Nugent snapped up the leftovers. The other clubs, in particular Branch Rickey's Cardinals, were glad to encourage this scrounging because Commissioner Landis wouldn't let them keep all their finds anyway. Landis wanted talent spread around, so to satisfy the Commis-

146

sioner, the Cardinals et al had some of their prospects groomed in Philadelphia rather than in the minors. It was Rickey who put the Phillies on to Klein, for example, though the Cardinals never did quite land him. (They already had a left fielder in a fellow named Joe Medwick.)

With this cozy arrangement, Nugent got his money and the rest of the league their players, and there was nothing that old Puritan, Judge Landis, could do about it. Jimmie Wilson, Lefty O'Doul, Pinky Whitney, Dolf Camilli, Bucky Walters, Claude Passeau, and Kirby Higbe, among the most notable, all came and went, and in cases such as Klein's, came and went again.

This bleeding of the Phillies to bolster the rest of the league lasted ten years before Nugent sold out. It was reported that he and his wife lived well, but apparently not on what they made from the ball club. A ballplayer negotiating salary with Nugent did best by holding out and getting himself dealt to a more generous outfit, as Kirby Higbe learned the hard way.

After winning 15 games for the last place Phillies in 1940, Higbe was offered $7,500 by the penurious Nugent. Higbe remembers, "I said, 'Mr. Nugent, if you're not going to trade me or sell me, I'll sign with you.' He said, 'I would just as soon trade my whole ball club. What have I got if I trade you?'"

Higbe learned the answer just after he signed: one hundred grand, Vito Tamulis, Bill Crouch, and Mickey Livingston.

A hopeful soul, the pitcher sent a letter to Nugent asking for some of the sale money. Nugent replied tersely, "It's all spent before I got it."

Through 1938, this decaying franchise subsisted in the decrepit Baker Bowl, built in 1887. Basically a wood structure, Baker Bowl was a firetrap. Ted Kessler, today the clubhouse attendant for visiting teams at the new Veterans Stadium, doubled as a volunteer fire fighter in his days as a batboy at Baker Bowl. "After the ball game, firemen would come in and put out the burning cigarettes," Kessler remembers. "They had barrels of water all over the park and buckets of water too, hanging on nails. If I or anyone saw a fire—there were lots of fires—we would take a bucket off the wall and douse the fire."

Baker Bowl could accommodate fifteen thousand spectators, but of course in the Phillies' and its declining years, the public did not care to test its capacity. In 1933, when the Phils won 60 games and finished seventh (they would go no higher in the next decade), 156,421 fans,

or an average of just over 2,000 per game, came to watch the paint peeling off the grandstand, cantilevered to afford the spectators a clear view of what they didn't particularly want to see. The Phillies did not command a fan's attention.

This was unfortunate because the stands were so close to the field that a patron need hardly have raised his voice to talk to or at a ballplayer. Baker Bowl could have been a haven for boo-birds, but like everything else there, criticism was pursued listlessly. A pointed assessment of the Phils was scrawled on an advertisement for Lifebuoy soap on the outfield wall: "The Phillies use Lifebuoy and they still stink." What more was there to say?

Ballplayers were of two opinions on the old bandbox. Batters loved it; pitchers dreaded it. The high right field wall, 280 feet from home plate, made left-handed batters drool and right-handed pitchers cringe. "It was a pleasure coming in there," glows Babe Herman. "I remember a curve ball I hit over the screen. It went across two wide sidewalks to the old railroad station. It went with the wind at least five hundred fifty feet. (They didn't measure in those days.) A kid brought it back in."

"It'd scare the heck out of you," shudders Jesse Haines. "When you'd stand on the mound and look around at those short fences, that was the worst sight a pitcher could have."

Kessler remembers that a lot of pitchers simply chickened out. "When they came to the ball park, they would suddenly develop sore arms," he grins.

The ball park dictated to the ball club its style of ineptness. In 1930, when no regular on the club hit worse than .280 and the team as a whole batted .315, the Phils won just 52 games and finished last, 40 games back. The pitching staff's ERA was 6.71. Including unearned runs (Philadelphia led the league in errors), the Phillies allowed an average of nearly eight runs per game. Not even a team that hits .315 can be expected to overcome that.

In 1938, the Phillies moved a few blocks away to the Athletics' Shibe Park, and Baker Bowl became a haven for other sports eccentricities, such as midget auto racing. The first year in their new home, the Phillies drew a bit better but played just as badly, finishing last again. "Them Phillies were brutal," Higbe says of his old teammates. "Man, what a bunch! We'd go into the ninth inning with the score tied and it'd seem people were more interested in getting home than in winning the game."

In 1942, Nugent sold the club to William A. Cox, but Commissioner Landis soon found the

The Phillies of the teens boasted Pete Alexander, bottom left, Earl Moore and Dode Paskert, top right, and a respectable record. By the time of "Jumbo Jim" Elliott and Dick Bartell, top left and bottom right, good players got their reward by being traded.

new owner unsuitable because he wagered on his Phillies (oddly enough, to win).

Robert M. Carpenter, Sr., chairman of the board of the DuPont Corporation, bought the team from Cox in late 1943. He entrusted it to his son, Robert, Jr., who immediately hired the former great American League pitcher, Herb Pennock, as general manager. At long last, management began to build a ball club.

The Carpenters spent more than half a million dollars for young ballplayers in the next five years. In 1947, they signed Curt Simmons for $65,000, and the next year they paid $25,000 for Robin Roberts. By 1946, the team had climbed to fifth, its best finish since 1932. In 1949, the Phillies were third.

The 1950 Phillies were a young team—only one regular, reliever Jim Konstanty, was over thirty—but more significantly they were a home-grown club. Six of the eight regulars and three of the four starters began their major league careers with Philadelphia. The Carpenters had taken a last-place team with no scouting system and in six years transformed it into a pennant contender that boasted the best young home-grown talent in the league.

"The Whiz Kids" won only 91 games in winning the pennant, and with a late-September swoon almost became "the Fizz Kids," as the Philadelphia papers were calling them before they finally clinched the flag. The Phils reached first place on July 25, and with less than two weeks to go led the Dodgers by nine games. Then they faltered, winning only two of eight while the Dodgers won eight straight. At the beginning of the final weekend, the Philadelphia lead over Brooklyn had shrunk to two games. Two games remained, both at Ebbets Field.

The Dodgers took the first one, 7–3, so the Phils were now just a loss away from falling into a playoff for the pennant.

To pitch the biggest game of the year, and probably in the history of the Phillies, manager Eddie Sawyer selected his ace, twenty-three-year-old Robin Roberts, even though this would be Roberts' fourth start in eight days. The 19-game winner had already failed four times to win his twentieth.

Don Newcombe opposed Roberts for the Dodgers. The year before, when Brooklyn needed to beat the Phillies in the season finale to clinch the pennant over St. Louis, Newcombe had started but lasted only three and a third innings. Roberts too had pitched in that game, also ineffectively. This time the match-up produced a thrilling pitchers' duel.

With two outs in the Phils' sixth of a score-less tie, Dick Sisler reached Newcombe for a base hit. Del Ennis, the Phils' leading hitter, followed with a Texas Leaguer to center that fell between Duke Snider and Jackie Robinson for a single, moving Sisler to third. He scored when Willie ("Puddin' Head") Jones rocked Newcombe's first pitch up the middle.

In the bottom of the sixth, the Dodgers tied it on a fluke homer. Pee Wee Reese sent a drive off the right field screen, but instead of rebounding onto the field, where it would have been in play, the ball dropped straight down onto the ledge of the wall below for a homer.

In the bottom of the ninth, Brooklyn almost won it. Cal Abrams opened with a walk and Reese singled him to second. The Phillies now played for the bunt, even though the hitter was Duke Snider, the third man in the order. Shortstop Granny Hamner moved close to second to shorten Abrams' lead; first baseman Eddie Waitkus charged from first; center fielder Richie Ashburn crept in to back up a possible play at second. Snider wasn't bunting, but it turned out that the Phils had defensed him perfectly anyway. Duke singled up the middle. Abrams, who had been held close to the bag, got a late start but was forced to try to score because Reese, who had been set free at first by the charging first baseman, was racing for third. Ashburn charged the hit and from shallow center fired a strike to catcher Stan Lopata, catching Abrams by ten feet.

It was only the first out of the inning, and the Dodgers had runners on second and third (Snider having taken second on the throw), but the play at the plate proved to be the turning point in the game. Roberts intentionally passed Jackie Robinson, retired Carl Furillo on a pop-up, and escaped the inning when Gil Hodges flied out. Some clutch fielding and a generous dose of luck had kept the Phillies alive.

In the top of the tenth, Sawyer allowed his obviously tiring pitcher to bat for himself, and Roberts singled. Waitkus contributed a bloop single, and the Phils had their first two men on with no one out. In a similar situation in the top of the inning, the Dodgers had spurned the bunt, gotten the hit, and killed their inning. The Phils tried the bunt, failed at it, but prevailed anyway.

Ashburn forced Roberts at third. Then came Dick Sisler, who already had three hits off Newcombe. Sisler took one strike, fouled one off, and resisted a fastball away. "The next pitch was a high fastball," he remembers. "I put the wood to it. I didn't know it was gone when I hit it, but after I rounded first base, I saw the ball go in."

Sensing the end, Roberts blew the Dodgers down in the bottom of the tenth. After 35 years of pathos, the Phillies had redeemed themselves.

Other than the tenacious Roberts, the key to the Whiz Kids was their old man, Konstanty. In 11 years in the majors, he won 66 games, 16 of them for the Phils in 1950. He compiled statistics that in other years were commonplace for star relievers, but in 1950, they were incomparable. He led the league with 74 appearances; the runner-up had 51. He had 22 saves, 14 better than the next best in the league. In short, Konstanty was the backbone of the Phils' pitch-

ing staff, which led the league in ERA but was only tied for fifth in complete games.

The hitting was balanced but unspectacular. Only one regular, Mike Goliat, hit less than .250. But only two, Ennis and Ashburn, hit more than .300. Ennis led the league in RBIs with 126, and three regulars, Hamner, Jones, and Sisler, had more than 80.

Obviously, the Whiz Kids were not a great team. The most exciting teams often aren't (the 1934 Cardinals, the 1951 Giants, the 1960 Pirates, for example). Perhaps the Phils were so popular precisely because they had to struggle

149

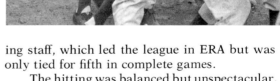

Top: *Chuck Klein led the Phillies' attack in the Baker Bowl, the quintessential hitter's ball park.* Above left: *Robin Roberts.*
Above right: *Greeting Dick Sisler after his pennant-winning homer.*

to win. Rags to riches and never very far from rags again, they were the true Cinderella team.

Midnight struck in the World Series against the Yankees. As in their first World Series, in 1915, the Phils lost four straight, tight, well-pitched games. "We were a more mature ball club," the Yankees' second baseman, Jerry Coleman, explains.

The next year the Phillies won 18 fewer games and dropped to fifth. Of the many Phillies who slumped, Konstanty was the most noticeable. He won 12 fewer games and saved 13 fewer than he had the year before. His ERA soared from 2.66 to 4.05. Whiz Kid young at thirty-three in 1950, he grew old in one year, and the club faltered without him.

By 1958, the Phillies were in the cellar again. Although the Carpenters had made a noble first effort in building the Whiz Kids, that team had simply not been strong enough to compete consistently against the powerful Dodgers and Giants of the early fifties. When the renova-

tions began, the team was destined for a few years in the second division. Management mistakes made the eclipse darker than it need have been. "The Phillies waited too long for trades," says Dallas Green, today the team's farm director, "and the farm system did not produce."

The team had stopped winning but not because it had stopped building. The pitching staff of the 1958 last-place Phils included some future stalwarts of the National League: Jack Sanford, Don Cardwell, and Dick Farrell, in addition to 1950 holdovers Roberts and Curt Simmons. Simmons had hurt himself in a lawn mower accident, but some of his best years were still ahead of him, though not as a Phillie. The experience of this edition of last-place Phils proved that signing talented ballplayers does not in itself produce a winner.

Gene Mauch succeeded Sawyer, in his second turn at the helm, after the Phils' Opening Day loss in 1960. Then the sinking ship hit bottom in 1961, when the Phillies set a modern major league record of 23 losses in a row and, with only 47 wins, finished last for the fourth straight year.

The young manager and his young players emerged from this cruel baptism a reborn team. Although the Phillies had lost Simmons, Sanford, Cardwell, Farrell, and Roberts through various transactions, the farm system had produced two other big winners of the near future, Art Mahaffey and Chris Short. Two young outfielders, Johnny Callison and Tony Gonzalez, were about to blossom into .300 hitters, and there was a howitzer arm at short in Bobby Wine. The futile Phillies of 1961 were, though their personnel was essentially unchanged, a .500 ball club in 1962.

People were starting to notice the Phillies they had scorned a year earlier. When the 1963 club won 87 games, though the biggest winner on the staff, Ray Culp, won just 14 games,

Phillies

Name of Park	Date 1st Game Played	Opponent & Score	Capacity
Athletic Baseball Grounds	April 22, 1876	Boston 6, Philadelphia 5	3,000*
Recreation Park	May 1, 1883	Providence 4, Philadelphia 3	2,000*
Philadelphia Baseball Grounds (Baker Bowl)	April 28, 1887	New York 4, Philadelphia 3	12,500
Shibe Park	July 4, 1938	Boston 10, Philadelphia 5 Philadelphia 10, Boston 2	33,000
Connie Mack Stadium**			
Veterans Stadium	April 10, 1971	Philadelphia 4, Montreal 1	55,581

Estimated attendance that day.
**Shibe Park renamed Connie Mack Stadium.*

Greg Luzinski deferred to teammate Mike Schmidt in home runs but led the National League in RBIs in 1975.

manager Gene Mauch, unknown when he was hired, was hailed as a strategic and psychological wizard. Mauch brilliantly martialed his forces when injuries and other setbacks threatened to abort the season. Mahaffey, a 19-game winner in 1962, hurt his arm and won just 7. Dennis Bennett, a southpaw rookie sensation, broke his ankle and won only 9. Don Demeter slumped miserably from his .300 and 100-plus RBI year of 1962. Don Hoak, picked up from the Pirates to plug a hole at third for a season, hit just .231.

Into the pitching breach Mauch hurled Culp, Short, and thirty-seven-year-old Cal McLish. Jack Baldschun won 11 and saved 16 in relief. Journeyman Wes Covington hit .300 in place of the faltering Demeter. In 1963, Mauch's pulsating baseball mind and blazing spirit showed the Phillies just how good they could be. Only the lack of a true ace for the pitching staff stood between them and the pennant.

For the 1964 season, Philadelphia traded Demeter to Detroit for Jim Bunning, who would win 74 games for the Phillies in the next four years, including a perfect game against the Mets in 1966. Bunning won 19 games for the Phillies in 1964, Short 17, Bennett and Mahaffey 12 each. Baldschun had 21 saves. The Phils unveiled a power-hitting rookie third baseman, Richie Allen, who batted .318, slammed 29 homers, and collected 91 RBIs. Gonzalez and Covington produced solid years at bat, and Callison had an outstanding one (31 homers, 104 RBIs). The weaknesses on the pitching staff, at third base, and in left field had become strengths. And yet the Phils lost the pennant.

With 12 games to play in the season, Mauch's team led by six and a half games. As it turned out, the Phils needed to win just four of the twelve. But they won only two, and those after they had already lost ten in a row and the pennant.

The loss of the pennant stung. But the greatest disappointment must have struck in the next few seasons, when it became clear that once again the best team the Carpenters had built was not good enough to challenge for the pennant. In 1965, Mahaffey and Bennett were through, and the Phils won 85 games, 7 less than in 1964. In 1966, though Philadelphia gained first baseman Bill White and shortstop Dick Groat from St. Louis and pitchers Larry Jackson and Bob Buhl from Chicago, the club won only 87, finishing fourth. "Because they were so close in 1964," says Dallas Green, "they tried to win through trades." They failed.

On June 15, 1968, Bob Skinner replaced Mauch as manager. "I had done all I could," Mauch said. "It was time for a change for me." Perhaps he sensed that yet another era of deprivation was about to ensue.

In the six years after Mauch's departure, the Phils won an average of fewer than 70 games a year. As they had after the pennant in 1915 and the pennant in 1950, they sank slowly but inexorably until in 1972, with 59 wins, they were one of the worst teams in baseball. But once again the phoenixlike Phils rose quickly to contention, and this time after a relatively brief eclipse.

Today, Steve Carlton, Jim Lonborg, and Tug McGraw supplement the youngsters on the pitching staff: Larry Christenson, Wayne Twitchell, Tom Underwood, Dick Ruthven—talented throwers all. Second baseman Dave Cash, procured from Pittsburgh, teams with little Larry Bowa at short for a sound keystone combination. Jay Johnstone, a disappointing hitter until he reached Philadelphia, and Garry Maddox, a budding star obtained from the Giants, fill two spots in the outfield unless and until the Phillies' own products, Mike Anderson and Jerry Martin, can replace them. Dick Allen, the prodigal son, has returned to finish his career in the city where he began it. But unquestionably, the titans of this Philadelphia contender are the best sluggers the farm system has ever produced: third baseman Mike Schmidt, National League home run champ in 1974 and 1975, and Greg Luzinski, the league's RBI leader in 1975.

If comparisons must be made, Schmidt, the taller and leaner of the two, strikes like a grenade launcher, Luzinski like the grenade. Schmidt's freer swing makes for more impressive sky-high homers when he connects. Luzinski's compact power delivers more reliably. Schmidt unloads; Luzinski explodes.

Today, for the first time in their history, the Phillies are drawing impressively. In 1974, nearly two million fans attended the home games. Partly, the renewed interest in the Phillies stems from a general sports revival in the city, led by the two-time Stanley Cup champion Flyers. Partly, the new Veterans Stadium, which the Phillies entered in 1968, is an attraction. But of course mostly, the team itself is the draw—a contender again after so many desperate years. No team has failed as badly and as often as the Phillies have, but that makes resurrection all the more exciting. In thirty years, the Phils have conquered not one but three eras of last-place despair. When they crown their latest ascension with a pennant, no loser will ever have been more triumphantly vindicated.

A Tradition of Victory
The Giants

One summer day in 1883, the saber-mustached manager of the New York National League baseball club, Jim Mutrie, got carried away. His boys were winning an important game, and Mutrie bellowed, "My big fellows! My Giants!"

Many of the players he so addressed were in fact big, as a seemingly disproportionate number of Giants have been since then. And, of course, there have been some giant-sized achievers. But in the many years since the nickname was first affixed to the team, "Giants" has broadened in meaning to encompass slightly built superpests as well as mammoth superstars, one-time heroes as well as abiding legends—the Leo Durochers and Eddie Stankys, the Bobby Thomsons, Dusty Rhodeses, and Billy Pierces, as well as the Mathewsons, Otts, Hubbells, Mayses, and Marichals. The Giant quality that covers them all has been a propensity for winning. Since the turn of the century, the Giants have won more games and have a better winning percentage than any other National League club. They also have won the most pennants. In their ten decades of National League life, the Giants have been imposing.

The most important of the early Giants was, as empire builders often are, a little man. John Joseph McGraw stood all of 5 feet 7 inches and weighed 155 pounds. When he took command of the Giants, on July 16, 1902, they were a last-

Opposite: *From Coogan's Bluff to Frisco Bay. The Giants now play on a promontory of the West Coast.* Above: *John Montgomery Ward, a player in the eighties, a manager in the nineties.*

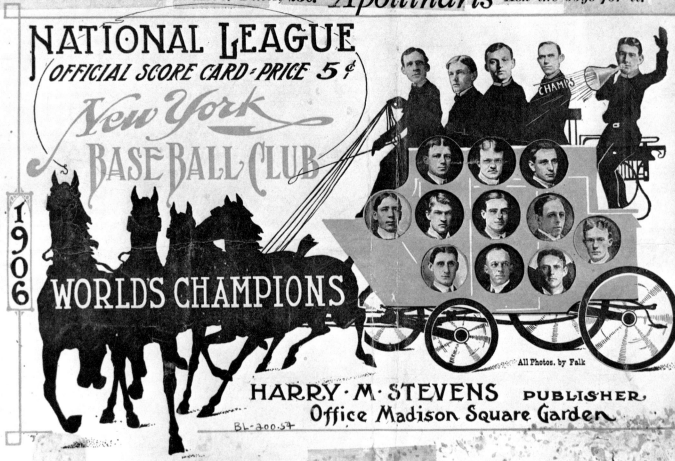

NATIONAL LEAGUE
OFFICIAL SCORE CARD • PRICE 5¢
New York
BASE BALL CLUB

1906

WORLD'S CHAMPIONS

All Photos. by Falk

BL-200-57

HARRY • M • STEVENS   PUBLISHER,
Office Madison Square Garden

place team. A parade of 13 managers had struggled unsuccessfully at their helm. McGraw came from the Baltimore Orioles, bringing with him such talented performers as Dan McGann, "Iron Man" Joe McGinnity, and fiery Roger Bresnahan. Upon taking control, the new manager's first act was to release half the players on the roster. "With my team, I'm absolute czar," he proclaimed, modifying slightly the title he was more commonly known by, "the Little Napoleon." Whether czar or emperor, McGraw reigned for thirty years, during which time he transformed his team into baseball royalty. His Giants won 10 pennants and finished second 11 times.

Their first pennant under the truculent Mr. McGraw came in 1904, less than two years after he arrived. In 1905, McGraw's Giants repeated as National League champs and disposed of Connie Mack's Philadelphia Athletics in the World Series on four shutout victories in five games. Three of the shutouts were the work of the star of the Series and of the decade for the

Giants, Christy ("Big Six") Mathewson. "It was a pleasure to watch Mathewson pitch," Mack observed, "when he wasn't pitching against you." Horace Fogel, the manager of the Giants before McGraw, had attempted to convert Mathewson into a first baseman, but McGraw was convinced that the big blond was a pitcher. As usual, he was right.

Mathewson was the ace of the Giants' staff from 1901 to 1914. With great control, stamina, and a fadeaway pitch akin to today's screwball, he won 20 or more games a dozen years in a row and 30 or more in each of four years, three of them consecutive. The Hall of Famer stands supreme in the Giants' record book with the most wins, shutouts, games, innings pitched, complete games, and strikeouts. "There was never another like Matty," McGraw proclaimed. "I doubt if there ever will be."

More than an uncanny talent scout and a loyal partisan, McGraw was a tactical baseball genius. He was the first manager to use pinch hitters and relief pitchers as specialists. He

154

Above: *With John McGraw holding the reins, the Giants drove to the top in 1905 but finished only second in 1906.* Opposite bottom: *McGraw, center, linked the old Orioles (Wilbert Robinson, left), with the Giants (Mathewson, right).* Opposite top: *"Bonehead" Merkle.*

began the custom of directing the team from the bench rather than from the coaching lines, as was traditional, though the opposition called him a quitter for leaving the playing field. Mathewson observed, "He knew he could pull the team through from the bench—concentrate better, see more of what was going on. And he missed nothing."

In 1911–13, McGraw made the bunt, the hit-and-run, and speed in general prime weapons in the baseball attack. On the legs of Josh Devore, Buck Herzog, Fred Snodgrass, Arthur Fletcher, and one of the era's most popular and flamboyant players, "Laughing Larry" Doyle, the Giants raced to pennants in those years. But they lost the Series each time, in 1911 and 1913 to the powerful Athletics, in 1912 to the Boston Red Sox on a rash of seventh-game miscues, the most notable of which was Snodgrass' tenth-inning outfield muff of a fly ball.

In those years, McGraw again illustrated his talent for discovering talent, and his perseverance. On McGraw's recommendation, the Giants purchased left-hander Rube Marquard from Indianapolis in the minors, though the price was $11,000, at the time the record for a minor league purchase. Marquard pitched erratically for the Giants and languished on the bench for a few seasons, but McGraw's judgment and patience proved justified. In 1911, the so-called "$11,000 Lemon" was 24–7, and in 1912, his record 19 straight victories were a major factor in the Giants' National League title.

In 1916, the Giants won 26 games in a row, still a major league record. Hall of Famer George ("Highpockets") Kelly, a young member of the team, remembers the weakest link in that chain of victories: "One time, we were really getting beaten, and McGraw kept trying to stall. Well, he finally won out, and the game was called before the end of the fifth. It was a great streak, but we were saved by rain."

The Stoneham era began in 1919, when Charles A. Stoneham bought the club. His son, Horace Stoneham, who succeeded him in 1936 and continued as owner through 1975, recalls how Stoneham, Sr., became the Giants' owner: "My father was born and brought up in Jersey City, and he liked a left fielder on their team who went to the Giants. He followed the left fielder to the Polo Grounds, became a Giant fan, and that's how he became involved."

"There were newspaper rumors that George M. Cohan was going to buy the team. Then at dinner one night my father said, 'Maybe I'll buy the club.' We didn't know he was serious. About a month later, he bought the Giants."

With Stoneham's cooperation and support, McGraw again changed the style of the Giants, remodeling them from speedy singles hitters into more powerful hitters, ideal for the short foul lines at the Polo Grounds. Trading, buying, shuffling personnel, McGraw, the giant force in baseball now, became a prolific talent broker. "The game meant more to him than individuals," Horace Stoneham observes. "He traded some people who were his good friends to help the team, and in some cases traded for them back to help the team again."

Highpockets Kelly left for Pittsburgh in 1917, then returned in 1919. McGraw also acquired pitchers Phil Douglas, Jesse Barnes, and Art Nehf, catcher Frank Snyder, and shortstop Dave ("Beauty") Bancroft. Emil ("Irish") Meusel came over from Philadelphia and meshed nicely in the outfield with George Burns and Ross Youngs. In 1922, Heinie Groh, the best third baseman in the league, was obtained from Cincinnati.

McGraw had a network of friends and old players who kept him apprised of gifted young ballplayers. He converted this informal scouting system into a talent pipeline, through which flowed players who would help produce pennants for him in four consecutive years, 1921–24. Frankie Frisch came from the Fordham campus to the Giants in 1919, shortstop Travis Jackson in 1922, first baseman Bill Terry in 1923, and third baseman Freddy Lindstrom in 1924.

As the class of the league, the Giants attracted New York's beautiful people—Broadway stars who would sit in the sun at the Polo Grounds and watch the imperious, strutting McGraw preside over his Giants like a movie director over his cast.

In the 1921 World Series, the Giants beat the Yankees in seven games, in the 1922 Series in four. These were the first World Series games staged completely in New York; indeed completely in one ball park, because the Polo Grounds was the home field for both clubs. In 1923, the Yankees moved into Yankee Stadium and finally beat the Giants in the Series, four games to two, despite a game-winning inside-the-park homer in the first game by an aging but still spritely outfielder for the Giants, Casey Stengel.

The 1924 World Series, between the Giants and the Washington Senators, turned on the famous "pebble play." In the seventh game, with one out and two on in the Senators' twelfth, Earl McNeely's seemingly sure double-play grounder hopped over the head of third baseman Fred Lindstrom, dooming the Giants. "That thing there, now, it was never written up the way I looked at it," Kelly contends. "Now it did hit a pebble, but Fred had backed up on it—inexperience, it was his rookie year. This allowed the ball an extra hop. The ball played Fred; he didn't play it."

Preventable or not, the pebble play foreshadowed a change in the fortunes of the Giants. After this, their tenth pennant under McGraw, they never won another for him. However, the Giants continued to be contenders, and the talent pipeline was still producing.

Upon arrival of the newest Giant in New

156

get results as soon as he learns about big league pitching."

McGraw was referring to the peculiar habit the kid had of lifting his right foot as he began his left-handed swing. Typically, McGraw could see in a seemingly awkward style the trademark of greatness. By 1928, McGraw's "baby" was the regular right fielder, a power-armed, power-hitting stalwart embarking on a brilliant 22-year career in the majors, all with the Giants.

The rise of Ott was one of the last of McGraw's monuments to the Giants. The end of the aging monarch's reign came on June 3, 1932, with the Giants just where they had been when he arrived, in last place. McGraw was broken by his team's misfortune as well as by his own poor health, but in abdicating, the dying king left a basically sound kingdom to his successor, "Memphis Bill" Terry, whom he recommended as manager. Thus, the McGraw legacy included not only the 10 pennants he won in his 31 years, but more to come. In 1933, as the old man watched the team from a center field clubhouse window, Terry led the Giants to the pennant.

As in McGraw's glory days, many of the giants on this team were pitchers. Left-handed screwballer Carl Hubbell could "kinda make a ball disappear," in the words of Garry Schumacher, former public relations director for the Giants. In 1933, Hubbell had a string of 46⅓

York in 1925, equipment manager Eddie Logan (today sixty-seven and still serving the club in that capacity, as his father had circa 1896) was sent to retrieve the recruit. Logan still gets excited when he tells the old story: "We had the Ninth Avenue El at the time. Mr. McGraw wanted somebody to go down and pick up this kid who was joining the club. He had been told to ride the El to the last stop, which was the Polo Grounds, but he took the El the wrong way and wound up at the Battery. I was supposed to be able to recognize him by his straw suitcase. I looked for it, and I found him. He was the same age as I was—sixteen. I said, 'C'mon boy, let's go.' He got the biggest thrill riding back on the train."

The gawky Louisiana boy with the straw suitcase entered the Giants' clubhouse and presented himself: "Mr. McGraw, I'm Melvin Ott."

From the beginning, McGraw knew Ott would be great. Questioned why such a youth was kept in the Polo Grounds, the manager responded, "He's too young to play big league ball, but I'm afraid to send him to the minors and have a manager there tinker with his batting style. The style is natural with him. He'll

scoreless innings and finished the season with an ERA of 1.66.

In the first game of a doubleheader on July 2, 1933, Hubbell bedazzled the St. Louis Cardinals with an 18-inning shutout, striking out 12 and allowing only six hits and no walks. In the nightcap, LeRoy Parmelee beat Dizzy Dean 1–0. Those 27 scoreless innings typified the power pitching and tight defense of the 1933 team. The Giants played for one run and made it decisive. Their slogan was a defiant "They Can't Beat Us!" More often than not they were right.

The Giants defeated the Washington Senators for the 1933 world championship. Hubbell hurled an 11-inning, 2–1 masterpiece in the fourth game. Ott's tenth-inning home run won the fifth.

After watching the beginning of another of the Giants' National League dynasties, John McGraw died, on February 25, 1934.

In the five years 1933–37, the Giants won three pennants, Ott supplying the power, Hubbell the pitching, Terry the guidance. Perfecting the style that McGraw had refused to tamper with, Ott was in his prime, well on his way to his 511 career home runs and 1,860 RBIs. Terry was finishing a formidable career, in which he compiled more than 2,000 hits and the all-time top career batting average for the team, .341. And Hubbell, in an era when uncertainty and fear gripped the country, was so reliable that he was aptly dubbed "the Meal Ticket." He produced seven consecutive 20-win seasons, and more triumphs than any other pitcher for the Giants but Christy Mathewson. The symbol of Hubbell's preeminence came in the 1934 All-Star

Game when he accomplished the incredible and historic feat of striking out in succession the best hitters in the American League: Babe Ruth, Lou Gehrig, Jimmie Foxx, Al Simmons, and Joe Cronin.

With the Giants on top again, the stars once more glittered in attendance at the Polo Grounds. Schumacher remembers, "The Broadway crowd, the nightclub people, would come out and sit together. There was Goodman Ace, George Raft, Tallulah Bankhead." Eddie Logan recalls that Bankhead, a rabid fan of the Giants, "would fill up a room with flowers if someone got hurt or sick." Horace Stoneham remembers the grand entrances of Milton Berle: "He would always come in the Eighth Avenue entrance. He was always the showman, and he timed his arrival so that the fans could see him."

In his first years as president of the Giants, Horace Stoneham presided over changes that would buttress the Giants of Hubbell, Ott, and the other McGraw holdovers. The team acquired infielders Dick Bartell and Burgess Whitehead, and outfielders Hank Leiber and Jimmy Ripple. The Giants won the pennant in 1936 and 1937, with Hubbell winning 16 in a row in 1936 and extending the string into the next year before finally losing, on May 27, 1937, after 24 straight victories (a major league record).

The 1937 Series was the Giants' last Series for 14 years. There were to be many changes at the Polo Grounds in the next few years, not all of them for the better. The biggest one came after the 1941 season, when Terry resigned to devote his time to the farm system he had begun and Mel Ott became the manager. Ott lasted seven years at the helm, never finishing better than third. In the beginning, the problem was the war and the aging of the veterans from the championship teams. In the end, there was no pitching, speed, or defense. But there was hitting. In 1947, Ott had a team in his image— "whackers," as Garry Schumacher called them. Huge Johnny Mize had 51 home runs, Willard Marshall 36, Walker Cooper 35, and a rookie named Bobby Thomson 29. In all, the Giants amassed 221 homers for the year, a record at the time. It was the first of the Giants' teams, so common in the decades to come, of raw power and not much else. The action delighted the fans, but it didn't win pennants.

In 1948, the fiery Leo Durocher replaced "McGraw's Boy." Actually, the contentious, controversial Leo was more in McGraw's image than either Ott or the other Southern gentleman, Terry, who had followed McGraw. In style and substance, the coming of Durocher marked

a new era for the Giants. "When Durocher replaced Ott," Eddie Logan remembers, "Mel and I sat in the clubhouse for about seven or eight hours telling each other the old stories."

Durocher announced, "This is not my kind of team," and he proceeded to change it. Alvin Dark and Eddie Stanky were obtained from the Boston Braves, and Durocher had his double-play combination. From St. Louis, he got Jim Hearn to use as a third starter behind Larry Jansen and Sal Maglie. The lumbering power

was gone, but Durocher had the kind of club he wanted. Westrum remembers the spirit: "He was all out to win. He'd get under your skin. He wouldn't care if it was tiddlywinks; he'd try to beat you." And the talent was there, led by the awesome, glowering Maglie. "I caught Maglie most of his games," Westrum says. "He had two or three varieties of curves he could get over. They called him 'the Barber' because once in a while he'd shave you with his fastball. He was uncanny."

In 1950, the Giants moved up to third place, victors in 50 of their last 72 games.

In May of that year, the team's coordinator of scouting, Jack Schwarz, sent scouts to look at a first baseman on the New York Cubans, a Negro team that was playing the Birmingham Black Barons. "We needed a first baseman," 159

Opposite: *In the early twenties at the Polo Grounds, the Giants* were *the show in town.* Above: *The glorification of "the Brat." Stanky's manager had a fancy for pugnacious little guys.*

Schwarz recalls. "The next day one scout and then another phoned me with the message, 'Forget about the first baseman. There's a little outfielder on the other club, Jack. You must get this fellow. He'll be in the Polo Grounds in two years.'"

In fact, he was there in one. Chub Feeney, then the Giants' vice-president, approved the price, $2,500 in cash and $7,500 if the outfielder were kept for 30 days, and the Giants set about trying to find a place in the minors for their latest acquisition. Sioux City didn't want him because the town was having racial problems, so instead he went to Trenton and lifted the team from sixth place to third by the end of the season. The next spring he was at Minneapolis and scheduled to play an exhibition game at Sioux City. By this time his fame had spread, and every light post in Sioux City had his picture on it, promoting the game on the strength of the player it had rejected the year before. He never did play in Sioux City. Durocher made a phone call, and nineteen-year-old Willie Mays, a .477 hitter, joined the Giants.

Perhaps Mays's greatest gift was his talent for conveying the joy he experienced in playing ball. This was not surprising, since he played the game so well and enjoyed it so much. But it takes more than talent and spirit to communicate the joy of the game. Jackie Robinson, for example, surely loved to play and had talent and spirit comparable to Mays's, yet for Robinson baseball was always a challenge; for Mays it was sport.

Chub Feeney says, "He did everything that could be done on the baseball field," but indeed he did more than that. He did what shouldn't be done, and did it so well and so naturally that he seemed to expand the limits of the possible. In fact, he only breached them, for what worked for Mays was at least impractical for everyone else, and most ballplayers had the instinctive sense to realize it. No one else even tried to emulate the way Mays caught a fly ball, in his famous basket, or the way he moved from first to third on a single to right—looking backward at the ball while cruising around second toward third.

Even more unique to Mays were the purely spontaneous spurts of genius. He could rescue a sun-plagued outfield partner on a fly ball with the aplomb he had for balls hit right to him. "Willie's territory in the Polo Grounds," quips former teammate Monte Irvin, "was second base to the center field monuments."

It seemed effortless, and perhaps much of it was, but it was rarely automatic. Like many superstars, Mays could flop as spectacularly as

he succeeded—particularly at bat. He hit a home run once in every 17 at-bats and struck out once in every 7. When he joined the Giants, he was hitless in his first 12 trips to the plate. Then, after some fatherly reassurance from Durocher, he got his first hit—a homer off Warren Spahn.

Months after gaining the man who was soon to become the most electrifying ballplayer in baseball history, the Giants produced baseball's most electrifying pennant. Mays was not the best of the Giants that year, though he was Rookie of the Year, but his style of play symbolized their season. As Mays would throughout his 22-year career, the 1951 Giants experienced setbacks only, it seemed, to make the victories that overcame them more glorious.

The low point was mid-August, when with two-thirds of the season gone, the Giants lan-

guished 13½ games behind the torrid Dodgers. Then, blessed by the managerial clairvoyance of Durocher, the Giants got hot. "Lco did one hell of a job," says Irvin. "He called the right shot so many times, moving a fielder here, bringing in a relief pitcher just at the right time."

According to Irvin, Durocher's magic buoyed the club. "We said, 'What the heck, we got a man who knows what he's doing—the least we can do is go out and perform.' I never will forget it. . . . We won sixteen in a row, and we beat everybody in the seventh, eighth, and ninth innings."

It took more than good fortune. In Irvin, the Giants had the top RBI man in the league. They had four men with 20 or more homers, led by Bobby Thomson with 32. And their pitching was the league's best, led by the league's top two

Clockwise from top left: *Hail the conquering hero—Thomson comes home; Jansen, Stanky, Irvin, and Durocher celebrate tying Dodgers for pennant; Dusty Rhodes, 1954 World Series star.*

Left: *Bobby Murcer shin to shinguard with
Cubs' catcher George Mitterwald.*
Above: *Jim Barr, a senior member of a young staff.*

winners, Maglie and Jansen, with 23 wins each. In the field, Stanky and Dark made the double plays, and Mays dominated the outfield. The Giants won 39 of their last 47 games (an .830 percentage), tying the Dodgers for the pennant.

"We beat them three–one in the first game," Irvin remembers of the three-game playoff, "and I hit a homer. The next day in the Polo Grounds, Billy Cox [Brooklyn third baseman] was like a magician. We hit them to the left, to the right. He was picking them off like a guy eating grapes. They beat us ten–nothing."

The finale pitted ace against ace—the Dodgers' Don Newcombe against the Giants' Maglie. Neither would finish. "Durocher told us if you stay close to Don you can beat him in the eighth or ninth," Irvin remembers. "But he was blinding us for eight innings."

With the Dodgers leading 4–1, Dark opened the bottom of the ninth by reaching on an infield hit. Inexplicably, the Dodgers' first baseman, Gil Hodges, held the bag against the runner, and Don Mueller singled past the first baseman. "Hodges was playing out of position," Irvin contends. "He should not have been holding him on—that run meant nothing. He would have had Mueller's hit if he hadn't been holding Dark on."

Irvin himself was next. "I tried to pull the ball and I popped up to Hodges." Two on, one gone for Whitey Lockman, the Giants' first baseman. Lockman delivered a slicing double down

the left field line, scoring Dark and finishing Newcombe. After consulting pitching coach Clyde Sukeforth, Brooklyn manager Chuck Dressen opted for Ralph Branca to face Bobby Thomson.

Because of what happened next, baseball fans, particularly New York baseball fans, tend to remember where they were at that moment, 3:58 P.M. of October 3, 1951. It was not just the dramatic come-from-behind race the Giants had run for the pennant, epitomized by this final rally. The unfaded memory of the moment is also a product of the fierce emotions that gripped the fans whenever the Giants played the Dodgers. Participants remember events more vividly than observers do, and at this game, as at all others between the Giants and Dodgers, there were no observers, only participants.

When Bobby Thomson faced Ralph Branca in the last inning of the last game of the season, it was the climax to baseball's fiercest rivalry as well as to its closest pennant race.

He hit a one-strike fastball. Like the original "shot heard 'round the world," Thomson's was a modest spark that ignited a mammoth explosion. It was a low, curving line drive that barely reached the seats, traveling a little more than 315 feet. Even before it ended its brief journey, the Polo Grounds was in bedlam. The Giants jumped up in the dugout. "Some guys banged their heads on the roof," Irvin recalls. "We knew that if it didn't get into the stands it would at least tie the score."

The first man out of the dugout was Eddie Stanky. While the fans screamed, cried, fought in disbelief, Stanky rushed straight to Durocher in the third base coaching box and jumped on him. Thinking it was a hysterical fan, Durocher turned to punch his second baseman, then saw who it was and for one of the few times in his life was speechless. By now Thomson had rounded third, and Durocher followed him home half carrying Stanky. In the broadcast booth, Russ Hodges screamed, "The Giants win the pennant!" eight times before subsiding in exhaustion. It was not a time for self-control. Only the Dodgers stood literally unmoved on the field.

After the Giants finally reached the clubhouse, a throng of some eight thousand fans laid siege to the shelter. "They wouldn't go away," Irvin says, "until Durocher and Thomson came out." Schumacher says, "They wanted the Papal blessing."

When it was over, the Yankees stood, as they usually did, between the National League champs and the world championship. They beat the Giants in six games. But it almost didn't

164

Above and opposite: *Superstar San Franciscans Willie Mays and Juan Marichal were the pillars of the Giants in the years after the move west.*

matter. There was nothing the Giants could have done to outshine their pennant-winning triumph, and it may have been just as well that they didn't come close.

The next two years, Mays was gone to the army and the Giants were in decline, finishing second and fifth. But in 1954, Willie and the Giants were back. Smashing 41 home runs, driving in 110, and leading the league with a .345 average, Mays was the runaway MVP. Don Mueller contributed 212 hits for a .342 average, and pinch hitter deluxe Dusty Rhodes hit .341, including 15 homers in only 164 at-bats. The Giants led the league in homers with 186 and in pitching with a composite 3.09 ERA. Former Brave Johnny Antonelli won 21 and led the league with a 2.30 ERA; Hoyt Wilhelm and Marv Grissom were stellar in relief.

This time the Giants won the pennant handily and saved their most dramatic heroics for the Series. Cleveland's Indians, winners of 111 games in the regular season, an American League record, lasted only 4 against the New Yorkers. The pivotal game was the first, in which Mays made the most famous catch of his career. With the score tied 2–2 in the top of the eighth inning, Indians on first and second, and none out, Vic Wertz lashed reliever Don Liddle's first pitch more than 400 feet to the base of the Polo Grounds' bleachers in center field. Mays scampered back and, with his back to the origin of the drive like a flanker catching an 80-yard bomb, plucked the ball two-handed just before he reached the warning track. Then, defying the laws of momentum, he maintained his balance, whirled, and fired the ball back to the infield. Two innings later, Mays squelched Wertz's next attempt to break the tie by cutting off his drive to left center, holding him to a double.

In the bottom of the tenth, pinch hitter Dusty Rhodes lofted a 260-foot, three-run homer, and the Giants won 5–2. Before the Series was over, Rhodes would have three more hits and four more RBIs in five more at-bats—an incredible efficiency ratio of more than one run produced per time at bat.

It was the first World Series victory for the Giants in more than twenty years, and the last as well. With a superstar and not much else, the Giants sank into mediocrity the next few years. Durocher left a sinking ship in 1955, and two years later the Giants abandoned their home in New York.

Following their rivals, the Dodgers, to the West Coast, the Giants began a new life in San Francisco and in five years won a pennant. There hasn't been one since, but the club has been a contender most years, thanks to a farm system that has stocked them (and, through unfortunate trades, the rest of the league) with fine ballplayers. The first of the non-New York stars was the 1958 Rookie of the Year, Orlando Cepeda, who batted .312 and clubbed 25 homers. The next year, Willie McCovey won the honor with a .354 average. Other future stars who came up through the Giants' organization in these years were Felipe and Matty Alou, Leon Wagner, Bill White, Mike McCormick, and Juan Marichal.

"I caught him when he first came up," Westrum says of Marichal, "and I told everyone, 'Here's your next twenty-game winner. . . .

Everything came natural to him. He had great control of four or five pitches. If he hadn't gotten hurt, he probably would have been one of the all-time greats."

The pitching of Marichal notwithstanding, the trademark of the Giants of the sixties was power. Throughout the decade, they had the top home run hitter in the league: Mays, McCovey, or Cepeda. In three straight years, 1962–64, they led the league in homers. Most years, the Giants were wanting in pitching, speed, and defense, but at least once it didn't matter. That was in 1962, when the go-go Dodgers lost Sandy Koufax in midseason and fell apart. The putt-putt Giants caught them in the stretch and beat them in another playoff. This time Ralph Branca was (under)played by Stan Williams, who walked Jim Davenport, forcing in the deciding run in the final game. This was the year Philadelphia alumnus Jack Sanford won 24 games, including 16 in a row, and thirty-five-year-old southpaw Billy Pierce found the fountain of youth in the winds of Candlestick. The left-field-to-right-field jetstream helped Billy keep right-handed power hitters at bay (even as it sailed left-handers' drives into the Bay), so Pierce was virtually unbeatable at home. Young Marichal contributed 18 wins, and veteran Billy O'Dell 19. It all proved that great hitting can make good pitching: the Giants' staff was sixth in ERA but first in complete games.

Then came the Yankees in the World Series and a heartbreaking loss. Somehow the National Leaguers snatched three games from the pinstriped smoothies, but in the end steadiness prevailed over spirit and sentiment. The Giants had the tying run on third and the winner on second in the last of the ninth, against Ralph Terry in the seventh game. But Bobby Richardson was, as the Yankees always were, in the right place at the right time, and McCovey's line shot went right to him for the final out. "They had just

Giants

Name of Park	Date 1st Game Played	Opponent & Score	Capacity
Union Grounds	April 25, 1876	Boston 7, New York 6	2,000*
Polo Grounds	May 1, 1883	New York 7, Boston 6	12,000*
Manhattan Field	July 8, 1889	New York 7, Pittsburgh 5	15,000
Polo Grounds	April 22, 1891	Boston 4, New York 3	15,000*
			55,131***
Polo Grounds**	June 28, 1911	New York 3, Boston 0	30,000
Seals Stadium	April 15, 1958	San Francisco 8, Los Angeles 0	23,750
Candlestick Park	April 12, 1960	San Francisco 3, St. Louis 1	42,500
			58,000***

Estimated attendance that day.
**Polo Grounds' stands destroyed by fire, April, 1911; rebuilt and opened, June 28.*
***Expanded capacity.*

Clockwise from above: Chris Speier awaits verdict on his drive; No-hit Halicki, left, shares a triumphant clasp with Gary Matthews; Derrel Thomas extends himself and ex-Giant Dave Kingman; Von Joshua's swing makes the ball park spin.

moved him over to the spot," McCovey ruefully recalls, "and just like magic I hit it right at him." Yankee magic.

Since the sixties, the Giants' empire has been in decline. Contenders if not winners throughout that decade, the club could not replace its mainstays as they grew old. In 1971, there was a divisional championship, but the next year the Giants plummeted to next-to-last and haven't been a contender since.

Once it begins, deterioration is not easy to check, much less reverse. The Giants' quest for ready cash and proven veterans to sustain them while the youngsters matured cost them two stars of the future in Dave Kingman and Garry Maddox. Nor have they fared much better in dealing veterans—witness Gaylord Perry for Sam McDowell. But the farm system's resilient, seemingly limitless capacity for producing talent may yet rescue the organization. The Giants' old empire builders would approve of the newest batch of young Giants because there are pitchers and speedsters as well as hitters. The leaders are hard throwers Pete Falcone, Ed ("No-Hit") Halicki, and loquacious John ("the Count") Montefusco; rifle-armed All-Star shortstop Chris Speier; and veterans Bobby Murcer, Willie Montanez, Gary Matthews, and fleet Von Joshua. The Giants are again following the formula of McGraw and Durocher that produced pennants and world championships. Tradition warrants more of them.

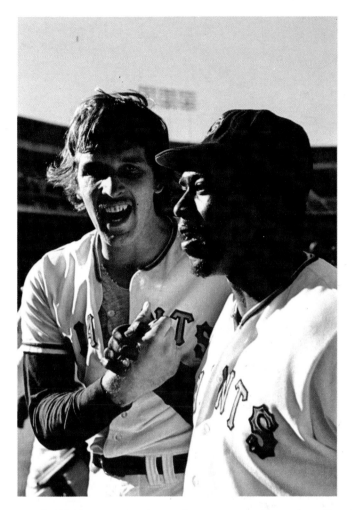

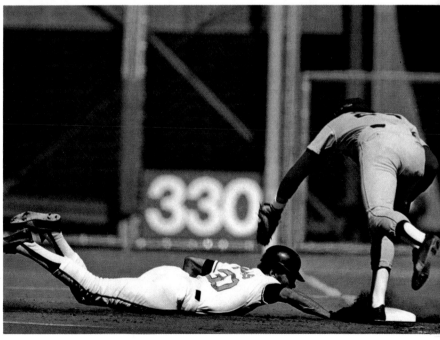

Affaire de Coeur
The Expos

Claude Raymond, former Montreal pitcher who is now one of the Expos' broadcasters, is a French-Canadian who played his last amateur game in Jarry Park when it could hold only two thousand fans. "The first time I came back here as a major leaguer was as a member of the Braves—May 16, 1969," says Raymond. "I came in as a relief pitcher in an extra-inning game, and when I came in, twenty thousand people gave me a standing ovation. I had tears in my eyes. I was so nervous, I dropped the ball thrown back from the catcher."

On August 19, 1969, the Expos acquired Raymond from the Braves on waivers, and the hometown boy had an even more satisfying homecoming. "When I first came here from Atlanta," he recalls, "it was coming home. The Braves were in first place, so being sent to Montreal cost me seven thousand dollars, but I was happy to produce in front of my own people. I was the first French-Canadian ballplayer to win as a major leaguer in Jarry Park."

Raymond's *affaire de coeur* (love affair) with the fans at Jarry Park—and theirs with him—was understandably intense. Hardly any of Quebec's native sons reach the majors, so the locals burst with pride over the ones that do. Even more remarkable is the affection with which the fans have adopted American ballplayers. In the Expos' first year, Mack Jones, a power-hitting journeyman outfielder from

Above: *Jarry Park, Expos' home since they began, is scheduled to be replaced by a domed stadium in 1977.* Opposite: *President of the Expos, John McHale, at the draft of the original team.*

Atlanta, Georgia; Coco Laboy, a twenty-nine-year-old rookie utility man from Ponce, Puerto Rico; and Bill Stoneman, a young, untested hurler from Oak Park, Illinois, all became instant local folk heroes. Jones hit two grand-slam home runs, and the bleachers were christened "Jonesville" in his honor. Laboy had an 11-game hitting streak and 18 home runs. Stoneman pitched a no-hitter, 7–0, against Philadelphia on April 17, and finished the year with five shutouts.

From the beginning, label-conscious, star-oriented Montreal wanted heroes of its own, even if they weren't yet on a par with the rest of the league's. Like most expansion teams, the Expos were originally stocked with names from the past—Mudcat Grant, Maury Wills, Larry Jackson, among others—but the fans' message was clear: they wanted more than good reputations. The letters to broadcaster Doug Van Horne said, "Don't talk about what players have done for other teams. Talk about what they are doing for Montreal."

Enter a star all Montreal's own. Rusty Staub was a Louisiana boy who came to Montreal from Houston, but almost from the beginning he was as effectively French-Canadian as his nickname, *"Le Grand Orange."* Staub hit 26 homers, batted in 79 runs, and was the Expos' first representative in the *Partie d'Etoiles*, the All-Star Game. For Montreal fans searching for an idol, no Yank was ever more welcome.

"He came here as an unknown, and not only was he our first big star, but he related to the people and had a sense of being a star," notes President John McHale. "His reddish hair, his stature, his unselfishness made him an easily identifiable figure. He was a very important factor in the success of this club."

As the city embraced the star, and vice versa, the bond extended to the whole country. Vice-president Jim Fanning observes, "Staub immersed himself in the community. He took French lessons. He became . . . the number-one baseball figure in Canada."

For those who remember the enthusiastic following Montreal accorded the Dodgers' old farm team, the Montreal Royals, the city's response to the Expos has not been surprising. After witnessing the maturing of many of the Dodgers' greatest stars, Jackie Robinson, Duke Snider, and Jim ("Junior") Gilliam, for example, the city had a firmly established core of baseball fans that the Expos could count on. If there was a surprise, it was the last-minute scrounging and scrambling before this successful operation could begin.

Just a few months before the team played its first game, a playing site had not yet been found. McHale explains, "The Autostade, a suggested site, was not controlled by the city but was Federal property . . . and there was no way it could be converted to baseball." McHale, National League President Warren Giles, Commissioner Bowie Kuhn, and Montreal Mayor Jean Drapeau came to tiny Jarry Park "as the last possibility," in McHale's words. "There was an amateur baseball game going on," the Expos' president remembers. "There was great enthusiasm. As we walked into the ball park, the people recognized Warren Giles. They stood up and cried, 'Le grand patron! Le grand patron!' That convinced Giles."

The amateur ball park was expanded in four months from a two-thousand seat facility to one able to accommodate twenty-eight thousand fans, and the Expos had a home.

Jarry Park was found, but "there was no money, no ownership," McHale continues, "except for Charles Bronfman and Lorne C. Webster. The first time I met Charles Bronfman, I told him all the negatives. He said to me, 'If you will stay here, run this, and be part of it, I will see to it that we get the money.' " McHale, then administrator of baseball, stayed to become co-partner and chief executive of the team.

Then there was the problem of assembling the baseball men to run the operation. Still racing the deadline of the 1969 season, McHale started pulling the Montreal organization to-

gether. Jim Fanning was the first man hired, joining the team as general manager. Gene Mauch, who had just left Philadelphia, became the manager. He would pilot the team for its first seven years.

That first year, using 42 players, the Expos won only 52 games, lost 20 in a row, and finished last, 48 games out. "Day after day you'd think you'd break it," recalls former pitching coach Cal McLish. "Some of the other clubs just had us overmatched."

Bobby Wine, who came to the Expos from Philadelphia when Larry Jackson retired, and was a mainstay at shortstop for the first couple of years, remembers that throughout the first-year adversity, the fans remained loyal: "The fans backed us one thousand percent. We waited until ten thirty one night to play—it was really raining. The game finally ended at one or two in the morning, and nobody had left."

In gratitude to the fans, the Expos inaugurated a ritual at the end of the first season that underscores the style of the team, the franchise, and the city. It has now become an annual custom in Montreal. "Each player is introduced individually, tips his cap, and leaves it on a table," John McHale explains. "As each player leaves, he runs from home plate down the left field foul line to the clubhouse, where he's accorded a great salute . . . and then there is a drawing for the caps."

In 1970, their second year, the Expos were able to give their fans more than memorabilia. Gene Mauch coined the slogan "70 in '70," and the Expos attained their goal. One bright and sunny Sunday, Ron Fairly hit a home run, clinching the Expos' seventieth win, and Jarry Park broke out in celebration as if the team had just won the World Series. That year, Staub slammed 30 home runs, batted .274, and participated in five outfield double plays. Bob Bailey had 28 homers. Pitcher Carl Morton, with 18 wins—the most in the history of the Expos—was *recrue de l'année* (Rookie of the Year).

There were three one-hitters pitched in 1971 by Montreal hurlers, two by Steve Renko and another by Stoneman, who racked up 251 strikeouts, 20 complete games, and five shutouts. The team climbed to fifth place, helped in large part by the preseason acquisition of gritty Ron Hunt. "Ronnie used to play wearing a rubberized suit under his uniform," notes Claude Raymond. "He said it was to make him lose weight, but I'm sure it was to absorb some of the knocks he was getting from the pitchers." Hunt was hit by pitches 50 times in 1971, setting the all-time

Opposite: *Le Grand Orange in striking form.*
Top right: *Dennis Blair catches a Giant.* Above right: *Jose Morales eludes one.*

record. "I saw him get hit on the head by Bob Gibson," continues Raymond. "He picked up the ball and threw it back to him as if to say, 'Here, that wasn't hard enough. Try it again.'"

By 1972, "Jonesville" and Mack Jones were gone. And, in a trade that shook Montreal, *Le Grand Orange*, Rusty Staub, was sent to the Mets for shortstop Tim Foli, outfielder Ken Singleton, and first baseman Mike Jorgensen. Foli batted .241 in 1972 and handled more chances than any other National League shortstop. Singleton and Jorgensen tallied 27 home runs and nearly a hundred RBIs between them. But Staub was hard to replace. "It was a very difficult trade," McHale acknowledges. "We had the star. We were able to trade him for three key people who made us competitors for the next two-three years."

Gene Mauch comments, "Staub in his three years here was almost legendary. But we needed to have numbers of young players. Over the years we've had to piece this thing together. All of it's been a stalling game—waiting for the kids, waiting for the kids."

Characterized by Fanning as "tough, determined . . . able to get average players to perform better than average, able to get through well in teaching young players," Gene Mauch was voted National League Manager of the Year in 1973. The Expos finished that season only three and a half games out of first, drawing their second highest road attendance and third highest attendance at home. Singleton scored 100 runs

Above: *Gene Mauch and Ron Hunt confront umpire Tom Gorman.* Right: *Bilingual baseball.*
Opposite: *Lefty relief pitcher Dan Warthen.*

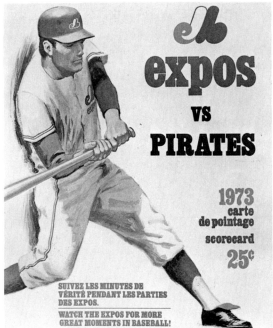

172

and drove in 103. Appearing in 92 games, pitching 179 innings, reliever Mike Marshall notched 31 saves and an earned run average of 2.66. After the season, Marshall was traded to the Los Angeles Dodgers for Willie Davis. "We're definitely proud of Mike's development," Mauch explained. "But I knew he had other things on his mind outside of baseball. Someday he's going to walk away from this game. I didn't want it to happen while he was at Montreal."

The half dozen years of sometimes colorful journeymen ballplayers came to a close for Montreal after the 1974 season. What the organization refers to as *la première phase* (phase one)—the "waiting for the kids"—was concluded.

Unfortunately, but inevitably, not all the kids made it. The first-round draft pick in 1969, Balor Moore, the pitcher some touted as the new Sandy Koufax, was also part of the memories of phase one. In 1972, Moore struck out 161 batters in 148 innings. He personified the early farm system—its promise and its disappointments. By the spring of 1975, the southpaw

was released outright, his options expired.

Montreal moved from the age of expansion to the era of respectability in 1974, its second straight fourth-place finish. The team completed the season 8½ games out of first with a percentage of .491, the highest in its history. Veteran Bob Bailey, the only original Expo still around, tallied 20 home runs and 73 RBIs. Montreal's top three minor league teams compiled a combined 242–172 won-lost record.

"At some point in every organization's life and history," McHale explains, "it has to make a decision when it wants to try to become great. We made that last fall [1974]. We won three pennants in our farm system. . . . We knew we'd have to sacrifice a year . . . but the treadmill of marking time stopped. We knew it was going to be painful . . . and that it would have some effect on attendance with all these new players. . . . A lot of people don't think our team today is quite as exciting as the same team we used to have. Pretty soon, though, several of these players are going to be household words."

La phase deux (phase two) for Montreal is geared to pitching, speed, and defense, with such players as Steve Rogers, Pepe Mangual, Larry Parrish, Gary Carter, and Barry Foote.

"With the players on the roster over fifty percent homegrown," McHale says, "phase two is well underway now."

"These players are just beginning," Cal McLish says, "and we'll be able to see a real fine team here." The future is on the field, not on the drawing board, for the Expos in phase two.

Meanwhile, the franchise is consolidating its position as Canada's representative in major league baseball. Although the Expos play before a basically French-Canadian audience, drawn from Quebec and Ontario, the team is a truly Canadian team, on national television from Newfoundland to Vancouver each week on the Canadian Broadcasting Corporation's game of the week. "We have gone from the point where we bought all the time," says McHale, "to the point now where we have one of the best con-tracts in baseball on a per game basis. Our ratings are nearly two million people. We represent the whole country."

By 1977, the Expos should be playing in the fifty-thousand-seat Olympic Stadium, and quaint Jarry Park, around which, McHale has said, "the soul and the spirit of this franchise are built," will become a memory—"for the people of Montreal what Ebbets Field is for the people of Brooklyn," says Claude Raymond. The new edifice will include underground parking, train stations, and most important of all, a convertible roof that will liberate the team from its perennial league lead in postponements.

Montreal baseball has come a long way since the early days, when the team lost a 2–1 decision to Bob Gibson and certain hockey-minded fans were cheered because the Expos had lost by only one "goal." Forgotten too is the frantic front-office maneuvering to start the team in the first place. "Everything was always an attempt to catch up," McHale explains. At

174

last the Expos have caught up, but the progress has entailed no loss of character. Today at Jarry Park, language is only the most obvious sign of a different flavor to Montreal baseball. The atmosphere is casual and cozy without the continual chanting, clapping, and cheering of many other major league ball parks. "The fans at Jarry Park seem to be waiting, politely waiting, for something to happen, almost as if they were watching a ballet or an opera," observes vice-president Fanning. "Then when something happens, they react, and they get excited. We must lead the league in standing applause."

Apart from the entertainment on the field, a fan can enjoy a fiddler on the (dugout) roof, the world's tallest man on stilts, and Les Grands Ballets Canadiens performing between games of a doubleheader. For the activists, there is dancing in the aisles between innings; for the girl watchers, beautiful usherettes to escort them to their seats. And always there is the language, not merely exotic but instructive. It allows an American fan to take a new look at his game, from a distinctly European perspective. For example, he learns that an outfielder is *un voltigeur*, from the French word *voltige*, for flying trapeze exercises. Or that the French word for pitcher, *le lanceur*, also applies to one who originates, launches, starts things going.

Such are the amenities of bilingual baseball. As long as Montreal remains the unique, bilingual, bicultural city it is, Montreal baseball will never lose its flavor.

Expos			
Name of Park	**Date 1st Game Played**	**Opponent & Score**	**Capacity**
Jarry Park	April 14, 1969	Montreal 8, St. Louis 7	28,000

Opposite: *Infielders Mike Jorgensen, left, and Pete Mackanin settle under a pop-up.* Top: *Jim Dwyer lunges for a liner.* Above right: *Woodie Fryman brings it.*

From the Borough of Churches to the City of Angels
The Dodgers

High above Chinatown and downtown Los Angeles, in the "paradise" of Chavez Ravine, tall palm trees peer like mawkish spectators over the outfield wall into Dodger Stadium and recognize, indeed epitomize, the new order. The palm trees are California's answer to the apartment buildings of Flatbush, as Elysian Park Avenue is to Bedford Avenue. A spacious, immaculate ball park nestled in a picturesque if not wholly convincing Hollywood setting has replaced grimy, congested, tiny Ebbets Field. The most conspicuous fans are now bronzed beautiful people, not brutally frank eccentrics. Brooklyn earthiness has given way to California gloss. The Dodgers are playing baseball three thousand miles away from Brooklyn.

Still, not all Brooklyn has been left behind. One remnant is Jim Gilliam, number 19. In the first base coach's box, he seems less than content as a relic. He kicks the ground, yells to the players, and looks as if he just might take the field himself instead of returning to the dugout when the Dodgers are retired. Walter Alston, broad and determined, the senior manager in baseball now, directs the game from the Dodgers' dugout as placidly as he did when he took over the club in Brooklyn. If it were somehow all undone and Ebbets Field by some miracle resurrected, it is difficult to imagine Alston any less secure or serene in Brooklyn than he is in Los Angeles today. After all, to him it has always

176

The Dodgers moved from a lower-middle-class home in Flatbush to spacious, immaculate Dodger Stadium in Chavez Ravine. They have prospered in the suburbs.

been the game, and not its trappings—whether the glitter of California or the grime of Brooklyn —that matters. "As far as I was concerned," he says of the biggest franchise upheaval in baseball, "it didn't make a whole lot of difference."

Perhaps he's right. In the front office, Al Campanis, now vice-president, still preaches the Dodger way, still bears down, in L.A. as he did in Brooklyn. Traveling secretary Lee Scott, who sits in his office surrounded by picture memorabilia, tells the old stories in barely reconstructed Brooklynese. And of course, the king of the holdovers, indeed of Dodgerdom, Walter O'Malley, presides with the same magisterial invincibility, even as he passes the scepter along to his son Peter.

From Daffiness Boys to Bums to suburbanites, the Dodgers *have* changed, of course, in an evolution that symbolizes the evolution of baseball. But it may be their continuity through all the upheavals that is the greatest trait they share with the national pastime. More difficult than imagining America without baseball is imagining baseball without the Dodgers.

They began in 1890, and during the first quarter century of their National League life, disposed of 11 managers. The team won only three pennants—one its first year in the league, under manager William H. McGunnigle, and again in 1899 and 1900. The turn of the century Brooklyn team was known as Hanlon's Superbas, for Ned Hanlon, majority stockholder and manager. Former president of the Baltimore Orioles, Hanlon brought his best players to Brooklyn, including Wee Willie ("Hit 'Em Where They Ain't") Keeler, who slapped out 179 singles in 1900, Hughie Jennings, Joe Kelley, and "Iron Man" Joe McGinnity, who paced the 1900 team with 29 victories.

Zack ("Buck") Wheat joined the team in 1909 and a half a century later joined the Hall of Fame. The wiry outfielder played until 1926 with Brooklyn, recording a lifetime .317 batting average on nearly 3,000 hits. Burleigh Grimes, the last man to throw a legal spitter, remembers the loyalty of the Brooklyn fans to Zack Wheat: "Nobody liked them—they'd climb all over you —but let some stranger come in and say anything about us and they'd tear him apart. Especially if he was knocking Buck Wheat, over there in left field. Those bleacher fans loved Buck."

In its early years, Brooklyn's National League team was also called the Dodgers, from the uncomplimentary "Trolley Dodgers," as Manhattanites sometimes referred to the residents of Brooklyn. In 1914, the team gained the nickname "Robins," after its new manager, fifty-one-year-old Wilbert Robinson. The stout "Uncle Robbie" presided over the team for the next 18 years, a period in which some of the game's most colorful and zany personalities and great individual stars displayed their talents in Brooklyn.

Scott remembers when " 'Beauty' Bancroft, who had just joined the team, wanted to know the signs. 'We don't have any signs,' Robinson growled. 'Just get up there and hit the ball.' "

With such brusque informality, Robinson guided the Robins to pennants in 1916 and 1920.

The stars of the twenties were Dazzy Vance and Burleigh Grimes. After a ten-year hitch in the minors, the broad-shouldered, tobacco-chewing Vance recorded his first major league victory at the advanced age of thirty-one. He was a late but bountiful bloomer. His big windup and dazzling fastball enabled him to lead the league in strikeouts for seven straight years. "Heck, you knew what he was going to throw," former Giant George ("Highpockets") Kelly said, "and you still couldn't hit him."

In 1928, at the age of thirty-seven, "the Dazzler" won 22 games and led the league in earned run average, though he was pitching for a sixth-place team. His best year, however, was 1924, when he compiled a 28–6 record, 262 strikeouts, and a 2.16 earned run average. "My God, he was great that year," exclaims Grimes. "One game he struck out fifteen Cardinals in nine innings, but the game was tied. Well, you know what he did in the tenth—just strike out Rogers Hornsby and Jim Bottomley, that's all, and he made them look bad. He had Bottomley looking like he was killing a snake. When he was on, which was most of the time that year, he was the best I ever saw." A pleasantly deferential statement from the man who won 22 games and led the league in complete games and innings pitched that year.

In 1926, Grimes's last as a player for the Dodgers, the team gained a player whose antics would characterize it for the next decade. The team was affectionately dubbed "the Daffiness Boys," and the crown prince was slump-shouldered, free-swinging Babe Herman, one of a group of Dodgers who could wreak havoc on friend and foe indiscriminately. Herman was one of a troika of Brooklyn baserunners who once wound up on third base at the same time. Uncle Robbie quipped, "Leave them be. That's the first time they've been together all year."

In 1930, "the Incredible Hoiman" had his greatest year, recording a batting average of .393 and a slugging percentage of .678. "I could've hit

The Los Angeles Dodgers of the sixties won with roughly this formula: two parts pitching, one part speed. Clockwise from opposite bottom: *Sandy Koufax, Don Drysdale, and Maury Wills.*

Meanwhile, St. Louis beat Cincinnati two straight, and the Giants were dead, killed by the club they had pretended wasn't in the league at the start of the season.

Larry MacPhail joined the Dodgers as executive vice-president in 1938. "You could say MacPhail was the father of today's Dodgers," notes Grimes. "He was a real doer. He put the lights in, started the radio announcing, and got money from the bank. Remember, the franchise was in real trouble then—no money—and MacPhail turned it around. The Dodgers owe a great debt to Larry; he was some promoter."

MacPhail was also a shrewd judge of baseball talent. He brought Leo Durocher in as manager, commenting, "I'm convinced that he will be just as good a manager as we can make him."

MacPhail started to stock the Dodgers with new personnel. One of his first moves was the purchase of Dolf Camilli from Philadelphia for $50,000. Camilli would lead the league in home runs and RBIs in 1941. Babe Ruth came over as a coach. "The Peepul's Cherce," Dixie Walker, who hit .300 all but one of his eight years at Brooklyn, and then Joe Medwick, Herman Franks, and Billy Herman became Dodgers. By 1940, the team had marched to a second-place finish. Skipper Leo Durocher said, "We need Kirby Higbe from Philadelphia and Mickey Owen from St. Louis and we've got the pennant." So MacPhail dealt for Higbe who won 22

four hundred," the Babe explained, "but I got tired."

After Wilbert Robinson departed, in 1931, Max Carey piloted the team for two years. Then, from 1934 to 1936, Casey Stengel presided. In 1937, Burleigh Grimes returned for a couple of years as manager. The managerial shuffling produced two third- and two fourth-place finishes, but otherwise the Dodgers spent the thirties mired in the second division.

It wasn't all dreariness and daffiness, though. Occasionally, the Dodgers rose to unaccustomed heights, particularly, it seemed, when they faced their crosstown rivals, the Giants.

The rivalry was unwittingly exacerbated at the start of the 1934 season when the Giants' manager, Bill Terry, asked, "Is Brooklyn still in the league?" Objective observers could forgive such a slight, for Brooklyn was hardly a contender—it hadn't been for years—but objectivity had nothing to do with it. Brooklyn didn't like being disdained, particularly not by Manhattan.

Sure enough, the Dodgers got their chance for revenge, and exacted it to the fullest. The two teams met at the Polo Grounds for the final two games of the 1934 season. As usual, the Dodgers had long since given up the pennant chase, but the Giants were in a first-place tie with St. Louis. Van Lingle Mungo won the first game, and Brooklyn triumphed the next day too.

180

Top: *William McGunnigle, Brooklyn's first pennant-winning manager.*
Above: *Hall of Fame outfielder Zack ("Buck") Wheat.* Opposite: *Uncle Robby, center, and his Daffiness Boys Herman, left, and Vance.*

games, and Owen, who recorded a .995 fielding average, the best in the history of Brooklyn catchers.

In 1941, 1.2 million fans crowded into little Ebbets Field and saw a Brooklyn team of speed and daring win its first National League pennant in 21 years. "Pistol Pete" Reiser, born the year before the Dodgers won their last pennant, batted a league-leading .343 and set a National League record by stealing home seven times. "He didn't know when to give up," Scott recalls. "I can still remember when he crashed into the outfield wall in St. Louis, and they took him to the hospital. All the ball parks have foam rubber now in the outfield because of him."

That disaster would not befall the Dodgers until the next year, however. This year they had another in store, the 1941 World Series. Trailing 2–1 in games, the Dodgers were on the verge of turning around the Series in the fourth game. They led 4–3 in the fourth game with two outs in the top of the ninth. Then Tommy Henrich swung at and missed a Hugh Casey spitter for strike three, but catcher Mickey Owen missed it too. Instead of becoming the final out, Henrich reached base, and the Yankees rallied for a game-winning four runs. Down 3–1 in games now, the Dodgers surrendered the Series the

next day. It was the first of five Series they would lose to the Yankees before finally winning, in 1955.

During the war years, the best of the Dodgers joined the service, among them Larry Mac-Phail. Branch Rickey replaced him, arriving from St. Louis with impressive credentials as a franchise builder. He continued the MacPhail policy of innovation, inaugurating tryout camps all over America and signing the best prospects for the Dodgers. He saw the black player as another untapped source of talent, and he mined it thoroughly. A parade of top black stars would come marching to Brooklyn in the next decade: Jackie Robinson, Don Newcombe, Joe Black, and Jim Gilliam—Rookies of the Year in 1947, 1949, 1952, and 1953 respectively—and Roy Campanella, Most Valuable Player in 1951, 1953, and 1955.

When World War II ended, the Dodgers stood at a crossroads. As the country plunged into a bash of baby-making and home building, deferred by a decade of depression and four years of war, the Dodgers began an era of the most exciting, most human, and most interesting baseball in the most receptive climate any baseball team ever had. Via the mellow, Southern-accented voice of Red Barber over the

Stars of the seventies.
Clockwise from above:
Jimmy Wynn, Dave Lopes,
and Andy Messersmith.

183

Top: *Ebbets Field was cramped by the boundaries of a city block.* Above: *Revolutionaries Robinson and Rickey.* Opposite: *Amoros' game-saving catch in 1955 Series finale.*

radio, news of the team would blanket Brooklyn from front stoops to candy stores to corner bars. On steamy summer nights, Brooklyn sweltered with pennant fever. In the autumn chill, it braced for the annual confrontation of a subway Series with the Yankees.

The great decade began, as such dynasties often do, with a heartbreaking defeat. Tied for the pennant after the 1946 regular season ended, the Dodgers lost two straight playoff games to the "chain-store" Cardinals Branch Rickey had built. Lee Scott recalls, "I had set up a big banquet room in the Hotel St. George in Brooklyn. We had about six hundred writers there the first night. They ate and they drank. On the second night, nobody came around. They all went to St. Louis."

But the riches of the future were coming around. On the farm in Montreal, the man who would propel the Dodgers' dynamo for ten years was preparing his dramatic entry into the big leagues. On April 15, 1947, Jack Roosevelt Robinson, the grandchild of slaves, became the first black man to play in the majors. The newest Dodger hit .297 and stole a league-leading 29 bases that year, overcoming taunts and racial epithets, hate mail, even threats of a strike by one National League team and a cool reception from some of his own teammates. He demonstrated daily the versatility of a superb athlete, playing 151 games at first base, though his best position was second. "Here is a man whose wounds you could not feel or share," Branch Rickey declared.

Led by Robinson, the Dodgers swept to the National League pennant and lasted seven games against the Yankees in the first nationally televised World Series. The Yankees won it, but the Dodgers produced the most memorable moments—Cookie Lavagetto's two-out, ninth-inning, pinch-hit double ruining Bill Bevens' no-hitter and giving the Dodgers a 3–2 victory, perhaps the most dramatic win in their history. Then in game six, little known outfielder Al Gionfriddo became an instant celebrity with a game-saving spectacular snare of Joe DiMaggio's bullpen-bound drive to left in the late innings.

Two years later, the Bronx bested Brooklyn again, this time after the Dodgers had squeaked into the Series by winning the pennant in the tenth inning of the final regular season game. Robinson was again the star, winning the batting title and the Most Valuable Player award.

Despite the losses to the Yankees in the Series, these were heady times in Brooklyn. Buzzie Bavasi, the former general manager of the Brooklyn Dodgers, now president of the

San Diego Padres, declares, "I wouldn't trade those years in Brooklyn for two pennants. Everybody knew one another. You'd call the fans by their first names. I don't think Walter O'Malley would give up one memory of Brooklyn for all the pennants he's won. Someday the borough of Brooklyn will get all the credit it deserves from baseball people. . . . A million and a half people could walk to Ebbets Field. You'd turn on the lights there, and fifteen thousand would come out just to see why the lights were on."

In 1950, Branch Rickey's last year as the club's president, the Dodgers lost the pennant in the tenth inning on the final day of the regular season to the Phillies, the team they had won it from in the tenth inning of the season finale the year before. Dick Sisler's three-run homer was the blast that doomed the Dodgers. Disappointing to be sure, but a birthday popgun shot compared to the shot that decided the pennant the next year.

Brooklyn born comedian Phil Foster calls October 3, 1951, "D-Day," that is to say, "Dat Day," when Bobby Thomson hit the home run that broke Brooklyn's heart. Lee Scott still seems shocked to recall the Dodgers' reaction: "Bang! The roof fell in. Into the clubhouse comes Ralph Branca. He leaned on the staircase like Jesus on the cross, only backwards, and he was crying to beat the band."

The next year, a return to normalcy—a pennant win, a World Series loss to the Yankees. In

Opposite: *The modernistic scoreboard structure at Dodger Stadium.* Above: *Steve Garvey, as MVP in 1974, the latest triumph of the Dodger way.*

1953, another pennant, by 13 games over Milwaukee, and another loss to the Yankees. Time for a change.

Walter O'Malley remembers that the response to Walter Alston's arrival as manager of the Brooks in 1954 was, "Who's he?" It was a question all Brooklyn was asking with trepidation, for the high-flying Bums seemed to need a weightier presence at the helm than a rookie skipper from the farm team where many of his players had been groomed.

One would have thought that this quiet man from rural Ohio was destined for anonymity, but the spotlight shines on unlikely faces. In 1955, in the fifty-fourth World Series, the Dodgers finally won one, and the fickle press suddenly found a master in the man it had tabbed a nonentity the year before. In the seventh game against the Yankees, spindly Sandy Amoros contributed an unforgettable, racing, stretching, one-handed grab of Yogi Berra's opposite field fly ball. Johnny Podres, a fresh-faced youngster from upstate New York, needed no more support. He twirled an immaculate 2–0 shutout, and at long last Brooklyn erupted in celebration.

Duke Snider recalls the festivities: "You had to pinch yourself to say it really happened. When we were on the bus back to Brooklyn from Yankee Stadium, it seemed as if everyone in New York City knew our route. The streets and sidewalks were packed with people. Everyone had a sign."

Alas, the glorious years in Brooklyn were almost over. As the postwar dynasty had begun its ascent with a bitter defeat in 1946, so it was beginning its decline in the celebration of its greatest achievement.

In 1956, Walter O'Malley sold Ebbets Field. He kept his Dodgers there as renters, but with a short lease and clear plans for bigger and better things. "I got worried about the location, the vandalism to automobiles, the molesting of women," O'Malley explained. The Dodgers played eight games that year across the river in Jersey City. "We tried to move the Dodgers to another location in downtown Brooklyn. I was interested in the Long Island Railroad terminus —it was to be the first domed stadium—but I couldn't win the political battle."

Other sites were suggested, one in Flushing Meadows, Queens, now the home of the New York Mets. O'Malley recalls, "I said then if I move from Brooklyn to Queens I might as well move to the West Coast, because we'll not be the Brooklyn Dodgers in Queens."

Even with everything arranged but the packing of equipment, it was hard to believe the

187

Bums were really leaving. "I went to the New York writers," Scott notes, "and I told them, and they laughed. They didn't believe me."

Fittingly, perhaps, most of the heroes of Flatbush withered into old ballplayers under the California sun, so Brooklyn kept as its own at least the memories of its Dodgers at their best. Duke Snider, Pee Wee Reese, Gil Hodges, Carl Furillo, Carl Erskine, Clem Labine, and Don Newcombe showed California only shadows of their former greatness. And the anchor of the great Brooklyn teams, catcher Roy Campanella, never made it to the West Coast as a player. A tragic automobile crash in January 1958 transformed him into a paraplegic.

Fortunately, Los Angeles was more than happy to receive the boys of summer in the autumn of their careers. Almost two million fans poured into mammoth Los Angeles Coliseum in 1958, including 78,672 for the first National League game, against the Giants. The Dodgers sank to seventh in 1958, their first second-division finish since 1944, but the next year a patchwork team of holdovers and newcomers captured the pennant. Against the White Sox in the World Series, reliever Larry Sherry recorded two wins and two saves in the Dodgers' six-game triumph. "I don't think our talent was as good as some of the other teams we had," Alston notes. "But I'm proud of that team. They helped each other out and had good morale."

In 1962, the team left the lopsided Los Angeles Coliseum, with its tiny left field and vast right field, and moved into Shangri-la, Dodger Stadium. Walter O'Malley had personally overseen every aspect of its design and construction, and his reward was a picture-perfect park, for which his team seemed to be a picture-perfect accessory. The Dodgers had little power with which to reach the fences in this difficult park for home runs; instead they had top flight pitching and jackrabbit speed to exploit the quickest

Dodgers			
Name of Park	**Date 1st Game Played**	**Opponent & Score**	**Capacity**
Washington Park	April 28, 1890	Brooklyn 10, Philadelphia 0	8,000
Eastern Park	April 27, 1891	New York 6, Brooklyn 5	12,000
Washington Park	April 30, 1898	Philadelphia 6, Brooklyn 4	18,000
Ebbets Field	April 9, 1913	Philadelphia 1, Brooklyn 0	24,000
			31,903*
Memorial Coliseum	April 18, 1958	Los Angeles 6, San Francisco 5	94,600
Dodger Stadium	April 10, 1962	Cincinnati 6, Los Angeles 3	56,000

* Capacity expanded.

and hardest infield in the pre-AstroTurf era. To the chant of "Go, Go, Go!", prompted by one of the first cheerleading scoreboards, Maury Wills stole 104 bases, smashing Ty Cobb's record, and won the Most Valuable Player award. Tommy Davis took the batting championship. Don Drysdale led the league in strikeouts and earned the Cy Young Award. Sandy Koufax topped all pitchers in earned run average. And the Dodgers set a major league attendance record of 2,755,184.

But not even this new, coolly efficient version of the Dodgers could overcome the disaster of an incapacitating finger injury to Koufax. Their ace fell out of the rotation in August. Like a child too stunned to cry, the Dodgers carried on nobly for a bit, but the tears came in floods in September. Leading by four games with seven to play, the Dodgers blew the lead, ended the season tied with the Giants, and in a blowup to rival the fiasco of 1951, lost the three-game playoff after entering the final inning two runs up.

Fortunately, bitter defeat would once again prove to be a prelude to glorious victory. The next year, with Koufax's arm sound again, the Dodgers were literally off and running, heading for perhaps their most impressive triumph ever. They swept the Yankees in four straight games in the World Series, thanks mainly to the pitching of Koufax and Drysdale, assisted by the hero of the last victory over the Yankees, Johnny Podres, and ace reliever Ron Perranoski. The mighty Bombers, who produced 714 runs over 162 games in the regular season, managed only 4 against the Dodgers' impeccable pitching. After it was over, the Yanks' Yogi Berra took a new look at Koufax's 25–5 regular season record and mused, "I can see how he won twenty-five, but I can't see how he lost five."

Before he was through, Koufax would lead the league in ERA five times, pitch four no-hitters, and three times surpass three hundred strikeouts in a season. His scowling, sidearming partner, Don Drysdale, would record 49 shutouts, 6 of them in a row during a record-setting 58⅔ consecutive scoreless innings in 1968. Together, Koufax and Drysdale accumulated four Cy Young awards. Only once in the eight-year period 1959–66 did one or the other of them fail to lead the National League in strikeouts.

In 1965, the Dodgers again won the pennant and World Series. Koufax declined to pitch the opening game because it was the Jewish High Holy Day of Yom Kippur; so he pitched the second and fifth, and when manager Alston tabbed him for the seventh, he had had only two days rest. "Deciding whether to pitch Kou-

WHO'S A BUM!

fax or Drysdale in that final game," Alston recalls, "was perhaps my toughest decision as manager." His curve having deserted him, the exhausted hero overpowered the Minnesota Twins with his fastball, clinching the Series with a dramatic 2–0 shutout.

One more year and Koufax had had enough. The man who coach Tom Lasorda said, "got so good that he was pitching to half the plate," was racked by pain in his pitching arm. And so at the end of the 1966 season, at the crest of his brilliance, Koufax retired.

It must have come as a grave disappointment that after the team's auspicious beginning in Los Angeles (four pennants and three world championships in 10 years) the Dodgers endured 7 consecutive years without so much as a divisional title. Not until 1974 did the Dodgers capture a flag. They were thoroughly Los Angeles Dodgers then, with none of the old Brooklyn players remaining, 17 years after the move. But, as they always will, traces of the old days remained. Steve Garvey, Most Valuable Player in the National League and Gold Glove winner in 1974 as well as the All-Star MVP, cast himself in the tradition of the old Dodgers. "Gil Hodges was always my favorite player," Garvey observes. "Playing first base here in Los Angeles, I'm trying to be here what Gil Hodges may have been to some little boy in Brooklyn."

A team with a new stadium in a new city, with new players and new fans, but still, seemingly forever, distinctly Dodgers.

189

Above: *The day after the Dodgers won the 1955 Series, the New* York Daily News *proclaimed the irony of the team's nickname.* Opposite: *The record-breaking crowd at the Los Angeles Coliseum for Roy Campanella Night and Yankees-Dodgers exhibition game.*

Big Red Machine
The Reds

The Cincinnati Reds were the first—not only the first professional baseball team, but the first one to have a farm system, the first to use a left-handed pitcher, the first to play night baseball, the first to travel by plane, and the first in dozens of other categories, from the momentous to the trivial. Until recently, however, the team was rarely first in the standings—in 1919 and only three times in the half-century thereafter. As baseball continued to proclaim Cincinnati the city of baseball firsts by beginning each new season there, it began to seem as if the citation at the start of the season was nothing but a consolation for the disappointment to follow at the end.

Then came baseball's contribution to the age of automation—the awesome Big Red Machine, programmed to win baseball games in profusion. In six seasons it produced an average of better than 95 wins a year. As a result, the cradle of professional baseball became a Middle American mecca for it. The faithful poured forth from the hinterlands not only of Ohio, but of bordering Kentucky and Indiana, even Tennessee and West Virginia. They came to see the team long acknowledged as the first at last lay claim to being the best.

It took until the last inning of the last World Series game, but the faithful were finally rewarded. After sweeping through the National

190

Mainstays of the Big Red Machine: Johnny Bench (above), Pete Rose (opposite left), and Don Gullett (opposite right). In 1976, Riverfront Stadium (opposite top) flew Cincinnati's first world championship flag since 1940.

League regular season and the championship playoffs, the Reds embarked on a roller coaster of a World Series with the Boston Red Sox that thrilled, chilled, and thoroughly exhausted both teams, before the Reds emerged the champions. They prevailed despite the best effort of Boston's wily Luis Tiant, slumps of the three, four, and five hitters in their batting order, a fantastic defeat in game six, and a 3–0 deficit as late as the sixth inning of the finale. They won the hard way—as chastened favorites overcoming inspired underdogs. And the baseball world saw the Big Red Machine at its human best.

Notwithstanding the other world championships, in 1919 and 1940, the last time the Reds were the best in baseball was when they began, in 1869. That year the original Red Stockings won all 69 of their games and the next year extended the streak to 92 before the Brooklyn Atlantics broke it. The stars of the team were baseball's Wright brothers—center fielder Harry, the first professional baseball player, and shortstop George, who earned $1,400 (tops on the team) that first season for batting .518, driving in 339 runs, and hitting 54 home runs. Flaunting such credentials, the Red Stockings left the brawling river town of Cincinnati and barnstormed a total of twelve thousand miles throughout the East and Midwest that first year. Wherever they went, they drummed up business with this musical pitch, written by one of the players:

> We are a band of baseball players
> From Cincinnati city.
> We come to toss the ball around
> And sing to you our ditty.
> And if you listen to the song
> We are about to sing,
> We'll tell you all about baseball
> And make the welkin ring.
> The ladies want to know
> Who are those gallant men in
> Stockings red, they'd like to know.

The performers won fame but little fortune. The Red Stockings capped that year with a private interview with President Ulysses S. Grant. Then they checked the bottom line and discovered a net profit for the season of $1.39.

By 1876, when they joined the National League as charter members, the Red Stockings had begun to accumulate firsts. They played in the first extra-inning game (a 1–0 shutout). In their first year in the National League, the Reds' Charley ("Home Run") Jones was the first player to hit two home runs in one inning. Two years later, the Reds had the first brother battery in baseball—pitcher Will White and catcher Deacon White.

One of their more provocative innovations led to their withdrawal from the league in 1881. The National League, particularly the Worcester, Massachusetts, team, objected to the Reds' practice of selling beer on Sunday at their ball park and tried to prohibit it. Already quarreling with the league over player raiding, the Reds decided not to submit and withdrew to the American Association, not without some defiant proclamations from their partisans. "Puritanical Worcester is not liberal Cincinnati by a jugful," trumpeted one Cincinnati paper. "What is sauce for Worcester is wind for the Queen City; beer and Sunday amusements have become a popular necessity in Cincinnati."

The breach lasted until 1890, when Cincinnati returned to the fold and finished fourth in an eight-team league. Obviously, the club was no longer the preeminent power it had been.

In the first 15 years of the new century, the Reds finished in the second division 10 times and disposed of 10 managers, including such notables as Joe Kelley, Ned Hanlon, Clark Griffith, Hank O'Day, Joe Tinker, and Buck Herzog. Next on the firing line, in 1916, was the old Giant, Christy Mathewson. He made an abortive attempt to contribute to the team as a pitcher when, in his first appearance for the Reds and the last of his career, he lost a pitching duel to the Cubs' Three Finger Brown. As a manager, Mathewson lasted only two years, but at least he presided over some improvement. Under him, the Reds rose to fourth in 1917 and third in 1918 with many of the players who would bring Cincinnati its first pennant and world championship in 1919. Two of the best came from the New York Giants—infielder Heinie Groh and the consummate outfielder, Edd Roush.

Groh, a slightly built right-handed batter, was a sub-.200 hitter his first year in the minors but lasted 16 years in the majors, 9 with the Reds. His trademark was a potent "bottle bat," which produced three straight .300 years, in one of which he led the league in hits. In addition to his impeccable fielding, Hall of Famer Roush hit .300 or better 11 years in a row for the Reds, winning two batting titles and missing another by just two points.

Hod Eller was another of the soon-to-be-champion Reds who blossomed under Mathewson. Eller began his brief but often brilliant career in 1917 with a 2.36 ERA overall, and a 1.62 ERA in relief.

For 1919, the Reds had a new manager,

Top: *1919 outfield, left to right—Sherry Magee, Edd Roush, Earle ("Greasy") Neale.* Above: *Palace of the Fans.* Left: *Pat Moran led 1919 world champs.*

193

Pat Moran, and two new pitchers who would lead the pennant charge: Dutch Ruether and Slim Sallee. Teaming with Eller (20-9), Ruether (19-6) and Sallee (21-7) formed the core of a pitching staff that led the league in shutouts.

Judged by winning percentage alone, the 1919 Reds were the best team Cincinnati has ever fielded in the National League. The Reds won 94 of 140 games, a winning percentage of .686. They did it mostly on pitching (least runs allowed) and defense (least errors), though in Roush they had the batting leader, too. The World Series should have capped this great year for Cincinnati; instead it tarnished it, even though the Reds won the Series.

Baseball was emerging from the hardships of the war years seemingly more vibrant than ever, particularly in the Midwest, the region that produced the 1919 pennant winners in the Reds and the American League champion Chicago White Sox. To capitalize on the game's growing following, the National Commission, the ruling body of the sport at the time, decided to extend the World Series from a best-of-seven to a best-of-nine playoff. Everyone profited from that arrangement: the fans, who got to see more baseball; the owners, who took in a record $722,414 in receipts; and the players, who divided $260,349, also a record. Unfortunately, the gamblers did well also.

No one ever proved that "the Black Sox Scandal" changed the outcome of the Series, but what the facts themselves didn't prove, the spreading stain of scandal implied. When it was announced that eight of the White Sox had conspired with gamblers to throw the Series, the Reds were branded the team that "won" a tainted Series, and those quotation marks have proved to be stubborn stains indeed to remove.

If "Shoeless Joe" Jackson and George ("Buck") Weaver of the Sox really were on the take, the Reds asked skeptically, how did they manage to hit .375 and .324 respectively? (Meanwhile, the Reds' best hitter, Edd Roush, slipped to a miserable .214.) True, the Sox' 29-game winner, Eddie Cicotte, one of the accused, was suspiciously unimpressive in the 9–1 pasting he took in the opener, but he hurled an impressive seven-hit win in the seventh game.

Fixed or not, the 1919 World Series was no romp. After Ruether and Sallee triumphed for the Reds in the first two games, the Sox won three of the next five before the Reds finally prevailed, behind Eller in the finale. Oddly, the most impressive Reds during the Series had been lesser lights during the regular season: Jimmy Ring hurled 14 impressive innings; outfielder "Greasy" Neale hit .357.

The Reds were not to win another pennant for 20 years, but they slipped rather than plunged into mediocrity. They finished third in 1920 and second to the Giants in 1922 and 1923. By this time, the leader of the pitching staff was gangling Eppa Rixey, who won 25 games in 1922.

The baseball depression mirrored the economic one in the River City during the late twenties and early thirties. Cincinnati sank to seventh in 1929 and 1930 and then, like so many others in America, seemed just to give up. There were four straight years of cellar dwelling, 1931–34.

The silver lining in this black cloud was sportsman-industrialist Powel Crosley, Jr., who purchased control of the failing franchise in 1934, when attendance was only 206,373—less than the Reds had drawn in eight World Series games with the White Sox in 1919. Crosley hired as general manager Leland Stanford MacPhail, who started Cincinnati on its five-year climb back to the top of the National League and replenished the club's reputation for bright new ideas. One of the first was lights. As a minor league executive in Columbus, Ohio, MacPhail had already produced night baseball. Now he approached the National League for permission to do the same in Cincinnati. Anxious to alleviate the Reds' desperate problem with attendance, the league readily agreed, and on May 24, 1935,

194

Above: *Double no-hit Johnny Vander Meer.* Opposite: *The Yankees won the 1939 World Series when the Reds committed three errors in the ninth inning of the seventh game. Here DiMaggio scores on a passed ball, sliding past Ernie Lombardi.*

in a typical MacPhail promotion, President Franklin D. Roosevelt in Washington flicked the remote control switch that turned on the lights. Then Cincinnati's Paul Derringer beat the Phillies 2–1. The spectacle attracted more than 20,000 fans, about ten times as many as the Phillies and Reds usually drew for a contest between them.

If night baseball seemed more like a stunt than a serious innovation, it was at least a tranquil one. The hearts of quite a few Reds must have fluttered when owner Crosley, a flying enthusiast, made the Reds the first team to travel by plane, in an era when commercial air travel was in its infancy.

Not quite flying high yet, the Reds gained a new general manager, Warren Giles, in 1936.

One of the first moves of the new man in charge was to hire Bill ("Deacon") McKechnie as manager. McKechnie came to Cincinnati as a manager who had already won more National League pennants (two) than the Reds had. He had won one with the Pirates and one with the

Cards. Now, he was about to win his third and fourth with the Reds, thus becoming the only manager to win pennants with three different clubs in the National League.

Like all successful managers, McKechnie had the knack of extracting the best from his players. Under him, Paul Derringer, a flop in 1937, won 21 games in 1938. First baseman Frank McCormick led the league in hits three years in a row, won the RBI crown in 1939, and took the Most Valuable Player award in 1940. Ponderous Ernie Lombardi, remembered by McCormick (no sprite himself) for "bad feet, bad legs . . . and those frozen rope line drives," won the batting title with a .342 average in 1938, and took the MVP award as well.

McKechnie polished the rocking-chair pitching style of Johnny Vander Meer, who in 1938 accomplished a feat not only unprecedented but yet to be repeated. On June 11 against the Boston Braves and June 15 against the Brooklyn Dodgers, the left-hander hurled consecutive no-hit games. "The first no-hitter I had pretty good control," he recalls, "even though I was known as a wild man. [He faced only 28 batters and walked only 3.] I had a fair curve and a good sinking ball, and was always ahead of the hitters."

The second game was more of a struggle. Vander Meer was wild, "throwing two or three balls to each hitter," McCormick remembers. "When you're out on the field, this can put you in a daze; we were always trying to stay on our toes."

"That game I threw only three curve balls through the first seven innings," says Vander Meer. "Until the last inning I wasn't going for the no-hitter, just the shutout. I didn't shake off [catcher] Lombardi in either game. Why should I? He was calling the right pitches."

That night, while Vander Meer and his teammates celebrated, Giles capped the day by acquiring right-hander Bucky Walters from the Phils. Walters won 11 games for the Reds that season, as the team climbed from last in 1937 to fourth in 1938. A year later, Walters led the league with 27 wins, and the Reds won their first pennant in exactly two decades. Paul Derringer (25–7) pitched the clincher, ending it by striking out the Cards' Joe Medwick and Johnny Mize on a total of six pitches.

The Reds' aces were good in the Series and every game was close, but the Yankees won them all. The deciding factor was power.

"They clobbered us," says Frank McCormick, at .400 the Reds' best hitter in the Series. "The only pleasant thing was in the last game. Jake Powell and Tommy Henrich were great needlers, and they'd been on me pretty good. After I lined a single off [New York pitcher Johnny] Murphy, I thumbed my nose at them. Judge Landis called umpire Bill McGowan, probably to get me thrown out of the game. Bill said to Landis, 'Oh, that's all right, Judge. That's just Frank's way of blowing his nose.' "

The next year the Reds were back in the Series, a better balanced team that had swept to the National League pennant by 12 games over the Dodgers. Derringer and Walters won 42 games between them, 10 fewer than the year before, but the addition of Jim Turner (14–7) and relief pitcher Joe Beggs (12–3, 2.00) more than compensated. The pitching staff was by far the best in the league. Buttressing the attack were newcomers Mike McCormick and Jimmy Ripple, both .300 hitters.

Derringer and Walters shone at their brightest in the Series, quelling the potent Detroit attack of Hank Greenberg, Rudy York, Charlie Gehringer, Pinky Higgins, and company.

196

The Cincinnati aces pitched in five of the seven games, winning four. The Series lasted seven only because potbellied, lumbering Bobo Newsom was just as brilliant as the Reds' pitchers. The Tigers' huge right-hander, who sweated and grunted on the mound like a beast of burden, hurled three complete games, two of them victories. But when he went to the mound against Derringer for a seventh-game showdown, the old war-horse was overtaxed. Weary after only a day's rest since his last start, Newsom faltered in the seventh, allowing two runs, and the Reds prevailed, 2–1.

When it was over and Cincinnati had its first world championship in 21 years, the Queen City lost its cool in saluting the Reds. Wild celebrants improvised on the conventional partying by lifting streetcars off the tracks. Perhaps they sensed that they would have an even longer wait for the next world championship party.

During the war, the Reds were so strapped

for manpower that they pressed into service a fifteen-year-old, the youngest player ever to compete in a major league game. He was pitcher Joe Nuxhall, today a radio broadcaster for the Reds. He entered a game on June 10, 1944, with Cincinnati losing 13–0. When he left, it was 19–0. "Players were scarce because of the war," he points out. "Bill McKechnie decided it was a good time to put me in a ball game. I guess a lot of the fans thought they'd never see that kid again." (In fact, Nuxhall lasted 15 years in the majors, most of them with the Reds.)

Two of the Reds' greatest stars of the postwar era were Ted Kluszewski and Ewell Blackwell. Blackwell was a sidearmer whose intimidating delivery and crackling fastball earned him the nickname "the Whip." In 1947, he hurled 16 straight victories, led the league in strikeouts, and very nearly duplicated Vander Meer's back-to-back no-hitters (against the same two teams Vander Meer had victimized, the Braves and the Dodgers). After no-hitting the Braves on June 18, Blackwell held the Dodgers hitless for eight and a third innings in his next start. Then Eddie Stanky slapped a single to center between Blackwell's legs, ruining the second no-hitter.

Kluszewski was a gargantuan first baseman. He was so musclebound that the short sleeves of the Reds' uniform shirt hampered his arm movement, so he wore a sleeveless uniform. In 10 years with the Reds, he hit .300 or better seven times and powdered 254 home runs. "In our day," he recalls, "they came out to see the home run because they weren't going to see much of anything else."

The Reds' resurgence began in 1956, when the man destined to be baseball's first black manager joined the team. "Frank Robinson was aggressive, as good players are," recalls Roy McMillan, the shortstop on that team and later a manager himself. "He was very quiet. He did

Reds

Name of Park	Date 1st Game Played	Opponent & Score	Capacity
Avenue Grounds	April 25, 1876	Cincinnati 2, St. Louis 1	3,000*
Bank Street Grounds	May 1, 1880	Chicago 4, Cincinnati 3	2,000*
League Park	April 19, 1890	Chicago 5, Cincinnati 4	6,000*
Palace of the Fans	April 17, 1902	Chicago 6, Cincinnati 1	12,000
Crosley Field**			29,488
Riverfront Stadium	June 30, 1970	Atlanta 8, Cincinnati 2	51,786

* Estimated attendance that day.
** Palace of the Fans renamed Crosley Field and capacity expanded.

197

Opposite top: *Bucky Walters, left, and Paul Derringer, aces of the Reds' 1940 world championship team.* Above: *Jim Maloney after no-hitting Houston in 1969.* Opposite bottom: *Fred Hutchinson was the Reds' spiritual leader in the sixties.*

his job, and he improved every day." Robinson played in every Reds' game that first season, cracked 38 home runs (tying a record for a rookie), and won the Rookie of the Year award. With a solid outfield (Robinson in left, Gus Bell in center, Wally Post in right), a deft keystone team (McMillan and Johnny Temple), and mainstays at first base (Kluszewski) and catcher (Ed Bailey), the Reds finished third in 1956, their best showing since 1944. There wasn't much pitching, but there was plenty of power—a record 221 homers in all, including 8 in one game against the Milwaukee Braves.

Fred Hutchinson took over as manager in midseason 1959, and in 1961, the Reds won the pennant, their first in 21 years, their fourth overall. Speedy Vada Pinson led the team in hitting with a .343 average, supplementing the power of MVP Robinson (37 homers, 127 RBIs), third baseman Gene Freese, and first baseman Gordy Coleman (26 homers each). However, the big difference between this team and the power teams of the fifties was pitching. The Reds found a 20-game winner in former Little Leaguer Joey Jay and a 19-game winner in fireballing left-hander Jim O'Toole.

The Yankees of Mantle, Maris, and Berra outgunned the Reds in a five-game Series. Joey Jay's second-game victory prevented a sweep. O'Toole pitched effectively, but the Yankees ace, Whitey Ford, was better, extending his Series scoreless string to 32 innings, a new record.

Through the rest of the sixties, the Reds finished as high as second, as low as seventh. Individual performances were more dramatic than the achievements of the team as a whole. Jim Maloney pitched three no-hitters, in one of which he struck out eight consecutive batters. Jerry Lynch banged 19 pinch hits two years in succession.

By far the most compelling individual drama, one that gripped the entire team—indeed, all of baseball—was manager Fred Hutchinson's ill-fated battle against cancer. Soon after the diagnosis, in early 1964, Hutchinson announced to the press with characteristic bluntness that he had cancer. He continued to manage the team, and as the season wore on, the Reds linked their struggle to his. He and his players rarely hid behind false pride or bravado, and the crusade that could have been maudlin became inspiring. The man's fierce will to win, now communicated to his ballplayers more poignantly than ever, found its most graphic expression in his battle to survive.

He lost. Wasted and disfigured by the disease, the once burly "Bear" left before the season

was through and died shortly thereafter. The Reds, emotionally drained themselves, caught and passed the faltering Phillies in the stretch, only to lose the pennant on the last day to the Cardinals. The fate of the team and its manager seemed intertwined.

The next year the Reds slipped to fourth when once again their pitching failed them. Right-handers Sam Ellis and Maloney had 20-win seasons, but only Maloney among the regulars managed an ERA under 3.00. The staff as a whole had an ERA worse than any other team in the league but the Mets. Thus, management looked for pitching in the off-season—a sound enough policy, but one that prompted one of the worst trades in the Reds' history. At age thirty, Frank Robinson was deemed prematurely aged and shipped to Baltimore for Milt Pappas, a twenty-six-year-old alumnus of the Orioles' Kiddie Korps of the early sixties. The Cincinnati attack was diversified enough to survive without Robinson, but Pappas hardly helped the pitching staff.

On January 22, 1967, after the Robinson-less, pitching-poor Reds had fallen to seventh and switched managers in 1966, the front office gained a new boss in Bob Howsam, imported from St. Louis. Under Howsam the parts of the Big Red Machine were assembled and the finishing touches applied.

Pete Rose, who had arrived in 1963, developed into a perennial contender for the batting championship, winning it in 1968 and 1969. The pugnacious, hustling switch hitter became another first for the Reds: the first $100,000 singles hitter. In 1967, Tony Perez blossomed into a 100-RBI man, and equally big and powerful Lee May broke into the lineup at first base and in the outfield. The next year, twenty-year-old catcher Johnny Bench became the league's top rookie with 15 homers and 82 RBIs, statistics that only suggested his promise.

In 1967 and 1968, the Reds were fourth, in 1969 third in the Western Division. And in 1970, in a surprising and delightful year for Cincinnati baseball, the Machine moved into high gear and took the pennant with 102 wins. The team had a new manager in Sparky Anderson and a new home in Riverfront Stadium, which opened on June 30, 1970, with a record-breaking crowd. Two weeks later, the All-Star Game came to town, and hometown boy Pete Rose scored the winning run in the bottom of the twelfth by blasting catcher Ray Fosse loose from the ball at the plate. By season's end the Reds had left the rest of their division, indeed the league, behind them, and in the playoffs they trounced the

Although somewhat less dramatic now in his contribution to the Reds because opponents have learned not to challenge his greatness, Johnny Bench remains one of the finest catchers in baseball history.

Below: *Pete Rose has mastered four positions in the field and continues to shine at bat.* Right: *Talented Dan Driessen has yet to crack the star-studded lineup.* Opposite: *Dave Concepcion fields like a shortstop but doesn't hit like one.*

200

Top: *Thirty-five years after celebrating its last world championship, Cincinnati turned out en masse to honor 1975 Reds.* Bottom: *After slumping early in Series, Tony Perez exploded for three homers.*

202

Pirates in three straight for the pennant.

Then came the World Series, and the masterful Brooks Robinson seemed to single-handedly dismantle the vaunted Machine. This Series was billed as the confrontation between the Reds and their expatriate, Frank Robinson, but Robinson's namesake stole the show. Brooks sealed the left side of the diamond against the right-handed power pull-hitting of the Reds with a breathtaking assortment of defensive gems. Diving to his left and right for smashes, charging up the line for dribblers, Brooks turned any ball hit near him into an out. "I never saw Pie Traynor perform," sighed a resigned Johnny Bench afterward, "but he had to be inhuman to be better at playing third than Brooks." Meanwhile, the Orioles were bombing Cincinnati's pitchers, who had no miracle workers in the field, and the Series lasted only five games.

The Reds would be back, but not the next year. After the exhilaration of near perfection in 1970, the Machine discovered that it was only human after all. Bench slumped to .238. Perez hit 15 fewer homers than he had in 1970. Tolan suffered a bad leg injury that hobbled him for the entire year. The team's batting average dropped nearly 30 points, from .270 in 1970 to .241 in 1971.

Here GM Bob Howsam stepped in to overhaul. He sent May, infielder Tommy Helms, and utility man Jimmy Stewart to Houston for second baseman Joe Morgan, pitcher Jack Billingham, outfielder Cesar Geronimo, outfielder Ed Armbrister, and veteran infielder Denis Menke. It was an inspired bit of dealing—insuring the 1972 pennant and probably quite a few more thereafter.

With the mainstays of the Machine—Bench, Perez, Rose, Bobby Tolan—back at their best in 1972, the retooled Reds reached first place on June 25, when Menke's extra base hit against the Astros capped a 5–4 Cincinnati win. In effect that was the end of the pennant race. By season's end, the Machine had accumulated another 102 wins and again far outdistanced the rest of the division. This time, the Pirates made it close in the playoffs, leading 3–2 in the bottom of the ninth in the fifth game before Bench bombed one for the tie and the Reds tallied another for the win. It was a thrilling comeback victory that seemed to portend great things in the Series.

It *was* a great Series, and the Reds made some great comebacks, but it ended in disappointment. The Reds met an equally fine team in the Oakland A's, who prevailed in seven games on the strength of just a bit more good fortune. Oakland took the first two games in Cincin-

nati, then the Reds won the third 1–0 in Oakland on Billingham's three-hitter. After a two-run rally in the eighth in game four, the Reds led 2–1 and were within three outs of tying the Series. But in the bottom of the ninth, Clay Carroll failed to hold the lead, surrendering three straight singles and the winning run.

It was discouraging enough to make an ordinary team fold, but the Reds were brilliant in adversity. Trailing 4–3 after seven in the fifth game, they tied it in the eighth and scored the winner in the ninth. Joe Morgan, who tallied the tying run, preserved the victory when, with men on first and third and one out in the bottom of the ninth, he nabbed a foul fly behind first and nailed the man from third trying to score the equalizer. Thus revived, the Reds thumped the A's 8–1 in the sixth game, back in Cincinnati, tying the Series.

In the thrilling finale, the Reds just ran out of comebacks. Behind 3–1 in the bottom of the eighth, they produced only one run, on Rose's single, Morgan's double, and a sacrifice fly. They might have had two, if Rose had not had to avoid the ball on Morgan's hit. As it was, Morgan was held to a double when Rose could advance only to third, and so the sacrifice fly was not enough.

The 1973 season came to naught when the Reds chased and caught the resurgent young Dodgers for the divisional crown, only to be upset in the playoffs by the New York Mets, who had finished the regular season with 82 wins, 17 less than the Reds. Then in 1974, the Dodgers couldn't be caught despite the Reds' best efforts again. Said Bench, "We were trying to catch the Dodgers all year. From about May every game—every pitch—was important. Despite all that, it was amazing we were there in September."

In 1975, however, the Reds once again dominated their division. Though the Dodgers were hampered by injuries to key men, it is doubtful they could have caught the Reds under the best of circumstances. Winning twice as many as they lost, the Reds surpassed their previous high in victories and in attendance. Then they capped the season with their dramatic World Series triumph.

The Big Red Machine today seems not only durable but indestructible, finding replacement parts even before it really needs them. First so often in the accessories to the game, first too with many individual feats and records, the Reds are finally becoming first in the category that matters most—winning. The Big Red Machine has sputtered some, but as the National League moves into its centennial year, baseball's first club celebrates it as the best.

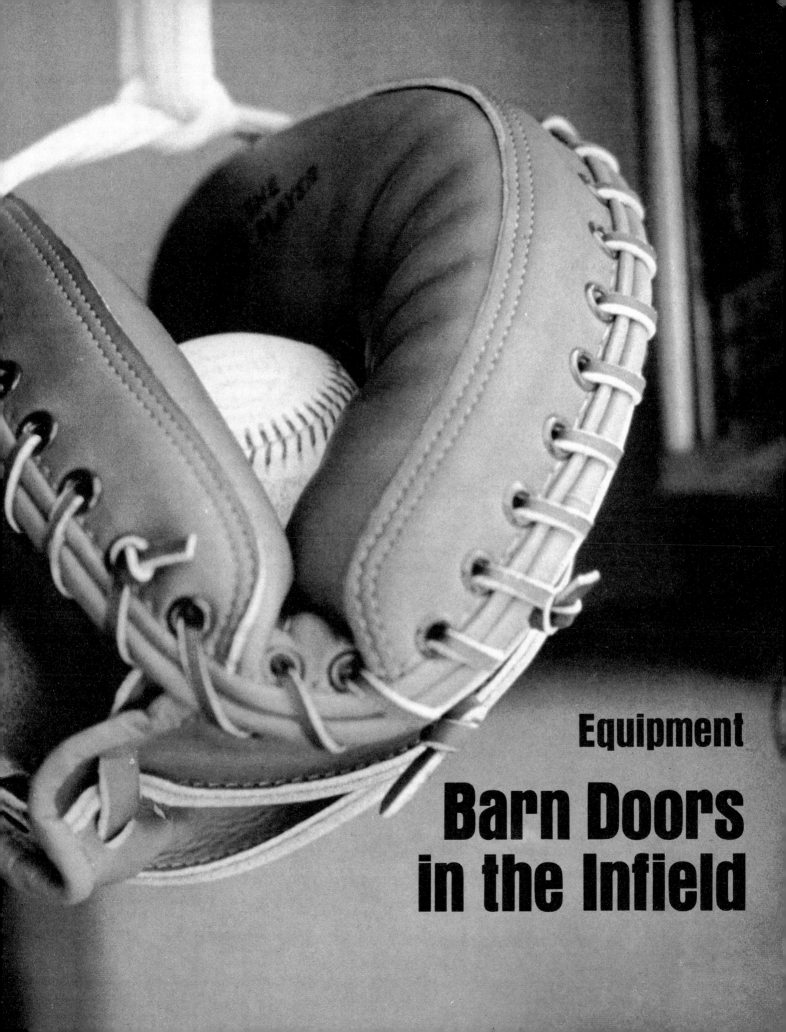

Equipment

Barn Doors in the Infield

hen he spoke to Roger Angell in the spring of 1975, Steve Blass was out of baseball, but he still remembered the day he was called to the big leagues. "I drove straight to Forbes Field," said Blass, "and went in and found the attendant and put my uniform on, at two in the afternoon. There was no *game* there, or anything—I just had to see how it looked."

By 1973, his career was in precipitous decline.

The major league uniform is the symbol of having made it into an exclusive fraternity of men who have kept on playing. It is the badge of belonging to America's greatest sporting tradition, belonging at the top. Whether made of flannel or Orlon, it has been woven of dreams.

The traditions of the uniform extend to the very founding of organized baseball. In 1851, the

Knickerbocker Baseball Club, established in 1845, appeared in suits patterned after those worn by cricket players: long blue woolen trousers and white flannel shirts with webbed belts and, of all things, straw hats. The impractical boaters were replaced in 1855 by flat-topped mohair caps, again copied from cricket gear.

Knee-length Knickerbocker pants were not invented by the Knickerbockers. They were introduced in 1868 by baseball's first professional team, known as the Red Stockings, from Cincinnati, Ohio. Lots of jeering and hooting greeted the players, but the fad caught on and influences the style of baseball pants today.

The Official Baseball Guide of 1878 recommended the use of white, and only one other color, as the "prettiest" for official National League uniforms. The promotional value of outfitting teams smartly was already recognized. Albert G. Spalding, first manager of the White Stockings, assigned a different color cap to each of his players according to position, to make it easier for fans to identify their heroes.

By 1882, the National League had adopted a rule providing an identifying color for each team in the league. The 1882 ruling called for all pants, belts, and ties to be white, but caps and shirts were to vary according to a player's position. By 1883, colors were specified only for stockings, which in this period were made of light weight silk. Curiously, the Chicago White Stockings wore maroon stockings at the opening of the 1899 season.

Although a team's positional hues were to be constant, color did not fade from the field. The 1901 Baltimore Orioles wore yellow stockings, black sagging pants, yellow belts, black shirts with a large "O" on the left breast, and double-breasted coats with wide yellow collars and cuffs. Two rows of enormous pearl buttons adorned the coats. (It wasn't until 1931 that glass buttons and metal objects were prohibited from the uniform as distracting. Ragged, frayed, or slit sleeves, colored tape or materials not of the uniform color, and anything suggesting the shape of a baseball are now also disallowed.) The Baltimore caps were pink, completing an outfit easily as remarkable as the current Houston Astros' rainbow array.

Cap Anson, who signed with Chicago in 1876, is held responsible for a change in uniform belt loops. It seems that Mike Kelly of Boston once grabbed Anson by the belt, preventing Cap from getting back to first to take a throw. Kelly, meanwhile, legged it to third before the ball was recovered. Anson persuaded a sporting goods house to try threading belts through the fabric of the pants so there wouldn't be enough leather for an opponent to grab. Today's Pirates, like many clubs, have eliminated belts entirely by wearing pull-on stretch knit pants.

The 1905 World Series pitted John McGraw's Giants against Connie Mack's Philadelphia Athletics. New York won four of the five shutout games, and it was speculated that their edge was at least partially psychological. McGraw decked his men in brand-new black uniforms with white trim, while Philadelphia, in the words of one reporter, "showed up in the same old suits—dirty, ragged, sweaty and torn."

Another story credits Connie Mack with a change in the uniforms worn by the Athletics. The players apparently played aggressively at home in worn uniforms, but when away were inclined to keep their outfits natty, even at the expense of not hitting the dirt in critical moments. According to the story, Mack equipped them with drab road uniforms they would not mind soiling, and team statistics soared. That this was the origin of the tradition of wearing whites for home games and grays on the road is unsubstantiated, but the idea must have worked. Differentiating between home and road suits at least made it easier to distinguish competing teams, and has been required in the major leagues since 1911.

Making comfortable, durable uniforms was not a simple matter. As late as 1912, major league ballplayers paid for their own uniforms. For about thirty dollars a year, they got suits of eight-ounce flannel, which amounted to several pounds of clothing, with an added five or ten pounds of absorbed sweat on hot days. As if that weren't enough of a burden, the material shrank with washing, so that when the season opened many men were seen in uniforms a full size too large. Laundering did more damage to the uniforms than slides and rough play, and even the newest uniforms soon became dull in addition to being baggy.

To streamline the uniform, a six-ounce flannel shirt was adopted in 1925, and by 1935 at least one team had reduced their shirts to four-ounce fabric. Pants were not lightened until 1946, when several teams tried a material that added rayon to the wool-and-cotton flannel.

From early days, the long-lasting baseball uniforms were handed down after a season in the majors. Typically, sixty whites and sixty grays were inherited by farm teams each year, and later, the well-laundered shirts and pants might be passed on for use in training camps.

During the mid-twenties, shirts became

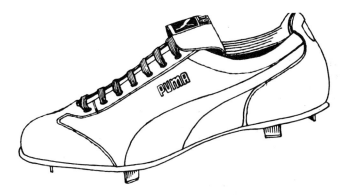

more colorful, with trim added down the front and at sleeve ends. A front-zipper shirt was introduced about 1930, and it remained popular until the early fifties. The newest shirts are knit, and pull over the head without buttons or zippers. Stripes outline the neck and sleeves.

The first recorded use of numbers on the backs of uniform shirts was June 2, 1916, when Robert McRoy, Cleveland's business manager, pinned numerals on his players in a game against Chicago. C. W. Murphy, president of the Chicago National League club, is also credited with having the idea as early as 1907, and Paul Graham, manager of Cincinnati's Tri-city team, apparently numbered his nine, as well as visitors, in that year. By 1931, the American League adopted universal player numbering. The National League endorsed the identification system two years later.

Tim McAuliffe of Boston began improving baseball uniforms in 1919, and in 1948 introduced a Dacron polyester fiber into the standard fabric. The new tri-blend had a tendency to pill, so his next experiment was to use 80 percent wool with 20 percent nylon, a lightweight and

flexible fabric used successfully by the Dodge–Davis Company until 1960.

In 1959, McAuliffe asked the Red Sox to try an Orlon-wool blend which, though practical, had a harsh, stiff feel. The team found the material softened considerably with laundering but lost neither its whiteness nor its strength. By 1963, a half-dozen teams—including the Giants and Dodgers—adopted the McAuliffe Orlon "flannel," which sold for $62.50 (hat, shirt, pants, belt, socks).

Just as Orlon improved the uniform's durability, knit fabrics have made the greatest impact on fit. Honus Wagner is memorable for trousers billowing around his knees. Steve Blass, in his finest moment, will be remembered in the Pirates' skintight knit knickers, which have been described as a cross between ski pants and long johns, with a drawstring at the waist and no fly. Blass himself thought getting out of the gear was like taking off a girdle, and much humor has resulted from between-inning delays when the Pirates are said to be changing. In fact, the trim, newer knits are modified in light of experience. Whether this streamlining is a matter of vanity, image, efficiency, or superstition, it is obviously a part of the colorful image of baseball as it approaches the National League centennial. Pinstripes, harking to Knickerbocker colors and the original Giants, could soon become the only remnant of uniform tradition.

Baseball shoes have also evolved with time. The 1877 Harvard team was the first to replace canvas shoes with leather, laced around the ankles. In the interest of speed, shoes became progressively lower cut, and by 1890, heel- and toeplates, originally sold separately, were attached to improve traction.

Adidas, a relatively new name in baseball shoes, introduced the first white models in 1967, shoes later adopted by players in both leagues. Their best shoes, of kangaroo leather, are known as the MVP and Triple Crown.

Each player receives two pairs of Adidas shoes, one with metal cleats for standard fields, and another with multiple cleats and soles made of heat-resistant polyurethane, designed for grip on artificial surfaces.

Although spikes came into general use in the late 1880s, and were designed to improve traction and speed, they were soon found ideal for other purposes. Patsy Tebeau, manager of the Cleveland Spiders in the 1890s, instructed his men to file their spikes before a game against the Orioles. "Give 'em steel and plenty of it!" he is reported to have shouted.

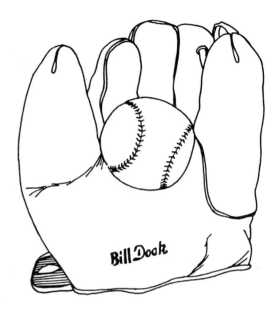

Bill Doak

The Spiders gained a terrifying reputation in the old National League until meeting their match in William Chase Temple's Pirates. In those days, visitors dressed in their hotel rooms and were driven to the ball park in horse-drawn hacks. Reportedly, as Tebeau's team neared the clubhouse, every Pittsburgh player was waiting, file in hand. Faced with equally sharp spikes, the Spiders at last moderated their base-running tactics.

Billy Fox, who managed Omaha in the Western League in 1910, suggested rounding off the corners and cutting deep, square notches in the sharp edges of the spikes. His spike, it was claimed, would bruise a shin but not break it open. Although improvements have been made in spike design with the advent of synthetics, the baseball shoe is still much as it was in the early days, and spikes are very much part of the game.

As the game became more dangerous and the players more skilled, defensive equipment was added and improved through experimentation. The cap is an example of a frivolous accessory developed slowly into the protective mechanism required by league rules. As mentioned, the Knickerbockers wore straw boaters for several years before adopting flat-topped hats. When the cap became formfitting, its protective function was recognized. The Reach Pneumatic Head Protector was patented in 1905 and worn on July 25, 1907, by catcher Roger Bresnahan, an innovator in the use of shin guards as well. While recovering from being hit by a pitched ball that knocked him unconscious, he decided that henceforth he would protect his head as well as his legs. The Reach explanatory literature said: "As the protector not only inspires the timid batsman with a sense of security, but guards against the loss of services of a valuable player by injury, every team should have two—one for right-handed, the other for left-handed batsmen." The protector was a half helmet worn on the side of the head exposed to the pitch.

Helmets composed of fiberglass and a polyester resin, in the formula used to produce bulletproof materials for the armed forces, were invented by Ed Crick and Ralph Davis, two Cleveland engineers, in 1950. By 1953, Pirates general manager Branch Rickey had formed American Baseball Cap to distribute the new plastic headgear, which weighed only 6½ ounces and came in three sizes. An airfoam lining was included as a sweatband and a method of adjusting the helmets to fit individual heads. The

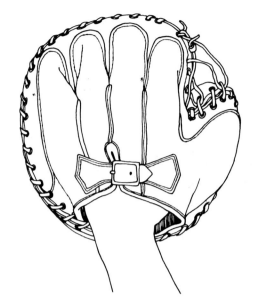

Rickey's helmet has received endorsement from the majority of ballplayers, and league rules now require all players to use some kind of protective helmet while at bat.

George Ellard captured the early catcher's pride in manning his position unprotected:

> We used no mattress on our hands,
> No cage upon our face;
> We stood right up and caught the ball
> With courage and with grace.

That spirit was soon to disappear. By 1901, rules had outlawed catching the pitch or foul balls on the first bounce and brought catchers into a squatting position close behind the plate. Injuries from wild pitches increased greatly along with damage from foul tips and from spiking by runners sliding in to score.

Knee pads were worn by catchers before the

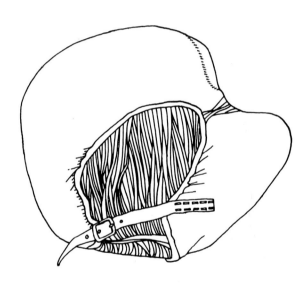

caps, sprayed with light-absorbing flocking and available in all team colors, cost roughly ten dollars each. They offered increased protection to blind-spot areas and sat lower over the temples and ears than did the traditional soft caps. Normally, batters turn or back away when threatened by a close pitch; Rickey's helmet covered more of the side and back of the player's head to compensate for this reflex. In 1954, Jackie Robinson of the Dodgers was struck on the side of the head while wearing the new gear and, thanks to the helmet, was able to stay in the game. A similar lightweight plastic and foam head covering was designed for catchers to wear under their masks.

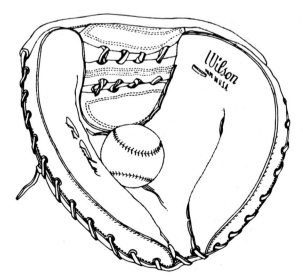

209

Top left: *Style of first glove ever used, circa 1877.* Top right: *Combination catching and throwing glove, circa 1885.* Middle left: *First webbed pitcher's–infielder's glove, circa 1901.* Middle right: *Unwebbed pitcher's–infielder's glove, circa 1901.* Bottom left: *Fielder's glove, circa 1905.* Bottom right: *Fielder's glove, circa 1915.*

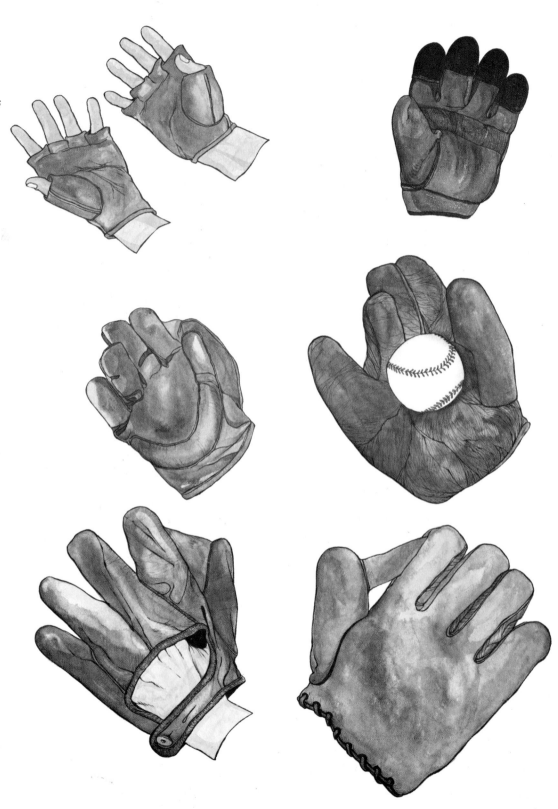

invention of shin guards, as were strips of felt under the stockings. The latter were popular with infielders, too.

There is a dispute over who invented shin guards. It may have been Charles ("Red") Dooin, catcher for Philadelphia in 1906, although John J. McGraw and Matthew Fitzgerald of the Giants also claimed credit. But there is agreement that Roger Bresnahan was first to don guards over his pants. On April 11, 1907, at the Polo Grounds, he wore a pair, becoming the object of overwhelming ridicule. Interviewed in Sarasota, Florida, in 1926, he remarked: "I didn't invent anything. I simply got a pair of shin guards, such as cricket players wore . . . and I strapped them outside my stockings. I was sick and tired of wild pitches, foul balls, thrown bats, and flying spikes bruising and cutting my legs."

The New York *Times* had this comment: "The white shields were rather picturesque in spite of their clumsiness and the spectators rather fancied the innovation. They howled with delight when a foul tip in the eighth inning rapped the protectors sharply. But Bresnahan, recollecting the many cracks on the shins he suffered last year, had slightly the better of the situation."

By 1910, Frank Chance, managing the Chicago Cubs, ordered his catchers to wear shin guards, despite the scorn Bresnahan continued to draw.

A Cleveland writer observed in 1912 that "With big men like Carrigan, Cady, O'Neill, Agnew, Meyers, Gowdy, Bresnahan, and Henry employing the tactics they have developed since the shin guard came into use, there is little chance for a runner to really try to score with a slide unless he takes a chance of getting a broken leg for his effort." Big league catchers had developed the knack of sticking their shielded legs in front of sliding runners to block the plate without danger of being spiked.

The shin guards used today, which come in team colors, are one piece—padded kneecap and leather knee connector, shin plate and side wings, padded instep connector, and three elastic straps to anchor the gear properly.

The first piece of protective baseball equipment was a mouth protector worn by George Wright, Cincinnati Red Stockings shortstop during the 1860s. The guard was patented and guaranteed not to have a disagreeable taste. In those days, most catchers lost their teeth after a season or two, but the mouth protector was not enthusiastically adopted and disappeared with the advent of masks and gloves.

Invention of the catcher's mask is attributed

*Albert Spalding
pre-1900*

211

to Fred W. Thayer, captain of the Harvard nine. It is said that in 1876 he produced a fencing mask for his catcher, James Alexander Tyng, who had threatened to quit rather than risk disfiguring his face.

Unique in annals of baseball is an out made by Mike Hines of the Red Stockings in 1884. With two strikes on the batter, a foul was tipped back right into catcher Hines's mask—and there it stuck, the mask's wires spread just far enough by the impact to hold the ball securely. Umpire Van Court called the Detroit batter out, saying Hines had caught the ball on the third strike.

Although masks were still ridiculed as muzzles, rattraps, and bird cages, their development continued. Reach and Spalding straightened the horizontal bars above the eyes and returned to Thayer's concept of continuous padding framing the head. An unnamed sportswriter of the period fumed: "There is a good deal of beastly humbug in contrivances to protect men from things which don't happen. There is about as much sense in putting a lightning rod on a catcher as a mask."

Today's masks resemble the platform mask, but are constructed of lightweight polycarbonate covered by strong glare-free padding that is easily cleaned or replaced. The amount of padding has significantly increased over the years. Modern masks utilize crossed vertical and horizontal ribs, leaving the area over the eyes clear.

In *Low and Inside,* Ira Smith and H. Allen Smith note that a secondary purpose of the umpire's mask is to protect his face from fists. They recall many an umpire, in the early days of frequent combat, taking off his mask, seizing it by the straps, and using it to beat an enemy's head. In Buffalo, umpire Hassett tried to throw a shortstop named Nattress out of the game for foul language, but Nat "rushed up to the official, took hold of his mask, pulled it out as far as the elastic straps would permit, then let it snap back onto Hassett's face. The free-for-all that followed ended with umpire Hassett forfeiting the game to Buffalo."

The chest protector was first used by John T. Clements, catching for the Philadelphia Keystones, in 1884. Called a sheepskin, it was worn under the uniform but still made the catcher an object of derision. Charles Bennett, Detroit catcher, claimed his wife made him the first version of chest protection, a garment strongly resembling the seamed and stuffed shield worn today. Henry Fabian claimed to have made the first body protector worn over a uniform for Tom Moran, a Dallas minor league catcher. It

fastened loosely around the neck and was stuffed with cotton. Moran appeared in it in 1903. Later vests were inflated with air and, by the thirties, filled with kapok for less bulk.

Today's body protector, in contrast to those worn at the turn of the century, is available in colors to match the uniform and wraps the neck area snugly to protect shoulder blades and collarbone. It is shorter than early models, extending only to waist level. The welting is horizontal rather than vertical, and the fit is much closer to the body, with armhole shaping.

Albert G. Spalding, while pitching for Boston in the 1870s, developed severe bruises on the inside of his left hand. "When it is recalled that every ball pitched had to be returned, and that every swift one coming my way, from infielders, outfielders or hot from the bat, must be caught or stopped, some idea may be gained of the punishment received," he wrote.

The first glove he encountered was worn in Boston by Charles C. Waitt, in 1875, playing first base for New Haven. It was flesh-colored, with a large round opening at the back for ventilation. Waitt admitted to choosing a flesh-colored aid because it might be inconspicuous, but when Spalding adopted a similar vented glove, he chose black. The great Spalding took no abuse from fans, teammates, or the opposition. He started a trend. "I found that the glove, thin as it was, helped considerably, and inserted one pad after another until a good deal of relief was afforded."

Henry Fabian, catching for New Orleans in 1880, had to snag pitches from 45 feet away. He

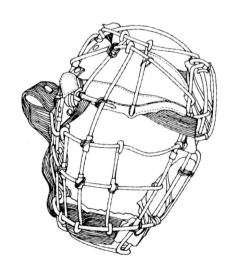

used two gloves on his left hand, inserting between the surfaces a small piece of sheet lead. Silver Flint, Cap Anson's catcher, used raw beefsteak between his thin leather catching gloves, and Anson himself wore kid gloves on each hand, with the fingertips stripped on the throwing hand.

By 1886, gloves with fingers were being sold, and players were using one glove more often than two. Among notable holdouts were Fred Dunlap, who led the league's second basemen in fielding in 1883, 1884, 1885 and 1889, and John ("Bid") McPhee, who signed with Cincinnati in 1882 and played for the next eighteen years, only consenting to wear a glove late in his career. McPhee led the league in fielding seven times.

The first pillow-type mitt is attributed to the New York Giants' famous catcher, William ("Buck") Ewing. He repaired his enormous glove himself and stuffed its palm continually, covering each soft addition with a new leather patch. Fans marveled at the growth of Ewing's many-hided patches, and the mitt became a ballpark feature as attractive as any present-day promotion.

Fielders' gloves came into general use later than did catching gear. Lave Cross, Louisville's massive catcher, joined Philadelphia in 1892 and was soon called upon to replace erratic Charles Reilly at third. With the shift, Cross took along his catcher's mitt. Grounders slammed at him just thumped into the big glove. His remarkable fielding brought forth howls. "They're playing infield with barn doors," critics protested. Fielders, as well as those at bat, were angry at the innovation.

Boston's Harry Schafer blasted the mitts in 1894: "The game of baseball is being spoiled by allowing players to wear those abominations known as mitts.

"It is all right for catchers to wear them. They are in an exposed position and likely to get hurt and they deserve protection. The same is true of the first-baseman; but there is where the line should be drawn.

"Players do not have to show skill in handling balls with those mitts on their hands. Those who cannot play without them should get out of the game and give way to those who can. There are plenty of players who can play splendid ball without using those monstrosities."

A Cincinnati paper editorialized in opposition to large mitts, saying fielders must have thought they were facing cannon balls instead of a yarn ball hit by a bat. The paper also suggested that some players might not draw their salaries without well-padded gloves, a position

prophetic of Lave Cross's fate at third once the league rule makers set limits to the character of fielding equipment.

The most innovative change in gloves came in 1919, when a right-handed spitballer from the St. Louis Cardinals approached William P. Whitley, Rawlings' production chief, with ideas for a naturally formed deep pocket and inner greased palm. The Bill Doak glove made its official bow in 1920 and stayed in Rawlings' line until 1953. It incorporated a multi-thong web laced into the first finger and thumb, and it influenced the redesign of catcher and first base mitts.

A former pro named Harry ("Bud") Latina joined Rawlings in 1922 and became known as "the glove doctor" for his numerous contributions to improved glove design. He is responsible for the Deep Well pocket, U crotch, laced pocket, Playmaker three-finger glove, V-anchored web, Edge-U-Cated heel, and many other strange-sounding modifications. Among his most famous developments are the Trapper Mitt, in 1940, and the Trap-Eze six-finger glove, brought out in 1959.

Gloves are manufactured both in the United States and in the Far East. First, tanned hides are graded and sorted for color, flexibility, and smoothness to determine which are shell or lining quality. The performance, appearance, and life of a glove depend on the character of its hides. A great glove has the correct feel (considering weight and pliability), is durable, and has a pocket shaped to trap the ball.

Gloves consist of as many as twelve pieces of leather, which are die-cut following blue-printed designs. The trademark, name, stock number, and similar means of identification are stamped on the shell, heel, and web before assembly. Fingers, palm, and thumb are joined wrong-side-out with welted seams. The glove is then turned right-side-out, and lining, pad, and heel are inserted. Binding and lacing are done by hand with cowhide or rawhide. The final shaping involves pounding the glove over a hot forming iron.

Gloves have come a long way since March 22, 1904, the day a patent was issued for the Base Ball Catcher. This cumbersome invention was a box of wood and wire built to reach from the player's chin to his waist—tied on, of course—with a screen on top to protect his face. The box had two wire doors, hinged to swing inward if struck by a ball. The ball entered the box through these doors, struck with a thud against a heavy pad backed by springs, and then dropped through a pipe at the bottom of the box. This

214

Christy Mathewson
1910s

215

pipe was closed at the end and opened instead on the side, so that the catcher could reach in to palm the sphere.

If gloves are the most sentimentally regarded pieces of baseball equipment, bats are given the most personal attention. Old-timers liked the feel of wood in their hands and depended on this sense in gauging a good swing. The seventies, however, have seen a new fad insulating the batter's hands from the bat, if only slightly. Golf gloves are being worn at the plate, and some players are even using them under their mitts in the field.

No two pieces of wood are alike. No two bats are alike. Precision is the key to making major league equipment, and the bat business is famed for painstaking attention to detail. Honus Wagner was said to be able to hit with anything big and heavy and did not complain about a variance in his bats of even two or three ounces. He was, nevertheless, a stickler about dimension and length, searching for sticks with identical handles and taper.

Bats differ in weight and balance, in overall length, in the shapes of both barrel and handle, in knob shaping, and in the character of tapering. The most capricious variable is the wood itself. Specially trained men search the slopes of Pennsylvania, the Adirondack Mountains, and the northern states generally for stands of straight ash. Hickory and Cuban Timber were also favorites in an earlier day, but are too dense to fashion modern lighter sticks. By judging the condition of a tree's bark, its height, and estimated age, a scouter determines whether or not growth has been regular enough to produce strength, durability, and straightness of grain.

Once a stand of timber is selected, the trunks are cut into bolts about forty inches long, sawn into squares or split, and turned into rounds for storage. These billets will be naturally dried for from ten months to two years, then stacked so that air circulates as they season. A bat with "no wood in it" is one that lacks resiliency, most likely due to improper drying or later exposure to heat.

The first of the famous Louisville Sluggers was made in 1884 for Peter Browning, one of the great hitters of the day. Browning is remembered to have seasoned timber for his bats in his own attic and to have expected three or four hits per game from the carefully formed sticks. Once, while playing for the Louisville nine, he broke his bat. There was an important game coming up the next day; Browning rushed to a local wood-turning shop and begged J. F. Hillerich to reproduce one of his bats exactly. Some say that Hillerich reached for a wagon tongue and set to work, but it is more likely that he used wood in stock, since he and his father manufactured bowling balls and pins. The following day, Browning got four hits off Hillerich's bat. It was the beginning of an empire. Hillerich & Bradsby became the world's leading producer of baseball bats, source of the famed Louisville Slugger. Today the company produces literally millions of bats for major leaguers and Little Leaguers alike.

Cap Anson, a leading figure in the National League from 1876 to 1897, never overlooked a piece of good wood that might be turned into a plate weapon. In corners of the Chicago ball park could be found Anson's collection of old logs and cart shafts, shipped there from as far away as New York. His locker was always filled with bats, and he never permitted anyone else to use his private stock. Rumor had it that 276 bats were hung like hams from the ceiling of Anson's basement. Some said the figure was closer to 500.

Another collector was named Perring. When the Ohio State Penitentiary was torn down about 1880, this scavenger obtained a piece of the hickory wood that had formed the scaffold. The wood was strong and obviously well seasoned, so Perring had it made into a bat. He used the bat for twenty years—until his retirement from baseball. It was 1906 when the bat passed from father to son. George Perring, playing for Kansas City in the old Federal League, made good use of the remodeled scaffold for another ten years.

Over the years, bats have been treated with tobacco juice, pine-tar rags, oil, and plastic washable sprays in the interest of maintaining good grip and an elegant, rubbed surface. Even Coke bottles have been used—rolled against the bat surface to compress the outer layer of wood, creating a harder hitting surface.

Heinie Groh's famous bottle bat is probably the most unusual legal weapon to have appeared on a diamond. In those days, before Ruth's style held sway, players choked up on their bats, sometimes taking less than a half swing in order to better direct hits through the infield. The weight in older bats was distributed more evenly than it is today, so the sticks felt less heavy than would be imagined. Giants' manager McGraw urged Groh to go to a larger barrel to improve place hitting. The third baseman was only 5 feet 7 inches tall, weighed 160 pounds, and his hands were too small to handle the big-barreled bats. At Spalding's in New York, he built up the barrel of a standard bat and whittled its handle until the finished product looked like a milk bottle. The barrel was full sized right above the long handle, so that if Groh hit an inside pitch, he would have some power. All 46 ounces of the bat seemed to be in its barrel, forcing Groh to chop at the pitches, his hands spread well apart. He used the weapon from 1912 on, and in the years 1917 to 1921 managed a .315 average. He hit .474 in the 1922 World Series and carried that percentage on his license plate thereafter.

Adirondack was founded in Dolgeville, New York, as the McLaughlin–Millard bat factory, using the Adirondack trademark to identify its ash, harvested from the nearby mountains. By the seventies, the company was sending a bat-mobile to spring training camps so that bats could be crafted on the spot to player specifications. In about thirty-five minutes, timber could be turned into a finished weapon, complete with a ring in the appropriate team color. Such service makes possible truly custom-made sticks and is invaluable to the firm in terms of experienced feedback on what does or does not contribute to a bat's success.

Players have been making pilgrimages to Hillerich & Bradsby in Louisville for years to maintain the same control over the production of their equipment. They are able to watch as raw billets are turned on a lathe and sanded; knobs of deadwood are knocked off the ends when the bat is removed from the lathe. The wood is then inspected and flame treated to harden the outer surface. (At this stage of the process, at least one company, Adirondack, applies a wood filler to improve color, accent grain, and fill any open pores.) After sealing, the bat is stamped with a code number on the knob, and the trademark and player's signature on the flat of the grain. A lacquer finish completes the job.

Since solid wood bats are subject to cracking, experiments have been made with substitutes not yet legal in the majors. The bamboo laminate bat consists of thin strips of bamboo bonded with epoxy under heat and pressure, much like plywood. The laminates run lengthwise and offer the same directional strength as solid wood. This bat resists cracking at the handle, but it has a tendency to bow when hit and connects with a "klunk" instead of the more satisfying "crack."

Aluminum bats are lengths of hollow pipe fitted with rubber plugs at tip and knob. They are stronger than wooden products, but the plugs can create problems by flying off at high speed.

Pitching machines, cuffs for pitchers' arms, lights and bells to ease the umpire's decisions on close base calls, even a bat shaped like a question mark have been invented over the years of baseball mania. Cartons of chewing gum and tobacco, stacks of towels and kimonos, soap, medicine, liniment, bandages; sweat shirts and rubber shirts, warm-up jackets and windbreakers, blankets; bases, a batting cage, gimmicks to record the count at the plate, the scoreboard; rakes, shovels, hose lines, sprinkling cans, grass seed, fertilizer, clay, topsoil, tarpaulins, artificial turf, benches, the stadium itself; equipment trunks, bags for bats and balls, rosin bags —the list of equipment required to stage a baseball game is endless. But all of it would be worthless without the ball.

Al Spalding reminisced about the first baseball games and quoted from the *Memphis Appeal* of a date unknown: "The ball was not what would be called a National League ball, nowadays, but it served every purpose. It was usually made on the spot by some boy offering up his woolen socks as an oblation, and these were raveled and wound round a bullet, a handful of strips cut from a rubber overshoe, a piece of cork or almost anything, or nothing, when anything was not available. The winding of this ball was an art, and whoever could excel in this art was looked upon as a superior being. The ball must be a perfect sphere and the threads as regularly laid as the wire on a helix of a magnetic armature. When the winding was complete the surface of the ball was thoroughly sewed with a large needle and thread to prevent it from unwinding when a thread was cut."

In one hundred years, the definition of a baseball has hardly changed. Official rules allowed the use of cowhide covers in 1975, following Spalding's research into an adequate substitute for dwindling horsehide resources, so that the ruling reads: "The ball shall be a sphere formed by yarn wound around a small core of cork, rubber or similar material, covered with two strips of white horsehide or cowhide, tightly stitched together. It shall weigh not less than five nor more than 5¼ ounces avoirdupois and measure not less than nine nor more than 9¼ inches in circumference."

It is hard to believe so much controversy could surround so little apparent change in an object, but in a game of contested plays, the ball could hardly reign unchallenged.

Today, big league umpires will toss in a new ball whenever the baseball is even slightly scuffed. It was not so on August 7, 1882, at the

Edd Roush
1920s

Chuck Klein
1930s

219

Polo Grounds. It was raining, as the Cleveland Spiders and the New York Metropolitans headed into the eighth inning, still using the first ball introduced that day. The wet and soggy sphere became plainly oval when hit foul or high into the air, and by the ninth inning it was sorely ripped. The umpire could not grant the request of the Metropolitans' captain for a new ball because the rules forbade a new ball until the beginning of a new inning. The ninth had begun. The game had to continue. But even with such economy, an estimated five million baseballs were used throughout this country in 1883.

In June, 1895, Rochester was playing Springfield on the Springfield diamond. The home team was half a dozen runs ahead in the seventh, when a Rochester player hit a homer past the outfield into the river. In the eighth inning, a ball broke when hit by a Springfield player; a new ball was needed. In those days, the home team was required to furnish all balls, but Springfield had brought only two and now those were gone. The umpire forfeited the game to Rochester.

Exclusive rights to manufacturing the National League ball were granted to A. G. Spalding & Brothers in 1877, but in the first few years the source and quality of balls in competition were not always regulated. Teams had been accustomed to playing with balls adapted to their strengths. A team of heavy hitters made certain to procure a hard, lively ball, but a superior fielding nine would use a softer ball.

A. J. Reach, Spalding's subsidiary, was granted manufacturing rights to the American League ball in 1901. That league had to enforce a rule calling for the umpire, not the home-team manager, to be custodian of balls. Connie Mack, manager of the Philadelphia Athletics, brought about the ruling. During a 1906 game in Philadelphia, he was discovered to be tossing soft balls to his pitchers whenever a New York batter fouled one into the stands. When the home-team Athletics were at bat, Mack was sure the New York pitchers had a good supply of hard spheres. From then on, home teams were to supply umpires with a satchel containing twelve new and twelve used balls. Any ball going out of play was to be returned to the home-team bench, but was not to be used again during that game.

Early balls varied greatly in weight (some weighed as little as 3 ounces) and were sometimes stitched in crescent-shaped sections. A less lively ball, standardized in 1872, remained remarkably uniform over the years. The 5-ounce Reach ball was 3 inches in diameter with a round 1-inch rubber core. A layer of ½-inch machine-wound woolen yarn covered the core. Two more layers of similar yarn were cemented to the first and to a cover of alum-tanned horsehide, stitched by hand with waxed cotton thread. One hide made about eighteen covers, and the leather was proudly compared to soft white evening gloves.

The present-day Spalding official league balls are made similarly. A cushioned cork center forms the heart, composed of a sphere of cork surrounded by a red layer then a black layer of soft rubber. Stretched tightly over the center (which must be ⅞ of an ounce) is yarn wound automatically by specially designed machines. The first layer consists of 121 yards of rough gray wool; the second is 45 yards of fine white wool; the third contains 53 yards of fine gray wool. One hundred fifty yards of white cotton complete the fourth winding. The ball is then dipped in rubber cement, and the cover is applied.

From 1877 until 1973, covers were made of horsehide. Spalding, working with the Tennessee Tanning Company, examined thirteen tanning processes before finding a way to make cowhide functionally equivalent to horsehide. The capacity for stress and abrasion was checked, as were the hide's friction characteristics, feel, and appearance. Since cowhide is strongest along the grain parallel to the backbone, the new covers are cut perpendicular to the backbone to take advantage of directional strength relative to the stitching pattern. This is a departure from the parallel cutting of horsehide covering.

Covers are dampened carefully and fitted over the completed centers before being stitched. Too much wetness will cause the cover to dry to a slick surface, too little is apt to make the seams gap or bulge, affecting the aerodynamics of the ball.

Stitching is done by hand using two needles, each threaded with 88 inches of waxed twine. One hundred and eight stitches are required by major league specifications. Finished balls are stamped with the Spalding trademark, "Official," the league identification, and the signature of the league president.

To be official, league balls are required to have an initial velocity of 85 feet per second and a rebound velocity of 54.6 percent of the initial velocity when tested on an indoor driving machine. The ball must retain its roundness after being pounded 200 times by a force of 65 pounds, and must be hard enough to distort less than three hundredths of an inch when compressed.

Such elaborate technical specifications have become necessary to guarantee balls of uniform resiliency. The first of many live ball–dead ball controversies occurred with the introduction of the cork center in 1910. Many had claimed that the low-scoring contests of the time were boring, so cork, covered with an eighth of an inch of rubber, was introduced to liven the ball. A decided effect on hitting was felt immediately. National League home-run production soared to 2,433 for the decade from 1911 to 1920, compared to 1,394 the previous decade. *The Sporting News* felt the public was being hoodwinked, but most fans liked the longer hits.

In response to increased hitting, pitchers began to develop special deliveries. The shine ball, spitball, emery ball, and others hopped out of reach of the batters and were outlawed by the league in 1920. (Soiling the ball had been prohibited as early as 1908.) A soft dry cloth was recommended for removing the gloss from new balls. Today, umpires rub game balls with canned river mud before the start of each game.

In 1919, the average ERA was 2.85, but by 1921, it had soared to 4.00, where the figure remained for another decade. The explosion in hitting was attributed to a livelier ball, though laboratory tests never proved the sphere had become any livelier. The end of the war and Babe Ruth's slugging spurred the rising statistics. In 1920, the year following the Black Sox scandal, baseball needed supermen, and the sluggers were happy to please. Other explanations for the spurt in batting are the restrictions placed on pitchers, better yarn made available from Australia after the war, and improved machines capable of winding the yarn tighter, adding resilience.

One sure statistic is that more new balls were in play after 1920. In that year, Ray Chapman had been struck by a pitched ball and killed. To reduce the danger of beaning the batter, a new ball was to be substituted whenever the ball in play became even lightly scuffed, on the theory that a ball with a rough spot can sail out of control. Pitchers had a harder time gripping the tight, fresh spheres, which were also easier for batters to sight. In 1925, teams averaged 2.5 more runs per game than in 1915.

The center of the ball was changed again in 1926, when the cushioned cork sphere now in use was introduced. By 1930, people were apt to tell you that if you held a ball close to your ear, you might hear a rabbit's heart beating within.

Twenty hitters that year batted .350 or better, and nine teams averaged .300 or better in hitting. Home runs in the league reached an unheard of total—1,565 for the season.

The last spate of home run hitting, in 1961, prompted the latest round in the debate over the liveliness of the ball. With Aaron, Mantle, and Maris slugging away, it was claimed that the ball had higher, wider seams than normal, and could travel 30 feet farther than earlier balls hit with identical force.

In 1973, when it was announced that balls were being assembled in the Republic of Haiti, statisticians went to work again. This time they claimed the ball was livelier because its seams were lower and less desirable to curveball pitchers. The flight of the 1973 balls was said to be more predictable than that of earlier models, and covers loosened with rubbing, it was claimed, because of an inferior type of bonding process.

In 1974, Spalding introduced the cowhide ball with great success over the season. Nevertheless, on March 12, in a Florida game between the Mets and Red Sox, two balls came apart at the seams, garnering much attention from players and press.

On March 29, 1975, the Mets and Cardinals experimented with a new Spalding ball using only 96 instead of the requisite 108 stitches. They reported getting more hits from fewer stitches.

In spite of the hullabaloo, Spalding seems to have done a remarkable job over the years, providing balls of equal quality and keeping players relatively content with their tools. After nearly one hundred years of supplying the major league official ball, the company announced, on June 20, 1975, that Spalding would discontinue supplying balls to the majors after the 1976 season. Rawlings would take over with the start of the 1976 season. Spalding makes 2.5 million baseballs annually, of which only 10 percent have gone to the major leagues. The manufacture of balls for schools and the general public will continue.

A great deal has changed in the American game these past hundred years. Improved play has been, at least in part, the result of improved baseball equipment. How the game is played 100 years from now could have a lot to do with the men and women supplying its equipment.

Stan Musial
1940s

222

Henry Aaron
1950s

Roberto Clemente
1960s

Cesar Cedeno
1970s

223

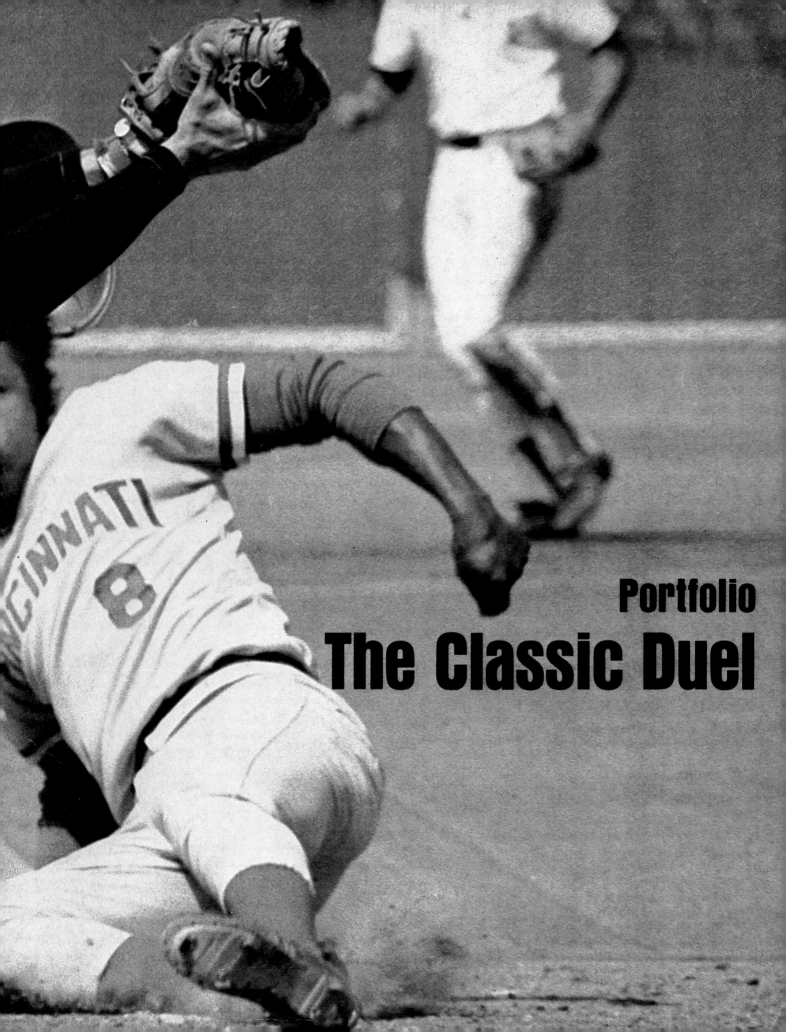

Portfolio
The Classic Duel

If anyone has trouble with his heart, just let him manage in the big leagues.
DANNY MURTAUGH

When I play the outfield or infield, it's almost like not playing at all. Catching is the most important job in baseball.

JOHNNY BENCH

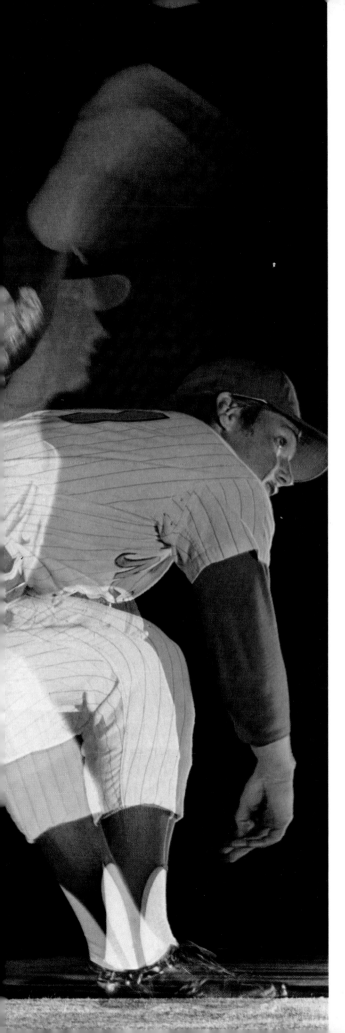

That classic duel between pitcher and batter is fascinating. No other team sport has such a dramatic and vivid confrontation. I live my life around the four days between starts.

TOM SEAVER

231

In a crucial situation, you've got to be able to say, "I hope the ball comes to me."

232   DARRELL EVANS

There's the pitcher, the ball, the situation. You figure the percentages. You narrow it all down. The ball is thrown. Everything you've figured will happen is happening. You put the bat on the ball and you can't even feel it. The ball jumps off the bat and you're running to first, drifting outside the line to start you on your way to second. The ultimate pleasure in baseball is that abstract moment when everything comes together and flows naturally.

TED SIMMONS

235

Show me a guy
who's afraid
to look bad,
and I'll show you
a guy you can beat
every time.
LOU BROCK

236

The second-base pivot is the hardest play in baseball. You don't see the runner, you sense the s.o.b. Half the time the second baseman doesn't even see first until after he's thrown, he's in such a hurry to get rid of the ball. There's three or four ways to cheat on the play so you don't wind up in the third-base boxes. You better believe we use 'em all.

CUBS' INFIELDER

714

Gulf

The Best

The All-Stars from Each Quarter Century

The four all-time, all-star teams that appear on the following pages were selected by a panel of baseball experts, which included, among others, presidents of the National League and members of The Society of American Baseball Research. Voting was on a point basis: five points for first choice, three points for second, one point for third. With the exception of the two ties, only the top vote getter is listed. In the extremely close votes, however, mention should be made that: Anson edged Brouthers; Hamilton beat out Thompson, Burkett, and Duffy; and Spahn outdueled Koufax.

1876–1900

First base	Cap Anson
Second base	Biddy McPhee
Third base	John McGraw
Shortstop	Hughie Jennings
Catcher	Buck Ewing
Outfielders	Ed Delahanty
	Willie Keeler
	Billy Hamilton
Right-handed pitcher	Cy Young
Left-handed pitcher	{ Ted Breitenstein
	Frank Killen

1901–1925

First base	Jake Daubert
Second base	Rogers Hornsby
Third base	Heinie Groh
Shortstop	Honus Wagner
Catcher	Roger Bresnahan
Outfielders	Edd Roush
	Zack Wheat
	Max Carey
Right-handed pitcher	Christy Mathewson
Left-handed pitcher	Eppa Rixey

1926-1950

First base	Bill Terry
Second base	Frank Frisch
Third base	Pie Traynor
Shortstop	Arky Vaughan
Catcher	Gabby Hartnett
Outfielders	Mel Ott
	Stan Musial
	Paul Waner
Right-handed pitcher	Dizzy Dean
Left-handed pitcher	Carl Hubbell

1951-1975

First base	Gil Hodges
Second base	Jackie Robinson
Third base	Ed Mathews
Shortstop	Ernie Banks
Catcher	{ Johnny Bench Roy Campanella
Outfielders	Henry Aaron
	Willie Mays
	Roberto Clemente
Right-handed pitcher	Bob Gibson
Left-handed pitcher	Warren Spahn

Chronology

1876 Ulysses S. Grant was in his eighth year as eighteenth President of the United States when, on Wednesday, February 2, men from eight professional baseball organizations met at the Grand Central Hotel, on lower Broadway in New York City. Their purpose: to break away from the National Association of Professional Baseball Players, the only pro league that had existed to that time. A 70-mile-an-hour wind lashed the streets of Manhattan as they deliberated and came to an historic agreement. The news wasn't published until the following Saturday—that the National League of Professional Baseball Clubs had been formed. It is the same National League that we know 100 years later.

The first game, the Boston Red Stockings against the Athletics in Philadelphia, drew 3,000 fans. The first man to come to bat was shortstop George Wright. The first man to get a hit was "Orator Jim" O'Rourke.

1877 In September, the Louisville Grays expelled four key players from their roster for throwing games—they had each received $100 a game from implicated gamblers. The National League later banished them for life.

Morgan G. Bulkeley, first elected president of the National League, resigned and was replaced by William A. Hulbert, the prime organizer of the league.

1879 On September 29, in a meeting at the Palace Hotel in Buffalo, New York, Arthur Soden, who had purchased three shares of the Boston club for $45.00 in 1876 and later was president of the team for 30 years, introduced the reserve clause, and it was adopted by the National League. In its initial form, only five players could be held "in reserve" by an owner.

1880 Cap Anson, one of the early great hitters in the game, managed the Chicago White Sox to the best won-lost record in baseball history. Their final tally was 67 victories and 17 defeats—a percentage of .798.

On June 12, a left-hander for the Worcester team, John Lee Richmond, pitched professional baseball's first perfect game, against Cleveland. He stood only 45 feet from the batters, but had to throw underhand.

To assure itself a solid financial base, the National League settled on a fifty-cent admission charge. In Syracuse, New York, there was a loud plaint that the single admission rate would "throw the entire assemblage into promiscuous relations . . . with drunken rowdies, unwashed loafers, and arrant blacklegs." The Cincinnati club was particularly offensive to the "higher social classes." It insisted on playing Sunday baseball and selling beer in the ball park (there were 27 breweries and distilleries in town). In October, the National League voted to forbid Sunday games and the sale of liquor on the grounds. Cincinnati dropped out of the league.

1883 A new rule was passed to stimulate baseball's offense: a foul ball caught on the first bounce was no longer an out. Cap Anson's stimulated Chicago sluggers scored 18 runs in one inning against Detroit.

1884 Pitchers were moved to 50 feet from home plate and were permitted to throw overhand. Ned Williamson, a hard-hitting shortstop with the White Sox, slugged a record 27 home runs. On that same team was Billy Sunday, who later made his name pitching from a church pulpit.

1887 Michael Joseph ("King") Kelly, a hard-drinking, hard-playing star who had batted .388 the year before to lead the National League, was sold from Chicago to Boston for the astronomical sum of $10,000. Kelly's salary was $2,000 annually, the ceiling figure for that period, but his new bosses gave him an extra $3,000 for the "use of his picture."

1890 Several years before, some of the Giants had joined in a Brotherhood of Professional Baseball Players and started chapters in other cities. The owners arbitrarily put in a salary classification system to which the players objected strenuously. Ignored, the players began the Brotherhood War, forming their own league. The revolt lasted only one year but ruined the American Association, almost buckled the National League, and created lasting bitterness.

1892 On June 10, Wilbert Robinson of the Baltimore Orioles rapped out seven hits in seven times at bat against St. Louis, a feat unequaled until 1975, when Rennie Stennett of the Pirates went seven-for-seven against Chicago.

1893 Two significant and lasting rules changes were adopted. The pitching distance from plate to mound, where a rubber slab was now mandatory, was set at 60 feet 6 inches, and all bats were to be completely round.

1894 The highest batting average (.438) in modern baseball history was achieved by Hugh Duffy, a 5-foot 7-inch outfielder with Boston. He led the National League that summer in home runs, doubles, slugging average, number of hits, total bases, and runs batted in. Teammate Bobby Lowe, a second baseman, the leadoff batter in a Decoration Day game against the visiting Cincinnati Reds, hit four straight home runs, the first man to do so.

1897 The Baltimore Orioles fielded a roistering crew that included John J. McGraw, Hugh Jennings, Dan Brouthers, and Willie ("Hit-'Em-Where-They-Ain't") Keeler. Keeler, a 5-foot 4½-inch outfielder, hit safely the opening game of the season, and kept hitting until his string of consecutive games was 44, a record topped only by Joe DiMaggio. Keeler batted .432 for the season.

Another remarkable player made his debut in the National League. He was bowlegged and had long scoops for hands. His name was John Peter Wagner, but everyone called him Honus. Ed Barrow (who later built the New York Yankees' dynasty), scouting for a Paterson, New Jersey, team, found him in a railroad yard outside Pittsburgh throwing lumps of coal to amuse himself. He was sold to Louisville for $2,100, and he reported to the Colonels on July 19—as a center fielder. (Not until 1901 did he play shortstop, a position at which many regard him as the best ever.)

1898 The monopolistic, autocratic National League staggered under a load of 12 teams. There was riotous behavior on the field, and the conduct of the players generally was deplored. A Purification Plan was introduced to monitor and suppress indecent or obscene language on the field. It was given up as hopeless; no case actually reached the appointed discipline board.

1900 The National League moved purposefully into the twentieth century. The total of 12 teams was reduced to 8: the Brooklyn Dodgers, New York Giants, St. Louis Cardinals, Cincinnati Reds, Chicago Cubs, Pittsburgh Pirates, Boston Braves, and Philadelphia Phils. These teams, unchanged, comprised the league until 1953.

The league was no longer without competition. Ban Johnson, a former sportswriter and bustling entrepreneur, organized a new circuit, the American League, and within a year he had it up to major league level.

1902 John J. McGraw started his career in New York as a baseball leader. He would remain on the job for 30 years and bring the Giants 10 pennants. McGraw arrived in mid-season, on July 7, under a cloud of controversy. The Baltimore

Orioles, whom he had managed, agreed to release him because they owed him $7,000 he had anted up to cover club debts. McGraw brought with him a brilliant battery of "Iron Man" Joe McGinnity and catcher Roger Bresnahan. McGinnity often pitched both ends of doubleheaders.

1903 Barney Dreyfuss, the owner of the Pittsburgh Pirates—managed by Fred Clarke and led on the field by both outfielder Clarke and Honus Wagner—was proud of the third straight pennant won by his club. He pushed for a postseason set of games with the Boston Pilgrims, who had won the American League championship behind pitcher Cy Young. This became the first World Series as we know it now. Back in the 1880s, for a period of seven years, there had been playoffs between the winners of the National League and the American Association (going to as many as 15 games between Detroit and St. Louis in 1887), but they were terminated with the demise of the Association. For three years in the 1890s, there was a Temple Cup competition between the first- and second-place teams of the league.

On October 1, this first World Series began, to be decided in a best-of-nine competition. Boston, with Young and Bill Dinneen each winning two games, was triumphant, five games to three. But the Pirates' players profited more. Dreyfuss let his players cut up the entire Pittsburgh share of the gate receipts. The losers received $1,316 each, the Pilgrims $1,182.

1904 Orator Jim O'Rourke, the man who got the first hit in the National League, was used as a catcher by John McGraw and, at the age of fifty-two, became the oldest man in the history of the National League to get a hit.

1905 The World Series was played after a one-year interruption. There had been a pause in 1904 because John T. Bush, who owned the champion New York Giants, vehemently hated the American League and refused to let his team take the field against the junior league's winner. He relented and, in fact, helped draw up the code which made World Series participation compulsory and a best-of-seven set.

Christy Mathewson, the ace of the Giants' pitching staff, shut out the Philadelphia Athletics three times, as the New York team won in five games. A crowd of 27,000 fanatics clustered under the veranda of the Giants' clubhouse, bellowing for a look at their heroes. *247*

1906 Chicago dominated the sports world; both baseball teams won major league pennants. The White Sox, on the South Side, gained fame as "the Hitless Wonders" of the American League with a collective batting average of .228. The Cubs, on the North Side, managed by Frank Chance, "the Peerless Leader," who also played first base and led the National League in stolen bases, won 116 games, the highest total in baseball history. In the horseless carriage World Series that followed, the White Sox upset the Cubs.

1908 On September 23, Fred Merkle, a nineteen-year-old first baseman for the Giants, made an error of omission that became baseball legend and haunted him the rest of his life. He neglected to touch second base.

In the last half of the ninth inning of a game against the Cubs, the score was tied at 1–1, two men were out, and the Giants had two men on base: Moose McCormick on second and Merkle on first. Al Bridwell laced a single to center field and McCormick scored easily. Merkle, on his way to second, saw Moose toe the plate and, to beat the fans rushing onto the field, turned before he reached second base and raced for the clubhouse. In the tumult that followed, Johnny Evers, Chicago's second baseman, retrieved a baseball—no one is sure where it came from—stepped on the bag, and appealed to umpire Hank O'Day that it was a force-out, nullifying the winning run. The Giants had already left the field. The umpires decided the game was a tie and had to be replayed. The National League president, Harry C. Pulliam, upheld their decision. Chicago and New York finished the regular season tied for first place. The disputed game was played over on October 8, and was won by the Cubs, 4–2, for the championship.

"Merkle's Boner," the most famous mistake in baseball history, came in his first full year with the Giants. He was to play in the majors 12 more seasons.

1910 William Howard Taft, a passionate fan, started the fashion of the President throwing out the first ball each season. He also complained about the lack of slugging, which led to the introduction of the first cork-center baseball.

Thomas Lynch was elected president of the National League. His predecessor, Pulliam, had committed suicide the previous summer.

The Chicago Cubs won their fourth league championship in five years. One of their avid followers, New York newspaperman Franklin P. Adams, immortalized their double-play com-

bination with eight lines of doggerel in the New York *Mail* that included the refrain "Tinker to Evers to Chance."

1912 Rube Marquard, once called "the $11,000 Lemon" (the price of his purchase from Indianapolis), left no doubt he was worth the highest money ever paid for a minor leaguer. Starting in early April, he won 19 straight games, still the record for consecutive victories. The Giants went on to win the pennant and meet Boston in the World Series.

It came down to the eighth game (the second ended in a tie because of darkness). At 1–1, the game went into extra innings. In the top of the tenth, Fred Merkle (remember him?) sent the Giants ahead with a run-scoring single. The great Christy Mathewson, his famed "fadeaway" pitch (a screwball) working perfectly, needed only three outs to secure the championship.

The first batter sent up a soft fly to the outfield. "While the ball is soaring its leisurely way," wrote the correspondent for the New York *Times*, "let us pause for a moment to think what hangs upon that fly . . . A President [Taft] is forgetting the bitter assaults that have been made upon him. . . . A campaign [by Woodrow Wilson for President] which may mean a change in the whole structure of the Nation's Government has been put into the background. What happens will be flashed by telegraph the length and breadth of the land and millions will be uplifted or downcast."

Fred Snodgrass, the Giants' center fielder, settled easily under the fly. The ball plopped into his glove. And out. The two-base error opened the floodgates for two Boston runs and triumph. A miserable winter and a lifetime of reminders lay in store for Snodgrass.

1913 John K. Tener, who had pitched for Chicago in the 1880s and went on to become governor of Pennsylvania, was elected president of the National League. He received a four-year contract for $25,000 annually, twice the salary of his predecessor.

1914 On June 28, Bostonians were oblivious to the tensions building in baseball. An outlaw circuit called the Federal League was organized with the backing of wealthy entrepreneurs. It raided the majors for talent, and the competition for players raised havoc with all baseball. Among the first to jump was Joe Tinker, who became player-manager of the Chicago entry.

The Braves were in last place, where they remained until July 19. Then, spurred by manager George Stallings and aided by Johnny Evers (who had been fired by the Cubs and joined Boston as a player for a $25,000 bonus), the Braves went on a winning streak. By September 8, they were settled in first place for good. They beat Connie Mack's powerful Athletics in the World Series four straight—another baseball first. They became known as "the Miracle Braves." (The Braves did not win another pennant for 34 years, and spent most of that time in the second division.)

1916 McGraw's Giants won 17 straight games on the road and then slumped drastically. On September 7, young left-hander Ferdie Schupp stopped the Brooklyn Dodgers, 4–1. The Giants went on to a record-setting 26 straight victories. The skein came too late; they still finished in fourth place.

1917 On April 6, Congress declared war on Germany. A few days later, the baseball season opened, with Major General Leonard Wood throwing out the first ball. Hank Gowdy, catcher for the Boston Braves, was the first major leaguer to enlist.

On May 2, before a sparse, chilled crowd in Chicago, one of the game's most memorable pitching duels was staged. Fred Toney was on the mound for the Cincinnati Reds against southpaw James ("Hippo") Vaughn of the Cubs. At the end of nine innings, neither team had a hit. The Reds managed a single and a run in the tenth inning to break the spell, and Toney got the side out to preserve his no-hitter.

1918 By May, more than half a million Americans were in France. There was not a club in the major leagues that did not have one or more players in the army. In June, a "work or fight" order was issued. Baseball owners decided to close shop for the regular season after September 1, though the World Series was later played. The pennant-winning Cubs lost to the Boston Red Sox, whose southpaw pitching star, Babe Ruth, extended his string of scoreless Series innings to 29.

John Tener resigned as president of the league and was succeeded, at the December meeting, by John A. Heydler, who had worked in the league office since 1902. Confronting Heydler was a gambling charge against Hal Chase, the best first baseman in the game, who had been suspended by Cincinnati on August 9. For lack of evidence, Heydler acquitted him of the charge, later found to be true. Chase drifted out of baseball after one more season.

1920 Baseball was rocked by the Black Sox scandal; Chicago allegedly threw the 1919 World Series to Cincinnati. On November 12, Judge Kenesaw Mountain Landis became the game's first commissioner. Landis had first come to the attention of the owners by presiding over an antitrust action brought against them by the Federal League in the United States District Court at Chicago.

Earlier in the year, at a February meeting of the joint rules committee of both leagues, the spitball and any other pitches that involved tampering with the ball were outlawed. Seventeen certified practitioners of the spitball were allowed to use that delivery until their careers ended. (Burleigh Grimes continued until 1934.)

On May 1, in Boston, the starting pitchers were Joe Oeschger for the Braves and Leon Cadore for the Brooklyn Dodgers. They each gave up a run. They each pitched 26 innings. The game was called on account of darkness— the longest major league game ever played. "I found myself growing sleepy at the finish," mumbled Cadore in the clubhouse.

1922 The National League featured a prodigious batter, reclusive in his habits, blunt, and aloof. The St. Louis Cardinals brought him up as a skinny shortstop in 1915, and didn't move him to second base until five years later. Rogers Hornsby batted .401, the highest National League mark since 1899. He also blasted 42 home runs with the new lively ball.

1924 Hornsby, who wouldn't go to the movies because the flickering lights might affect his batting eye, reached his zenith as a hitter. He batted .424 for the Cardinals.

The National League resolved baseball's last major gambling scandal. The Giants had bought a fine young outfielder, Jimmy O'Connell, from San Francisco for $75,000, and he was beginning to contribute as the team pushed for an unprecedented fourth straight pennant. Before a September game against the lowly Phillies, O'Connell approached their shortstop, Heinie Sand, and said, "I'll give you five hundred dollars if you don't bear down too hard." Sand reported the bribe offer to his manager, who relayed it to the commissioner's office. Three days before the World Series, Landis banned O'Connell and Cozy Dolan, a Giants coach who was implicated, from baseball for life.

In the Series, the Giants lost in the seventh game, a twelve-inning thriller, when a grounder by Earl McNeely struck an infield pebble and bounced over the head of the Giants' eighteen-year-old rookie third baseman, Fred Lindstrom.

1926 It was a staggering year on the diamond. Grover Cleveland Alexander, weary from evening the World Series at three games apiece on October 9, staggered out of the bullpen on October 10 to face Tony Lazzeri of the New York Yankees. The Cardinals held a slim one-run margin. The bases were loaded, there were two outs. Pete struck out Lazzeri on three pitches and hurled two more scoreless innings to win the Series.

On December 20, it was announced that Rogers Hornsby, the player-manager of the world champion St. Louis team, had been traded to the New York Giants for second baseman Frankie Frisch and pitcher Jimmy Ring. Hornsby had wanted a three-year contract at $50,000 a year. Owner Sam Breadon refused. Breadon was also upset because, earlier in the season, Hornsby threw the owner out of the Cardinals' clubhouse.

1927 Pittsburgh played a brilliant brother combination in its outfield. Paul Waner, playing right field in his second season with the Pirates, was joined by rookie center fielder Lloyd Waner. Paul, called "Big Poison", batted .380 to lead the National League. Lloyd, called "Little Poison", batted .355 to finish third. Little Poison, at 5 feet 9 inches, was half an inch taller than Big Poison.

1929 In the seventh inning of the fourth game of the World Series, the Chicago Cubs sailed blithely along with an eight-run lead. The almost sure victory would be their second in a row, and would even up the Series against Connie Mack's Philadelphia Athletics. But the A's scored 10 runs in the bottom of the seventh and won the game. In the bottom of the ninth inning in the next game, the Cubs again led, 2–0. And again the A's rallied dramatically, with three runs.

1930 Everything was depressed but batting averages. The entire National League went on a hitting rampage. Seventy-one players, an average of almost nine per club, batted over .300. They were led by Bill Terry, the first baseman of the Giants, who finished at .401, the last .400 hitter in the National League. The Giants had a team batting average of .319, a modern record. Lewis ("Hack") Wilson, who was 5 feet 6 inches tall and looked nearly as wide, hit a league high of 56 home runs. That atoned for the fly ball that he had lost in the sun during the ten-run binge

by the Athletics in the 1929 Series. Hack also set a major league record of 190 runs batted in. Floyd ("Babe") Herman, a colorful Brooklyn outfielder, was the only man ever to bat .393 and finish second.

1931 After the season's final averages were released, a few men would have given anything for an extra hit. Chick Hafey, with the first place St. Louis Cardinals, was the batting champion with an average of .3489. Bill Terry was edged out at .3486. Hafey's teammate, "Sunny Jim" Bottomley, was third at .3482.

The ensuing World Series, against the Philadelphia A's, belonged to still another of the Cardinals, John Leonard ("Pepper") Martin, "the Wild Hoss of the Osage." He had become the regular center fielder—a guy with a perennially dirty uniform, who throve on headfirst slides. He ran the A's crazy, and batted .500 for the Series, which St. Louis won in seven games.

1932 Ill, losing control of the players, and unable to operate as he wanted to, John J. McGraw resigned as manager of New York on June 3. A doubleheader scheduled for that day was rained out. On the clubhouse bulletin board, a typed message notified the players that McGraw had resigned and would be succeeded by Bill Terry. McGraw died a year and a half later.

1933 Prodded by the Depression, baseball searched for new ways to display its product. The minor leagues tried baseball under the lights. Doubleheaders were scheduled as regular dates rather than just to make up for rained-out games. On July 6, at Comiskey Park in Chicago, the first All-Star Game was held, a brainchild of Arch Ward, the energetic sports editor of the Chicago *Tribune*. John J. McGraw was appointed manager of the National League team, his last appearance in a dugout.

Bill Terry quickly brought the Giants to a top perch again. They won a memorable doubleheader on July 2 that put them on the path to the pennant. The opener went 18 innings and was won by Carl Hubbell, 1–0. In the second game, LeRoy Parmelee bested an exciting new young pitcher for the Cardinals, Jay Hanna ("Dizzy") Dean, 1–0.

Hubbell had salvaged his career by perfecting a screwball that broke away from right-handed batters. He also pioneered a new sartorial note for players, who customarily rolled their pants up just below the knee—Hubbell let his hang down almost to his ankles.

1934 Any doubt about the appeal of the All-Star Game was dispelled by a remarkable pitching feat. The game was played, on July 10, in New York's Polo Grounds, which made starting pitcher Carl Hubbell feel right at home. He responded by striking out, consecutively, Babe Ruth, Lou Gehrig, Jimmie Foxx, Al Simmons, and Joe Cronin—five of the greatest hitters in baseball.

The pennant race that summer was dominated by an irrepressible group of individuals called "the Gashouse Gang." Operating out of St. Louis and managed by Frankie Frisch, the gang included such disparate people as Dizzy Dean and Leo Durocher. Dean, ribald and bragging, was joined on the pitching staff by his younger brother Paul. Between them, they won 49 games. Dizzy's contribution was a startling thirty-win season.

On September 21, while pushing to overtake the league-leading Giants, the Cardinals came into Brooklyn's Ebbets Field for a doubleheader. Dizzy spun a 13–0 shutout in the opener. Paul pitched the second game and made it a no-hit, no-run 3–0 victory.

Dizzy pitched two shutouts in three days the final week of the season to bring the Cards the title. The Giants faltered against the Brooklyn Dodgers, managed by a jug-eared character named Casey Stengel. Earlier, manager Terry had asked loftily, "The Dodgers—are they still in the league?"

In December, John Heydler resigned after 16 years as president of the league and was succeeded by Ford Frick, a baseball writer who had joined the league earlier in the year as head of its publicity bureau.

1935 The legendary Babe Ruth became a National Leaguer. It was, at the age of forty, a brief and poignant experience. The Babe, thwarted in his ambition to become a manager, drew his release and signed with the Boston Braves as a part-time player and assistant manager. He was successful in neither. The Braves finished last with 115 losses, the most until the expansion era of the 1960s.

Ruth, however, did have one last hurrah. On May 25, in Pittsburgh, he hit three home runs in one game, the last one a towering drive over the right field roof, which had never before been cleared. It was his last homer in the majors. Ruth quit a few days later and showed up only once again in uniform officially, as a coach with the Brooklyn Dodgers for part of the 1938 season.

In Cincinnati, Larry MacPhail, a talkative colorful baseball executive who took part in a wild scheme to kidnap the Kaiser in World War I, signaled the future for baseball. He installed lights in Crosley Field. On May 24, the Reds played the Philadelphia Phillies under the arcs in the first night game in history. President Roosevelt turned on the floodlights from a switch in his Washington office.

1938 Johnny Vander Meer, a left-hander who was just wild enough to keep batters from digging in at the plate, pitched consecutive no-hit, no-run games. Vander Meer had flunked trials with Boston and Brooklyn, but harnessed his speed enough to stick with the Reds. He pitched a hitless shutout against the Braves in Cincinnati on June 11. Larry MacPhail, who had moved on to become general manager of Brooklyn, turned on lights for the first time at Ebbets Field on June 15, Vandy's next turn on the mound. Vander Meer picked the occasion to blank the Dodgers without a hit, surviving a crisis in the ninth when he walked the bases full with one out. Vander Meer's double no-hit effort is unique in baseball.

The drama of the pennant race centered on a red-faced catcher named Gabby Hartnett. The Pittsburgh Pirates led most of the season. The Cubs, managed by Hartnett, entertained them for a crucial three-game series late in September. It opened with a doubleheader. The Cubs won the first to move within half a game of the Pirates. The second was tied, 5–5, in the last of the ninth, with dusk creeping over Wrigley Field, and the umpires about to call the game. Hartnett stepped up to the plate with two out and nobody on. Pitcher Mace Brown slipped two strikes past him in the enveloping darkness. Hartnett hit the next pitch into the left field bleachers, and the Cubs took over the league lead. They won again the next day, and continued to the championship.

1939 The Baseball Hall of Fame, which had been inducting men since 1937, opened officially for public view at Cooperstown, New York.

1941 Baseball was beginning to feel the impact of the world at war. The first United States peacetime draft had been enacted. On March 8, Hugh Mulcahy, an excellent pitcher for the Philadelphia Phillies, was drafted at the peak of his career and would miss five years.

The Brooklyn Dodgers rose to the top in the last "normal" season of 1941. The Dodgers' team, shrewdly put together by GM MacPhail and managed by Leo Durocher, included young outfielder Pete Reiser, who led the league in hitting—and running into outfield fences.

The Dodgers were dueling the mighty Yankees on even terms in the World Series—were, in fact, about to tie it up in the fourth game—when catcher Mickey Owen let a third strike, which would have made the last out of the game, slip by him. The batter, Tommy Henrich, reached first, and the reprieve led to a New York rally that won the game.

1942 On January 15, President Roosevelt sent Commissioner Landis "the Green Letter," in which he said, "I honestly think it would be best for the country to keep baseball going."

1945 Baseball struggled through the war years without curtailing schedules. Only the All-Star Game was dropped, in the summer of 1945. Players were scrounged from everywhere. A fifteen-year-old pitcher appeared in a game for the Cincinnati Reds—at twenty-four, Joe Nuxhall made it back to the club and stayed in the big leagues 15 years. The majors had a one-armed outfielder and a pitcher with an artificial limb.

With Larry MacPhail in the service, Branch Rickey moved from St. Louis to Brooklyn. On August 28, he brought a black athlete, Jackie Robinson, into his office for an interview.

1946 Peace came briefly to the world, but not necessarily to the National League. The Pasquel brothers of Mexico decided this would be a good time to upgrade the caliber of Mexican League baseball and reached across the border for talent. They were particularly successful in luring players from the St. Louis Cardinals, the dominant team in baseball, and the New York Giants. A. B. ("Happy") Chandler, who had become commissioner in 1945 after the death of Kenesaw Mountain Landis, suspended the jumpers, among them Max Lanier of the Cardinals and Sal Maglie of the Giants, for five years. He lifted the suspension in 1949.

The National League race ended in a dead heat between the Cardinals and the Brooklyn Dodgers. In the first league playoffs, the Cardinals won the pennant by taking two straight.

Harry Brecheen won three games to pace the Cardinals' triumph over the Boston Red Sox in the ensuing World Series. In the eighth inning of the seventh game, Enos Slaughter scored the winning run by sprinting home from first base on Harry Walker's double, while shortstop Johnny Pesky of the Red Sox hesitated on the relay from center field.

1947 A tumultuous year for the National League.

On April 10, the week before the season opened, Commissioner Happy Chandler suspended manager Leo Durocher of the Dodgers for the entire season. The charge: "conduct detrimental to baseball." "The Lip" was accused of consorting with gamblers, and had received unfavorable publicity for marrying movie star Laraine Day amidst legal complications. Burt Shotton succeeded Durocher. (He and Connie Mack of Philadelphia were the last managers to work in street clothes.)

The day after Durocher's suspension, the Dodgers bought the contract of Jackie Robinson from their Montreal farm club. He played first base that inaugural season. On May 9, President Ford Frick announced that a threatened strike by the St. Louis Cardinals over Robinson's presence in the game had been averted. Robinson broke in with a .297 batting average and led the league in stolen bases, with 29.

The dominant pitcher in the game was Ewell Blackwell, known as "the Whip," a side-armer for Cincinnati. He had a league high of 22 victories and, in mid-season, came within two outs of duplicating Johnny Vander Meer's double no-hitter feat. Mel Ott, manager of the Giants, bowed out as an active player with 511 career home runs, at the time second only to Babe Ruth.

Brooklyn, despite the turmoil, won the pennant. In the fourth game of the World Series against the Yankees, the Dodgers collected only one hit. It came with two out in the ninth inning: a two-base blow by Cookie Lavagetto off the right field wall that scored two runs and deprived pitcher Floyd Bevens of both a no-hitter and a victory. In the sixth game, Al Gionfriddo made a miraculous catch of a drive by Joe DiMaggio that helped the Dodgers even the Series. But they lost the decisive game.

1948 The resurgent Boston Braves brought a new cry to the game: "Spahn and Sain and pray for rain." Spahn was a classy, mature left-hander. Sain, a curveball specialist, won 24 games. Their arms carried the team to its first pennant since the Miracle Braves won in 1914.

Stan Musial, who had turned to the outfield when his arm went dead as a minor league pitcher, hit a career high of .376. He led the league in number of hits, two-baggers, three-baggers, runs, runs batted in, and slugging average, and his total of 39 home runs was just one shy of the top.

Leo Durocher came back to Brooklyn, only

to be sent to the Giants in an amazing mid-season managerial switch.

1950 The Philadelphia Phillies, without a pennant since 1915 and out of the second division only twice in 23 years, climbed to the National League championship. They won it on the last day of the season, over the Brooklyn Dodgers; Dick Sisler hit a three-run homer in the tenth inning to give Robin Roberts the triumph on the mound. It was his twentieth victory of the campaign, the first of six straight twenty-game seasons for "the Whiz Kids' " top pitcher.

1951 On May 25, the New York Giants called up twenty-year-old Willie Howard Mays from their Minneapolis farm club. He was hitting .477 for the Millers. Willie was soon playing stickball with the kids in Harlem, hollering "Say, Hey!" to everybody, and using his glove like a basket to catch fly balls in center field.

On August 11, the Giants trailed the league-leading Dodgers by 13½ games. Inexorably, the Giants crept up and finally tied the Dodgers on the last day of the season, leading to the second playoff in National League history. Each team won one game. The decisive third game was held at the Polo Grounds, on October 3. The Dodgers, behind 20-game winner Don Newcombe, scored three times in the eighth inning to take what looked like an insurmountable 4–1 lead. The Giants, in their last time at bat, routed Newcombe with three hits that accounted for one run, placed men on second and third, and brought Bobby Thomson to bat. Manager Charley Dressen brought in Ralph Branca from the bullpen. Branca fired one strike. On the second pitch, high and inside, Thomson looped a drive that barely reached the short lower left field stands, 315 feet away. It was the most dramatic home run in history.

A new commissioner presided over the World Series. Ford Frick was elevated to the job on September 20. Exactly a week later, Warren C. Giles, the president of the Cincinnati Reds, took Frick's place as the league head.

1953 The first big league franchise shift of the twentieth century was announced at a league meeting in St. Petersburg, Florida, on March 18. The Boston Braves would move to Milwaukee and Boston would be without a National League team for the first time since 1876. The Braves felt impelled to move because they drew only 281,000 spectators in 1952.

1954 One of the most sensational catches in baseball history sent the New York Giants on their way to a four-game sweep of the World Series over the Cleveland Indians. It came in the eighth inning of the opening contest in the Polo Grounds, on September 29. The score was tied, 2–2. The Indians had two runners on base. Vic Wertz, who had four hits in the game, lashed a drive to the deepest part of the park, 450 feet to straightaway center field. Willie Mays turned and raced with his back to the plate. Just before he reached the green fence, he looked over his head, stretched, and gloved the ball. In the tenth inning, pinch hitter Dusty Rhodes hit a three-run homer for the Giants' triumph.

1955 The Brooklyn Dodgers, after seven futile tries, finally won a World Series, defeating the Yankees in seven games. A part-time outfielder from Cuba, Sandy Amoros, saved the finale with a spectacular running catch at the left field foul line.

1956 Don Newcombe, winner of 27 games for Brooklyn, was the winner of the first Cy Young Award, established this year. But the hitters in the league weren't quelled. The Cincinnati Reds hammered out a club total of 221 home runs to tie the record set by the New York Giants in 1947. Walter F. O'Malley, president of the Brooklyn Dodgers, shifted eight of his team's home games to Jersey City, a portent of the future.

1958 The National League became truly national, coast to coast. The transfer of the Dodgers to Los Angeles and the Giants to San Francisco, a jointly conceived move, became a *fait accompli*. On April 19, they faced each other in the Los Angeles Coliseum and introduced major league ball to the West Coast. The Giants played their home games in tiny Seals Stadium. Both teams awaited the construction of their own new ball parks.

1959 On May 26, a lean Pittsburgh pitcher named Harvey Haddix faced the Milwaukee Braves, a team of pennant-winning caliber, and for nine innings he allowed neither a hit nor a walk, and none of his teammates made an error: perfect baseball. Haddix kept his string going through the twelfth inning, the most phenomenal pitching performance ever. Haddix's perfect performance was broken when the first man up in the thirteenth reached first base on a throwing error. A sacrifice bunt was followed by an intentional walk, and Joe Adcock broke up the classic by barely clearing the right center field fence with a three-run homer.

1960 In the last half of the ninth inning of the seventh and last game, the Pittsburgh Pirates won the World Series over the Yankees on a home run by second baseman Bill Mazeroski. Downtown Pittsburgh was a mess that night.

Less than a week later, at a special league session, the senior circuit announced expansion to 10 teams in 1962. Entries in Houston and New York would be added to the existing eight.

1961 Warren Spahn pitched the second no-hitter of his long career, a 1–0 classic over San Francisco, on April 28 in Milwaukee. It came just five days after his fortieth birthday.

1962 The Los Angeles Dodgers moved to their new stadium in Chavez Ravine, and set a major league attendance record of 2,755,184. Many were drawn by the exploits of shortstop Maury Wills, who broke Ty Cobb's forty-seven-year-old mark of 96 by stealing 104 bases.

No team in history ever lost more than the 120 games dropped by the New York Mets in their first year of existence.

1965 The pitching of the Dodgers' Sandy Koufax was peerless. On September 9, he pitched his fourth no-hitter in four years, a perfect game against the Chicago Cubs. A month later, Koufax rallied Los Angeles to a Series triumph over the Minnesota Twins by tossing two shutouts.

1968 The National League completed its expansion to a 12-team loop by granting franchises to San Diego and Montreal, with play to begin in those cities in 1969.

Bob Gibson set the existing earned-run record, yielding 1.12 runs per nine innings pitched over the course of the season. He struck out 17 batters, also a new record, in the opening game of the World Series, against Detroit. Four days later, he achieved his seventh straight Series pitching victory, another record.

1969 The amazing New York Mets astonished the baseball world by bringing a world championship to Shea Stadium. The Mets were the first expansion team to win either the pennant or the World Series.

Charles ("Chub") Feeney, vice-president and general manager of the San Francisco Giants, a man who had spent all his adult life in baseball, succeeded Warren Giles as president of the National League, in December.

1971 The National League set an all-time attendance record of 17,324,857.

1972 Baseball was rent by the first general strike in its history, over the issue of an increase in player pensions. The strike lasted thirteen days and delayed the opening of the regular season by ten days. All teams missed at least six games, and many missed nine. Baseball kept its house in order by reaching a compromise raise of $500,000 in the pension fund.

1973 The Baseball Hall of Fame waived its five-year rule and, on March 20, inducted Roberto Clemente, for 18 years a great outfielder with the Pittsburgh Pirates. Clemente had been killed New Year's Eve, in a plane crash off the coast of his native Puerto Rico, while taking relief supplies to the victims of a terrible earthquake in Nicaragua.

The New York Mets, with Willie Mays joining them for spot duty, made it to their second World Series but were toppled in seven games by the Oakland Athletics.

1974 On April 28, before 53,775 fans in Atlanta Stadium and a national television audience, Henry Aaron drove a fourth inning pitch over the left center field fence—home run number 715 of his illustrious career—to pierce the supposedly inviolate mark set by Babe Ruth. The ball was caught by Atlanta relief pitcher Tom House, in the bullpen, against the auxiliary scoreboard. The pitch was delivered by Al Downing, who wore the same uniform number, 44, as Aaron.

Left fielder Lou Brock, of the St. Louis Cardinals, at the age of thirty-five, stole 118 bases, surpassing Maury Wills's record.

Mike Marshall, the bullpen specialist of the Los Angeles Dodgers, appeared in a record-setting 106 games—he pitched in 13 consecutive games at one point—and became the first relief pitcher to be voted the Cy Young Award.

Bob Gibson, the ace of the Cardinals for 16 seasons, ran his strikeout total past 3,000. The only pitcher in baseball history with more was Walter Johnson.

1975 On July 15, the finest in the National League won their twelfth All-Star Game in thirteen years.

Later the same month, the league reached the half billion mark in attendance—since 1901, when figures were first recorded.

Tom Seaver of the Mets became the first pitcher in major league history to strike out 200 or more hitters in eight straight seasons.

Cincinnati won its first World Series since 1940, beating Boston by scoring a run in the ninth inning of the seventh game.

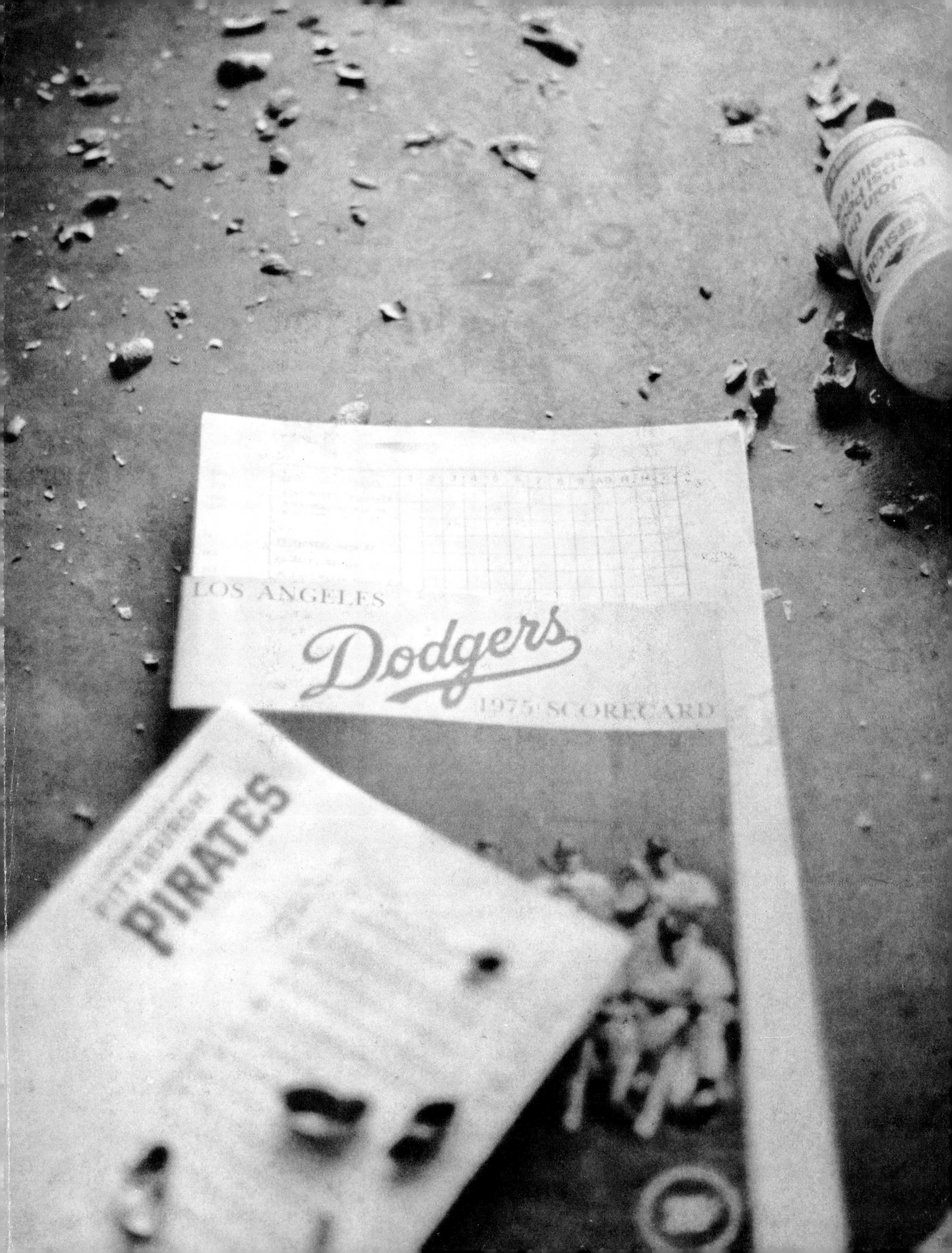
LOS ANGELES
Dodgers
1975 SCORECARD
PIRATES

Credits

Acknowledgments

The publishers wish to thank the following people who contributed their time and thoughts:
Richie Ashburn, Yogi Berra, Joe Black, Bobby Bragan, Lou Brock, Max Carey, Larry Chiasson, Fred
Claire, Jerry Coleman, Harry Craft, Blake Cullen, Alvin Dark, Art Santo Domingo, Don Eaddy,
Darrell Evans, Chub Feeney, Eddie Ferenz, Jim Ferguson, Fred Fleig, Marni Frommer, Carl Furillo,
Joe Gallagher, Ralph Garr, Bob Gibson, Bill Giles, Hy Goldberg, M. Donald Grant, Mickey Grasso,
Burleigh Grimes, William Guilfoile, Jesse Haines, Billy Herman, Kirby Higbe, Bob Hope, Monte
Irvin, Cliff Kachline, George ("Highpockets") Kelly, Dave Kingman, Al Laney, Harry ("Cookie")
Lavagetto, Al Lopez, Jerry Lovelace, Joe McCarthy, Frank McCormick, Andy Messersmith, John Mil-
ner, Van Lingle Mungo, Stan Musial, Lindsey Nelson, Al Oliver, Paul Owens, Harold Parrott, Patrick
Quinn, Jack Redding, Merv Rettenmund, Bobby Risinger, Pete Rose, Ed Routzong, Mike Ryan, Hal
Schumacher, Fred Shaffer, Larry Shenk, Charles Shriver, Ted Simmons, Cathi Sivyer, Ken Smith,
Don Sutton, Dick Wagner, Harold Weissman, Glenn Wright, Charlene Yoritsune

Authors

Roger Angell 18-21; Henry Berry 22-39; Bob Cooke 40-55; Mercer Field 204-23; Dr. Harvey Frommer 56-203; Murray Olderman 244-54

Illustrators

Merv Corning jacket 244-45; George Smith 42, 72, 80 right, 96, 121, 122 top, 124, 127 left, 144 bottom
right, 146 bottom left, 149 bottom left, 180 bottom, 194, 204-23

Photographers

David Bier Studios 168; George Brace 25, 26, 27, 30, 31, 34, 35 right; Pat Capone 68; Alan Carr, courtesy of
Patrick Quinn 28, 44, 52 right, 53, 119 bottom, 123, 124-5, 159; Dennis Desprois 76-77, 165, 200, 224-5, 228, 232
top, 237; Melchior DiGiacomo 45 bottom, 78, 90, 98, 99, 105 top, 110, 117, 143 top left, 191 bottom right, 201,
226 top and bottom right, 232 bottom, 233, 235, 236 bottom; James F. Flores 182; Focus on Sports 14–15, 67
bottom, 71, 79, 106, 226 bottom left, 229 bottom, 240-1; John Garetti, courtesy of Henry Berry 10, 11, 94 top
right, 146 top left and bottom right; Steve Goldstein for Spectra-Action 43, 51, 69, 89, 104, 105 bottom, 118, 131,
134, 135, 150, 191 bottom left and top; Ellen Griesedieck 176, 186, 227, 234, 255; Dennis Huls, San Diego Union
136-7; Fred Kaplan 111 bottom left, 142, 143 top right and bottom, 162-63, 166, 167, 171, 174, 175, 183, 187,
229 top, 239; Gene Kelly 39; Los Angeles Dodgers 178, 179; Library of Congress 37; Montreal Expos 168, 169,
173; National Baseball Hall of Fame and Museum, Inc., photographed by Frank Rollins 2, 3, 6-7, 22-23, 24
top and bottom, 29, 35 left, 43, 48-49, 50, 52 left and center, 62, 75 top, 80 left and middle, 81, 82, 84, 85, 88 top,
94 bottom, 100, 101 right, 109, 119 top, 125, 127 right, 144 top, 146 top right, 153, 154, 156, 172 right, 180 top,
184 top, 193 bottom left and bottom right; National League from the 1876 original minutes 1, 4, 5, 8, 9, 12, 13;
New York Daily News, Copyright 1955 New York News Inc., reprinted by permission 189; Philadelphia
Phillies 149 top; Pittsburgh Pirates 82-83, 88 bottom; Lewis Portnoy for Spectra-Action 74, 75 bottom, 236 top;
John Sammis 128 top; San Diego Padres by Ron McClendon 137; Sports Illustrated photo by James Drake ©
Time Inc. 140; Sports Illustrated photos by Walter Iooss, Jr., © Time Inc. 67 top, 238 bottom; Sports Illustrated
photo by Fred Kaplan © Time Inc. 111 bottom right; Sports Illustrated photo by Heinz Kluetmeier © Time Inc.
130; Sports Illustrated photos by Neil Leifer © Time Inc. 66, 70, 107, 111 top, 152, 230-31; Sports Illustrated
photo by Herb Scharfman © Time Inc. 170; Sports Illustrated photos by Sheedy & Long © Time Inc. 132, 138,
139; Sporting News 60, 64, 65, 83, 87 top, 92, 93, 94 top left, 95, 97, 101 left, 128 bottom, 144 bottom left, 155,
157 top, 161 bottom, 172 left, 181, 184 bottom, 188, 193 top, 195, 196 top; Tony Tomsic 190, 199, 202 bottom;
United Press International 45 top, 46, 54, 55, 63, 73, 86, 87 bottom, 114, 115, 122 bottom, 157 bottom, 158,
160-1, 161 top, 164, 185, 196 bottom, 197, 202 top; Herb Weitman 102-3; Wide World Photos 58, 149 bottom
right; Michael Zagaris 116.